David Rennie-Massey

RITSCHL
& Luther

RITSCHL
&Luther

A Fresh Perspective on
Albrecht Ritschl's Theology
in the Light of His Luther Study

David W. Lotz

Nashville • ABINGDON PRESS • New York

Ritschl and Luther

Library of Congress Cataloging in Publication Data

LOTZ, DAVID W. 1937—   Ritschl and Luther:
a fresh perspective on Albrecht Ritschl's theology
in the light of his Luther study. Bibliography: p.
1. Luther, Martin, 1483-1546—Theology. 2.
Ritschl, Albrecht Benjamin, 1822-1889. I. Title.
BR333.2.L67   230   73-14962

ISBN 0-687-36449-3

Quotations from *Luther: Lectures on Romans,*
LCC, Vol. XV, newly translated and edited by
Wilhelm Pauck, copyright © MCMLXI by W. L.
Jenkins. Used by permission of The Westminster
Press and SCM Press Ltd.

Quotations from *Luther's Works*, edited by Jaroslav Pelikan and H. T. Lehmann, Vols. 12, 13, and
26 by permission of Concordia Publishing House;
Vols. 31, 32, 34, 35, 36, 40, and 43 by permission of Fortress Press.

MANUFACTURED BY THE PARTHENON PRESS AT
NASHVILLE, TENNESSEE, UNITED STATES OF AMERICA

TO MY FATHER

The Rev. Walter J. Lotz

PREFACE

This essay represents a critical investigation of Albrecht Ritschl's interpretation and use of Luther's theology, with a view to providing a fresh perspective on Ritschl's own theology in the light of his intensive Luther study. This linkage of Ritschl's name with Luther's may well elicit a response of surprise, if not suspicion and skepticism. I hope to show, however, that the theme "Ritschl and Luther" is not only defensible, because warranted by the evidence, but is also particularly useful as a propaedeutic to the study of Ritschl's entire theological system. Thus the scope of this book is considerably broader than its title might initially indicate. I have called my approach a "fresh perspective" on Ritschl's theology by way of express rejoinder to that "standard" viewpoint which largely reiterates Karl Barth's overly severe criticisms.

Three further points of clarification should perhaps be noted. First, it would be both mistaken and presumptuous to suggest that the approach I have adopted is a decidedly new one. The older (pre-Barth) literature on Ritschl regularly calls attention to Ritschl's self-acknowledged indebtedness to Luther and Reformation thought. More recently, Ritschl's Luther interpretation has found a cordial, albeit critical, reception in important works by Otto Wolff (*Die Haupttypen der neueren Lutherdeutung*, 1938) and Walther von Loewenich (*Luther und der Neuprotestantismus*, 1963). My indebtedness to these two books will be evident throughout this presentation. To the best of my knowledge, however, the present study is the first full-length treatment of Ritschl's Luther interpretation, and is also the first sustained attempt to show how Ritschl's involvement with Luther actually informed his comprehensive theological enterprise. While it has become somewhat commonplace to say that the leitmotif or inner impulse of Ritschl's thought is summed up in the motto "Back to the New Testament by way of the Reformation," the precise meaning and significance of Ritschl's commitments to Reformation Christianity have heretofore not been accorded detailed attention. In this limited sense, then, the following pages may be said to offer a "fresh" perspective on Ritschl's theology.

In the second place, I should not wish to give the impression that I simply reject out of hand those critical strictures on Ritschl's theology which in the main have their provenance in neo-Orthodoxy. In fact at various points I find myself in significant agreement with a number of these criticisms. Yet all too often they seem to me to be lacking in the necessary rigor and precision: they are not sufficiently nuanced or properly qualified and so end up being quite misleading. More regrettably still, these criticisms—particularly the familiar and, in my opinion, untenable claims that Ritschl's theology is anthropocentric and that it succumbs to a rationalistic moralism—have become so stereotyped through heedless repetition as to obstruct a truly impartial investigation of Ritschl's thought. Indeed the bulk of Ritschl criticism appears to be based more on familiar catchwords and polemical slogans than on a careful reading of Ritschl's own works. It must be granted, however, that to some extent Ritschl himself is responsible for this disturbing state of affairs. His thought can be so opaque, his language so obscure, and his precise meaning so difficult of apprehension that even his most sympathetic interpreter must perforce resort to explanatory categories which frequently involve questionable generalizations and oversimplifications. Indeed I am convinced that Ritschl's theology, stylistic matters apart, has repeatedly elicited inordinately severe criticisms precisely because it is so *complex* a phenomenon. That is, it lends itself to caricature because it is such a dense combine of biblical, Reformation, and modern components that the incautious critic is virtually compelled to oversimplify in order to render a supposedly luminous judgment and to assign Ritschl his "proper place" in the spectrum of modern Protestant thought. In pursuing my own work of historical revisionism, therefore, I have consciously sought to avoid the pitfall of simply replacing certain dubious, simplistic judgments with others open to precisely the same charge. In brief, I have endeavored to do justice to the aforementioned complexity of Ritschl's theology by presenting a suitably nuanced exposition, analysis, and critique of his Luther interpretation.

Finally, I should like to emphasize that my basic intention in this book is to use Ritschl's Luther interpretation as a meaningful point of entry into Ritschl's own theology, as a heuristic device for uncovering the central impulses of the Ritschlian system. Hence, for present purposes, the *evaluation* of the accuracy and adequacy of Ritschl's Luther interpretation has a secondary or derivative importance, although I do devote two chapters to this topic. No doubt for some readers this evaluative issue will be of supreme interest and import. I certainly have no quarrel with this concern as such, since I share it myself, yet it is not my major preoccupation in the following pages. In fact any thorough assessment of Ritschl as a Luther scholar would call for a separate study of substantial proportions. I am also acutely aware that Luther interpretation is an immensely complex matter in its own right and has proved to be a lifetime's labor for many scholars. I cannot pretend to such massive involvement and expertise, but I have attempted to give a reading of Luther's theology which is warranted both by Luther's works themselves and by the findings of responsible Luther interpreters. Indeed one of my most challenging procedural problems was that of not allowing the intricacies (and intrinsic excitement) of Luther research to turn me aside from the primary task at hand. I append these various remarks not to disarm criticism in advance (a futile gesture in any case), but simply to spell out my intentions and to indicate my awareness of some of the difficult interpretive problems involved in such an undertaking. The introductory chapter also takes up these concerns at greater length.

In its present form this study is a revised and expanded version of a dissertation originally submitted to the faculty of Union Theological Seminary, New York. The major alteration is the inclusion, in appendix form, of a translation of Ritschl's "Festival Address on the Four-hundredth Anniversary of the Birth of Martin Luther," delivered in Göttingen on November 10, 1883. Besides its obvious importance for my theme, this essay possesses intrinsic significance as perhaps the clearest and most concise expression of Ritschl's self-understanding as a reformer of Protestantism. It should also prove of special interest to scholars engaged in a study of how the sixteenth-century Reformation was interpreted and appropriated by the leading representatives of modern theological liberalism. In this connection I might note that while the contributions of Adolf von Harnack, Ernst Troeltsch, and Karl Holl to the general thematic of "the Reformation and the Modern World" are widely known, it is often overlooked that Albrecht Ritschl's Luther study actually posed many of the formative problems with which these historians subsequently wrestled, particularly the pressing question of a "scholastic residue" in Luther's theology and the extent to which the Protestant Reformation thus remained "more medieval than modern."

My scholarly debts are legion. To record them all would require the proverbial river of ink, yet some are too great to go unmentioned. In particular, I should like to express sincere gratitude to my friend and colleague Professor Paul L. Lehmann for many fruitful suggestions from which I have benefited greatly. His painstaking reading of the original manuscript has provided me a model of careful scholarship. Three Ritschl scholars—Professors Brian Gerrish, Philip Hefner, and Darrell Jodock—have since read this study in its revised form and have materially aided me with their thoughtful, detailed responses. Obviously I do not wish to burden any of these individuals with responsibility for the errors and shortcomings that remain; frequently their counsel was better than my ability to act on it. A special measure of thanks is also due my esteemed colleagues in the province of historical studies at Union—Professors Cyril C. Richardson, Robert T. Handy, and Robert W. Lynn—for their sustained interest in this project and unfailing encouragement. And I especially want to thank my wife, Norma, for her salutary neglect of this entire enterprise and for the gentle reminder that there are more things in heaven and earth than dreamed of in a scholar's study.

New York, N. Y.   **D. W. L.**

CONTENTS

ABBREVIATIONS

J. & R. I
: *Die christliche Lehre von der Rechtfertigung und Versöhnung.* Erster Band. *Die Geschichte der Lehre.* Bonn, 1st ed., 1870, 2nd ed., 1882 = 3rd ed., 1889. Trans. from the first ed. by John S. Black, *A Critical History of the Christian Doctrine of Justification and Reconciliation.* Edinburgh, 1872.

R. u. V. I, 2nd ed.
: Second edition of *Die christliche Lehre von der Rechtfertigung und Versöhnung.* Erster Band. *Die Geschichte der Lehre.* Bonn, 1882.

J. & R. III
: *Die christliche Lehre von der Rechtfertigung und Versöhnung.* Dritter Band. *Die positive Entwickelung der Lehre.* Bonn, 1st ed., 1874, 2nd ed., 1883, 3rd ed., 1889 = 4th ed., 1895. Trans. from the third ed. by H. R. Mackintosh and A. B. Macaulay, *The Christian Doctrine of Justification and Reconciliation: The Positive Development of the Doctrine.* Edinburgh, 1900. (Reprinted, Clifton, N. J., 1966.)

Instruction
: *Unterricht in der christlichen Religion.* Bonn, 1st ed., 1875, 2nd ed., 1881, 3rd ed., 1886 = 4th ed., 1890 = 5th ed., 1895. Trans. from the fourth ed. by Alice Mead Swing, *Instruction in the Christian Religion,* printed in Albert T. Swing, *The Theology of Albrecht Ritschl* (New York, 1901), pp. 171-286. [Paragraph numbers are supplied in parentheses.]

Festrede
: *Festrede am vierten Seculartage der Geburt Martin Luthers, 10. November, 1883,* in *Drei akademische Reden* (Bonn, 1887), pp. 5-30.

13

Pietismus	*Geschichte des Pietismus*, 3 vols. Bonn, 1880-1886.
Leben	Otto Ritschl, *Albrecht Ritschls Leben*, 2 vols. Freiburg i. B., 1892, 1896. [Vol. I covers the years 1822-1864; Vol. II, 1864-1889.]
WA	*D. Martin Luthers Werke*. Kritische Gesamtausgabe. Weimar, 1883- .
LW	*Luther's Works*. American Edition. General editors, Jaroslav Pelikan and Helmut T. Lehmann. St. Louis and Philadelphia, 1955- .
Romans Lectures	*Luther: Lectures on Romans*, ed. and trans. Wilhelm Pauck. Vol. XV in the Library of Christian Classics. Philadelphia, 1961.
BC	*The Book of Concord: The Confessions of the Evangelical Lutheran Church*, ed. and trans. Theodore G. Tappert, in collaboration with Jaroslav Pelikan, Robert H. Fischer, and Arthur C. Piepkorn. Philadelphia, 1959.

[For recent translations of the "Prolegomena" to *The History of Pietism; Theology and Metaphysics*; and *Instruction in the Christian Religion*, see *Albrecht Ritschl: Three Essays*, trans. and with an Introduction by Philip Hefner. Philadelphia, 1972.]

INTRODUCTION: RITSCHL AND LUTHER

1. A FRESH PERSPECTIVE ON RITSCHL'S THEOLOGY

During the past two decades there has transpired a discernible renascence in Ritschl scholarship. This renewed attention directed to "the last of the Lutheran Church fathers," as Adolf von Harnack styled him, is evidenced in the increasing volume of monographs, dissertations, and journal articles devoted to various aspects of Ritschl's theology.[1] There has been growing recognition, in the wake of the so-called dialectical or neo-orthodox theology, that the great liberal theologians of the later nineteenth and early twentieth centuries, among whom Ritschl was certainly preeminent, have continued relevance for present-day theological endeavors. In an insightful manner they encountered and came to grips with certain problems which are still very much with us, such as the relation of Christ to culture, faith to history, and Christianity to the world religions—problems which have in fact become even more acute in our contemporary context. Indeed the theology of neo-Orthodoxy has been found wanting on precisely these issues (being accused, for example, of acosmic and ahistorical tendencies).[2] At the same time this Ritschl renascence has largely been occasioned by a pervasive scholarly concern to give Ritschl his historical due, and so to hasten the exit of that "passing cloud" under which his work has languished so long.[3]

With the advent of dialectical theology and the attendant decline of liberalism and the Social Gospel, Ritschl's theology (which in America was primarily associated with Henry Churchill King, A. C. McGiffert, William Adams Brown, and Walter Rauschenbusch) also passed from the scene or, more accurately, was peremptorily dismissed.[4] Karl Barth's atti-

[1] See the bibliography for a listing of recent studies of Ritschl's theology. Harnack's remark is to be found in his essay "Zur gegenwärtigen Lage des Protestantismus," in *Reden und Aufsätze*, II (Giessen, 1906), 139.

[2] See, for example, Jürgen Moltmann, *Theology of Hope* (New York, 1967), esp. Chapter I ("Eschatology and Revelation"), pp. 37-94.

[3] Already more than thirty-five years ago H. R. Mackintosh wrote in his *Types of Modern Theology: Schleiermacher to Barth* (London, 1937): "Ritschl at the moment belongs, like Tennyson, to the 'middle distance,' too far for gratitude, too near for reverence. He is behind a passing cloud to-day" (p. 141, n. 1).

[4] See Kenneth Cauthen, *The Impact of American Religious Liberalism* (New

tude toward Ritschl, for example, has bordered on the overtly hostile and is reflected in the harsh, cursory treatment accorded him in Barth's history of nineteenth-century theology.[5] Ritschl's theology is there considered but a passing phase in modern Protestant thought, a transitional phenomenon in a century which began and ended with the regnant influence of Schleiermacher. Ritschl's significance is seen in the enthusiasm with which he returned to "the theoretical and practical philosophy of the Enlightenment in its perfected [i.e., Kantian] form," so that his theology marks the actual fulfillment of the Enlightenment's preoccupation with man in himself.[6] Ritschl is charged with the *Verbürgerlichung* or acculturation of Evangelical theology, namely, its conformation to the bourgeois ideals of the age of Bismarck. Until the recent reappraisals Barth's critique has largely shaped the course of subsequent Ritschl study, supporting that reading of his theology which finds therein foremost instances of religious subjectivism, moralism, anthropocentrism, etc.

The present study, by contrast, attempts to disengage itself from this still widespread neo-orthodox critique and to return to the "original" Ritschl through the medium of his explicit interpretation and general use of Luther's theology. Thus it also purports to afford a less polemical and more intrinsic point of entry into Ritschl's theological program by examining, elucidating, and evaluating the central, determinative significance which Ritschl accords Luther's theology. This particular approach to Ritschl has grown out of the conviction that heretofore justice has not been done to his avowed commitments to Reformation theology. And this conviction, in turn, has been reinforced by some brief remarks of Jaroslav Pelikan in his editorial preface to a recent study of Ritschl's theological methodology. Pelikan calls attention to the necessary ingredients of any fair and adequate reappraisal of Ritschl's place in modern theology:

> For Ritschl to be rediscovered and his role in the making of modern theology to be reassessed, it is necessary to look not only at the constructive proposals he made for the theological interpretation of the Christian message, but at the foundation of those proposals in his own interpretation of Christian history.[7]

York, 1962), for an indirect assessment of Ritschl's influence on American theology. Samuel L. Akers, *Some British Reactions to Ritschlianism* (Yale Studies in Religion, Number 8, Scottdale, Pa., 1934), offers a parallel treatment of Ritschl's reception in Great Britain.

[5] Karl Barth, "Ritschl" (Chapter XI), in *Protestant Thought: From Rousseau to Ritschl* (New York, 1959), pp. 390-97.

[6] *Ibid.*, pp. 391-92.

[7] Jaroslav Pelikan, "Editor's Preface" to Philip Hefner, *Faith and the Vitalities of History: A Theological Study Based on the Work of Albrecht Ritschl* (New York, 1966), p. ix.

Previous Ritschl scholarship has, of course, primarily concerned itself with his constructive proposals, particularly his important contributions to the philosophy of religion (his anti-metaphysical bias and theory of value judgments) and his widely influential social-ethical interpretation of the cardinal Christian teachings. As a result much less attention has been directed to Ritschl's interpretation of Christian history, his profound and far-ranging historical labors, and the concomitant grounding of his theology in the tradition of classical (Reformation) Protestantism. This study attempts, therefore, to redress this deficiency and so is offered as one further contribution to the current reassessment of Ritschl's theological achievement.

I shall have to demonstrate, of course, that Ritschl himself acknowledged Luther's theology (in whole or in part) as a norm for his endeavors, lest it appear that his achievements are being measured by some alien or purely arbitrary standard. The simple fact that Ritschl was a German Protestant theologian initially suggests that Luther would hold a prominent place in his thought. As John Dillenberger wryly observed:

> The inner compulsions of practically every German historian of theology, and of theologians who are not primarily historians, to study Luther and to use him for systematic purposes is hard for Anglo-Saxons to understand. But without accepting this fact, little can be understood of German theology.[8]

In addition there is certainly abundant prima facie evidence for Ritschl's depth involvement with Luther's theology. Even a cursory reading of the first and third volumes of his magnum opus reveals numerous careful expositions and analyses of Luther's central teachings, while shorter works such as the *Instruction in the Christian Religion* and the *Christian Perfection* repeatedly invoke Luther's support. H. R. Mackintosh justly noted that "no modern German theologian has ever been more eager to have Luther on his side." [9] Yet the secondary literature, while generally acknowledging Ritschl's relation to Luther, has failed to examine this relationship in detail and depth.[10] To this latter task I address myself.

[8] John Dillenberger, *God Hidden and Revealed* (Philadelphia, 1953), p. 37.

[9] Mackintosh, *Types of Modern Theology*, p. 157.

[10] A notable exception is Otto Wolff's excellent study, *Die Haupttypen der neueren Lutherdeutung* (Stuttgart, 1938), which devotes a lengthy and perceptive chapter to Ritschl's Luther interpretation (Dritter Abschnitt, "Der Typ der idealistisch-reformatorischen Synthese in seiner Selbstauflösung," pp. 121-236). I gratefully acknowledge my indebtedness to this sympathetic appraisal for numerous fruitful insights and bibliographical references. Wolff, however, does not analyze the significance of Ritschl's Luther study for his historical researches, nor does he examine it in light of Ritschl's own contemporary apologetic and polemical requirements.

17

I propose, therefore, to offer a fresh perspective on Ritschl's theology by approaching it in light of his critical dialogue or *Auseinandersetzung* with Luther's theology. I certainly do not contend that Ritschl's encounter with Luther supplies the only correct perspective, or even the most important one, for the study of his theology. Such claims would scarcely befit an investigation so restricted in scope and intention. But I do maintain that this viewpoint helps to uncover essential features of Ritschl's theological undertaking which might otherwise be overlooked or minimized: the actual nature and extent of his indebtedness to his Reformation heritage; the indisputable congruity (as well as incongruity) between his leading theological themes and Luther's major motifs; the basic coherence of his historical and systematic labors; his remarkable vocational self-understanding as a "reformer" of Protestantism, impelled to that task out of intended fidelity to Luther's original but long neglected insights; his status as a defender of the "Protestant principle" in the face of contemporary attacks on the viability of Reformation patterns of life and thought. In summary, my fundamental contention is that Ritschl's Luther interpretation is a decisive factor in his overarching theological enterprise and affords an adequate, if limited, basis for appraising his specific goals and accomplishments; that Ritschl's involvement with Luther provides a significant interpretive key to his total theological program, both historical and systematic; and that to study Ritschl in light of his creative encounter with Luther and Reformation thought is to enter into the heart of his own theology and, most importantly, to do so on its own terms.

From these brief introductory remarks it will be seen that I am actually undertaking two primary and interrelated tasks in this presentation. In the first place, I hope to make a substantive contribution to contemporary Ritschl scholarship by approaching and analyzing Ritschl's total theological system from the viewpoint of his involvement with Reformation thought, particularly Luther's theology. I am persuaded that this latter viewpoint is neither an arbitrary, artificial one nor of merely tangential significance, but is at once integral to Ritschl's own understanding of his labors and productive of valuable insights into the structure and content of Ritschl's historical and constructive theology. I have labeled this viewpoint a "fresh perspective" on Ritschl's theology in explicit opposition to a veritable host of stereotyped criticisms which still abound in the province of Ritschl study and which in fact seem to turn on the unexamined assumption that "Ritschl" and "Reformation" are two utterly distinct and irreconcilable magnitudes. In articulating this revised *Ritschlbild*

I have eagerly and gratefully seized on various suggestive clues and hints provided by earlier Ritschl interpreters, foremost among them Otto Wolff. Perhaps I should add that my fundamental aim is not the revivification of Albrecht Ritschl's theological system—for that is neither possible nor desirable—but rather the rehabilitation of his theological reputation, which has been not only needlessly tarnished but also frequently distorted beyond recognition.

Secondly, I propose to explicate in detail, and at length, the major features of Ritschl's Luther interpretation. In this sense the present essay is offered as a contribution to the history of modern Luther scholarship. I am also persuaded that Ritschl's Luther interpretation has given a vital impetus to modern Luther research and actually stands in the immediate background of the twentieth-century Luther renaissance, although for a variety of reasons Ritschl's contributions in this realm have been generally overlooked or accorded only cursory notice. In any case, even if one were to discount Ritschl's role as a precursor of Luther study today, it is obvious that a specific knowledge of his Luther interpretation is requisite for any informed study of the Luther scholarship of such figures as Wilhelm Herrmann, Adolf von Harnack, Ernst Troeltsch, and Karl Holl.

2. REMARKS ON PROCEDURE AND METHODOLOGY

As indicated previously, it is my intention to investigate both Ritschl's explicit interpretation and general use of Luther's theology. By "general use" I mean the way in which Ritschl takes up his Luther interpretation into the total fabric of his theology, rather than his full-scale elaboration of any single theme derived from, or informed by, his Luther study. To attempt to pursue the latter course—e.g., to examine and criticize in detail Ritschl's doctrine of God or his theological epistemology in light of his Luther research—would in effect transform this investigation into a form of systematic theology. My primary interest has been the more modest one of determining what was in fact Ritschl's understanding of Luther's theology and what role if any that understanding played in his own theological enterprise. Of course, since the focal point of his Luther scholarship was the doctrine of justification by faith, my exposition, analysis, and critique necessarily revolve around Ritschl's interpretation and use of this central idea. But such a procedure is dictated by historical-textual rather than systematic considerations.

In line with these historical-textual considerations, and by way of a careful examination of Ritschl's literary corpus and relevant secondary sources, I have sought in Chapters I and II to determine Luther's overarching place in Ritschl's theology. A number of preliminary questions have guided this inquiry: Why is Luther important for Ritschl, even of decisive significance? What are the major ingredients of his Luther interpretation, i.e., on what aspects of Luther's thought does he concentrate? And how does he take up into his dogmatics and historical-critical labors the results of his Luther study? In order to answer such questions with a degree of completeness, I first present in Chapter I a summary statement of the general features of Ritschl's interpretation, with particular attention to Luther's place in his systematic theology. There the focus is on Ritschl's relation to nineteenth-century Luther scholarship, his use of the primary sources, his appropriation of major motifs in Luther's thought along with his basic critique of Luther's presumed inadequacies, and his impetus to Luther studies among his disciples. The purpose of the first chapter is not to criticize Ritschl's findings but simply to present them in some detail in order to show that Ritschl both followed Luther on important points and at the same time defined his own position as a necessary corrective to Luther's failings.

This study of Ritschl's Luther interpretation is not limited, however, to a specification of Luther's place in Ritschl's systematic theology. Chapter II is accordingly devoted to an exposition of Ritschl's Luther interpretation within the larger framework of his interpretation of the Reformation and the subsequent history of Protestantism. While many historians of modern religious thought have correctly remarked on Luther's significance for Ritschl's constructive theology, few have indicated, much less analyzed, the way in which Ritschl's interpretation of Luther and Reformation theology informed his massive historical investigations. For that reason it is of utmost importance to see that Ritschl did not merely approach Luther as a seminal thinker in the history of Christian thought, from whom he could appropriate various leading themes. It is no less true that he viewed certain features of Luther's theology as determinative for the inner life of Protestantism, as an index to Protestantism's vitality in both thought and practice. Thus Luther informed Ritschl's theology in a decidedly authoritative or normative fashion.

As is further elaborated in both Chapters I and II, Ritschl's approach to, and appropriation of, Luther's fundamental ideas exhibit a recurrent pattern or typical *modus operandi*. That is, he constantly attempted to move behind the various "Luthers" of the received and current theological traditions in order to lay hold of the authentic Luther (or young

Luther) who stood at the inception of the Reformation. Ritschl was convinced that the seminal practical ideas of the young Luther had never come to fruition in the historical course of Protestantism. Therefore he envisioned his own task, a decidedly reformatory obligation, as that of revitalizing Protestantism by reappropriating and restructuring Luther's original insights. It is obvious that his projected work of reformulation actually presupposed the successful recovery of Luther's leading ideas in their original form. Hence in Chapters III and IV I pursue my dominant historical interest by examining this latter process of recovery (rather than that of systematic reconstruction). To this end I inquire into the adequacy of Ritschl's comprehension of Luther's "practical root ideas," in particular his interpretation of Luther on justification.

In Chapter III, after presenting a brief summary of Ritschl's primary findings, I specifically consider the accuracy of his portrait of the young Luther. Since Ritschl repeatedly played off the early Luther (*ca.* 1515-1520) against the later Luther (and Lutheranism), confidently asserting that he had finally recovered the original Luther, the validity of his entire Luther interpretation depends greatly on the accuracy of his findings regarding the young Luther. In Chapter III, therefore, I test these findings by closely examining Ritschl's comprehension of both the young Luther's doctrine of justification and his distinction between law and gospel. In Chapter IV I then pursue the critical judgments reached in Chapter III and seek to determine the fundamental defect of Ritschl's interpretation. I suggest that the basic failing of this interpretation, from which its other limitations derive, is its obfuscation of Luther's theology of the cross as the latter comes to expression in Luther's understanding of God's dynamic word. The summary critique presented in these two chapters especially addresses the larger question: In the process of supposedly recovering the real Luther (in contradistinction, for example, to the "Melanchthonized" Luther of Orthodoxy), did Ritschl in fact apprehend the integral Luther? I do not thereby intend to suggest that he should have taken over in massive fashion the whole of Luther's theology into his own (which in any case would have been a manifest impossibility). I do ask, however, whether he correctly pinpointed Luther's seminal thoughts, as he claimed to have done, and whether he appropriated the full range of those thoughts. In answering such a question one might be led to conclude that Ritschl himself, no less than his opponents, failed to recover the authentic Luther.

Chapters III and IV are essentially negative in tone and intention, centering as they do on the patent shortcomings of Ritschl's interpretation. Chapter V concludes my investigation with a positive appraisal of Ritschl's achievements in the light of his own historical situation. That is to say, the ultimate significance of his interpretation and use of Luther's theology does not wholly depend on the accuracy of his scholarship or the tenability of his claims. Indeed at numerous points he could quite legitimately call Luther to his support. More importantly, however, as I shall seek to demonstrate, his failings as well as successes assume a meaningful logic of their own once they are sympathetically examined in the context of the pressing theological problems with which he was constrained to grapple.

Having thus outlined the substantive course of the argument, I must now indicate more precisely the scope and methodological assumptions of this essay:

(*a*) This treatise does not purport to be an exhaustive study of either Ritschl's or Luther's theology. Therefore no attempt is made to provide a detailed comparison-contrast of a whole complex of individual doctrines or leading ideas in both men. While such an approach might be of interest, it tends to be atomistic and would really fail to uncover Luther's fundamental import for Ritschl. I am primarily concerned with an act of historical appropriation: the creative interpretive venture whereby Ritschl seeks to re-present, or render contemporaneous, a past phenomenon. Hence I am interested in a dynamic interaction between two theologies, not a static juxtaposition of one theology alongside another (where both would be viewed as self-contained totalities which could then be compared point for point).

(*b*) A certain ambiguity attaches to the word "interpretation." It can refer both to a process or development (the process of finding something out) and to an end product or result (the "findings" themselves). Here the focus is on the actual results of Ritschl's Luther interpretation, with a view to their specific function in the system. Thus I do not undertake a genetic approach to the problem, i.e., a chronological tracing of the development of Ritschl's understanding of Luther in an attempt to reconstruct this process of appropriation. Ritschl began his depth study of Luther early in 1857, and so I assume that by the period of the major works (1870 ff.) his Luther interpretation was basically complete.[11]

---

[11] See Otto Ritschl, *Leben*, I, 294 ff. "While Ritschl was still in the process of publishing the second edition of his *Entstehung der altkatholischen Kirche* [1857], he directed his interests to a new field of labor where they were firmly to remain for many years. He began his studies on the doctrine of justification, commencing specifically with his researches into Luther" (p. 294).

(c) I am also concerned with determining the adequacy of Ritschl's interpretation. But how is such adequacy to be measured? What criteria are to be employed and what assumptions control this act of appraisal? The problem of historical evaluation raises a variety of complex issues. What does it mean, for example, to hold that Ritschl is "faithful" (or "unfaithful") to Luther's own position? Some critics might maintain that only a demonstrable repristination of Luther's theology would be the truly adequate interpretation. On this model Luther's theology stands as a self-contained whole which must be taken over *in toto* if it is to be faithfully reproduced. Such a position is rejected here, however, because it in effect denies or at least evades the hermeneutical problem, namely, that new historical contexts inescapably require new perspectives on any past phenomenon precisely if that phenomenon is to have continued validity and relevance. This latter proviso means that Ritschl's Luther interpretation does not merely belong to the long history of Luther scholarship but at the same time discloses Luther's theology as itself a present force operative in history. Thus Luther's theology is known *in actu*, just as we often best comprehend some past phenomenon in terms of what it has become. It may well be true, therefore, that Ritschl gives noteworthy expression to elements of Luther's theology which in Luther himself (or in the sixteenth-century setting) did not fully come to expression. Similarly one may also employ Ritschl's Luther interpretation to clarify central features of Ritschl's own theology which might otherwise remain unclear.

The dominant historical-textual concern of this essay determines the leading criteria in the light of which Ritschl's Luther interpretation will be evaluated. These are principally three in number:

1. *Ritschl's reading of his primary sources.* Is Ritchl's summary of the young Luther's theological position warranted by the primary sources? Has he correctly reconstructed the development of Luther's original views on justification? Does he do justice to various statements of the young Luther which might serve to call his interpretation into question or require significant modifications? And has the more recent Luther scholarship confirmed Ritschl's reading of the sources, especially in light of the recovery of Luther's earliest biblical lectures and commentaries?

2. *The impact of polemical considerations.* Ritschl was a theologian much given to controversy, as might be expected of a theological reformer. One often discerns a polemical intent, as distinct from purely expository interests, underlying his interpretation and use of Luther. He values Luther as a bulwark against past and present deformations of Protestantism; he criticizes Luther at those points where he discovers

continuity between these deformations and the Reformer himself. Thus Luther stands forth in Ritschl's outlook as both alien and ally. This intense polemical tendency raises the critical question: Did Ritschl perhaps too hastily identify Luther's position with either his own viewpoint or that of his adversaries, without sufficient regard for Luther's uniqueness and possible independence of *both* viewpoints? The threat of historical anachronism always attends such a reading of the remote past in the light of the present or less remote past.

3. *The impact of a new historical situation.* Between Ritschl and Luther stand the Enlightenment, Kant, Schleiermacher, and the representatives of classical German idealism, as well as the subsequent breakdown of the Hegelian synthesis in left-wing critics such as Strauss and Feuerbach. In short, during the intervening centuries those revolutionary movements of thought transpired which have decisively shaped the so-called modern mind. And Ritschl at all events considered himself a modern man! At stake was not only the truth of the Christian message but also its truthfulness to the situation of contemporary man.[12] Hence Ritschl's Luther interpretation as a matter of course exhibits a dialectic between his adherence to the "tradition" (of which Scripture and the Reformers were the foremost representatives) and his apologetic concerns vis-à-vis the modern world. There is accordingly a decided tension between the tradition and Ritschl's own *Sitz im Leben,* a tension which is the ineluctable correlate of the hermeneutical problem. Methodologically considered, however, such a dual commitment to past and present should entail some form of interpretive procedure which distinguishes between the descriptive task (what *did* a given historical entity mean in its own context?) and the hermeneutical task proper (what *does* that past entity now mean in a new context?). It is helpful to inquire whether Ritschl was sufficiently aware of such a tension between these two tasks (or tenses) and, if so, whether he actually succeeded in maintaining it. Or did he perhaps neglect or otherwise overcome this tension before it could pose any serious problems for his interpretation? In other words, if a past phenomenon is actually to be re-presented, then it must first be comprehended in its own historical integrity before it can be translated into a new context. Historians have thus often remarked on the need for empathy in all acts of historical interpretation, for the patient endeavor to live within a past phenomenon before pronouncing on its present relevance and meaning.

[12] See Christoph Senft, *Wahrhaftigkeit und Wahrheit: Die Theologie des 19. Jahrhunderts zwischen Orthodoxie und Aufklärung* (Tübingen, 1956), esp. Chapter IV ("Ritschl: Der Glaube als Gabe und Tat"), pp. 124-66.

1 LEADING FEATURES OF RITSCHL'S LUTHER INTERPRETATION

1. RITSCHL THE LUTHER SCHOLAR

In 1921 Wilhelm Herrmann, who along with Adolf von Harnack is justly regarded as the greatest of Ritschl's disciples, assessed the master's theological achievement in these terms:

A. Ritschl had the power to rescue Luther's work from that ruin into which it had fallen, even among those who comported themselves as the most loyal of Luther's heirs. For he once more brought the Christian faith into plain view as that life set free for earnest men through the person of Jesus. . . . He himself welcomed the duty of saving Luther's work from the corruption into which it had fallen, particularly among those who supposed themselves the Reformer's most faithful successors.[1]

Thus Herrmann, in what must at first glance seem a surprising judgment, focused unhesitatingly on Ritschl's preoccupation with Luther as the key to his greatness and the basis for his lasting contributions to theological scholarship. Whereas today we think immediately of Ritschl the historian of theology or the systematician, Herrmann has memorialized Ritschl the Luther scholar. In Ritschl's relation to Luther he discerned the underlying dynamic of his mentor's labors. More specifically, he pointed to Ritschl's self-imposed task of rescue—his vocational sense of performing a reformatory duty, especially vis-à-vis contemporary Lutheranism—as the heart of the Ritschlian program. For Ritschl attempted the revalidation of that evangelical view of life, grounded on the person and work of Christ, to which Luther gave classic expression, but which subsequent Protestantism had failed to make its own. Hence, on Herrmann's view, Ritschl like Luther himself and in conscious dependence on Luther aimed at the restoration of the authentic evangelical *Lebensideal*.

[1] "Albrecht Ritschl, seine Grösse und seine Schranke," in *Festgabe von Fachgenossen und Freunden A. von Harnack zum siebzigsten Geburtstag dargebracht*, ed. Karl Holl (Tübingen, 1921), p. 405. Cf. Ritschl's explicit disdain for those "exclusivistic Lutherans" who indeed "loudly proclaim the fact that they belong to the Lutheran Church, but in reality are attached only to the interests of a quasi-conservative party within that Church," and who thus debase "the genuine orthodoxy [i.e., catholicity] of Luther" himself. J. & R. I, 159-60, 164.

Herrmann's evaluation will sound strange or narrow or even perverse only to those accustomed to view Ritschl primarily as the father of the now discredited Social Gospel and of a moribund liberalism, or as the foremost representative of nineteenth-century *Kulturprotestantismus*, or as the prime mover in the back-to-Kant movement within late nineteenth-century theology, or particularly in terms of Barth's caricature of him as "the very epitome of the national-liberal German bourgeois of the age of Bismarck." [2] Herrmann's assessment, of course, might be attributed to an uncritical party spirit or suspected of outright inaccuracy. Yet eminent non-Ritschlian scholars have echoed his estimate of Ritschl's significance. Horst Stephan, for example, also claimed: "It was primarily Ritschl's relationship with Luther that, alongside the power of his theological thinking, secured his ascendancy over all other theological leaders of his time." [3] In a similar vein Otto Wolff contended that "Ritschl, for the first time since Schleiermacher, led dogmatic thinking in its multisided totality back to Luther." Indeed, concluded Wolff, "the 'Lutherness' of the Ritschlian theology is the native soil for the fully ripened Luther understanding of our own day." [4] And more recently Walther von Loewenich, the Erlangen Luther scholar, has affirmed that "Ritschl is the first of the modern systematicians to make Luther's thought the foundation of his own theological system. . . . With Ritschl Luther research achieved general significance for the first time in the nineteenth century." [5]

In fact the majority of Ritschl's critics, including a significant number of British and American scholars, have found some occasion, if only in passing, to allude to Ritschl's intensive and extensive involvement with Luther.[6] Nevertheless there have been few noteworthy attempts to examine

[2] Barth, "Ritschl," p. 392.

[3] *Luther in den Wandlungen seiner Kirche*, 2nd ed. (Berlin, 1951), p. 80.

[4] Wolff, *Die Haupttypen*, pp. 176, 234-35.

[5] *Luther und der Neuprotestantismus* (Witten, 1963), pp. 92, 109.

[6] Cf. Robert Mackintosh, *Albrecht Ritschl and His School* (London, 1915), p. 14: "Definitely, then, Ritschlianism is a Protestant, a very Protestant, theology. It appeals to the spirit rather than the letter, but is to give us a distillate of the genuine Luther. . . . Is it not of interest that the whole Protestant world should be stirred by a theology built neither on the lines of radicalism nor on those of reaction, but seeking to go back to Luther's best teachings, while employing for the exposition and defence of old principles all the resources of modern knowledge?" So also Albert T. Swing, *The Theology of Albrecht Ritschl* (New York, 1901), p. 35: "The relation which Ritschl sustains to Luther is the most important of all for the understanding of our subject. It is Luther who is Ritschl's greatest helper, and he seeks to turn the young men of Germany from the later scholastic Lutheranism to the earlier religious Luther." Most recently David Mueller, *An Introduction to the Theology of Albrecht Ritschl* (Phila-

the precise ingredients of Ritschl's Luther interpretation, showing how he took up Luther's central themes into the fabric of his own theology. Surely one of the major ironies of recent theological history is that Ritschl's Luther scholarship should have prepared the way for the eventual dissolution of his own system by giving a decisive impetus to twentieth-century Luther research, and so to that neo-orthodox attack on his theology conducted in the name of the Reformers, only for Ritschl himself to be neglected as a leading Luther scholar and an important forerunner of the Luther renaissance. Not only is memory short, but theological warfare has not infrequently been total warfare and the victors (even when they proclaim the *pax Dei*) are not customarily inclined to acknowledge the indispensable aid of the vanquished. In any event, a judicious and more dispassionate evaluation of Ritschl's total accomplishment certainly demands a closer scrutiny of his creative encounter with Luther's theology. The remainder of this chapter will be devoted to a survey of the leading features of this encounter.

2. RITSCHL'S LUTHER STUDY IN ITS CONTEMPORARY SETTING

Among the major theologians of the nineteenth century Ritschl occupied a unique place in that he constructed his system in conscious dependence on the fundamental motifs of Luther's theology.[7] While Luther scholarship clearly attained new levels of scholarly completeness and precision in that history-minded century, as evidenced in the text-critical Erlangen and Weimar editions of Luther's collected works, only Ritschl set out by design to bring Luther's theology to contemporary expression in a multifaceted, comprehensive, and coordinated statement

---

delphia, 1969), has also called attention to Ritschl's "continuing involvement with the theology of the Reformation as it came to expression in various movements in nineteenth century Germany such as Lutheran confessionalism and Lutheran Pietism— neither of which he could acknowledge as the legitimate extension of the intention of the Reformers" (p. 17).

[7] In addition to the previously cited studies by Stephan, Wolff, and von Loewenich, see the following for a treatment of Ritschl's place within the larger framework of modern Luther scholarship: Heinrich Bornkamm, *Luther im Spiegel der deutschen Geistesgeschichte* (Heidelberg, 1955); Friedrich Wilhelm Kantzenbach, "Lutherverständnis zwischen Erweckung und Idealismus," *Luther* (Zeitschrift der Luther-Gesellschaft) 36 (1965): 9-30; W. von Loewenich, "Wandlungen des Evangelischen Lutherbildes im 19. und 20. Jahrhundert," *Wandlungen des Lutherbildes: Studien und Berichte der Katholischen Akademie in Bayern*, ed. Karl Forster, 36 (Würzburg, 1966): 51-76; Ernst Wolf, "Luthers Erbe?" *Evangelische Theologie* 6 (1946-47): 81-115; 310-12.

of the Christian faith. The Luther of popular piety and national sentiment had received fervent acclaim in the Reformation jubilee of 1817. Luther the hero of faith lived on anew in the theological representatives of the Awakening following the national wars of liberation. Luther the *Kirchenvater*, the confessional Luther, was reappropriated by the theologians of so-called neo-Lutheranism (Vilmar, Löhe, Kliefoth). Groundbreaking histories of the Reformation portrayed Luther within the broader context of his age in order to underscore his far-reaching significance for sixteenth-century socio-political developments, no less than for religious and churchly affairs.[8] Penetrating monographs devoted to Luther's cardinal doctrines appeared in ever-increasing numbers, along with several noteworthy studies of Luther's total theology.[9] And libraries and archives were searched for original manuscripts of the Reformer's lectures as part of the Rankean inspired scientific return *ad fontes*. It remained for

[8] Foremost among these histories was the epoch-making work of Leopold von Ranke, *Deutsche Geschichte im Zeitalter der Reformation*, 6 vols., 1839-1847. This work directed German historical writing on the Reformation well into the twentieth century.

[9] Ritschl's most frequently cited secondary source on Luther's theology was Julius Köstlin's comprehensive study, *Luthers Theologie in ihrer geschichtlichen Entwicklung und ihrem Zusammenhange*, 2 vols., 1863 (2nd ed., 1883). Köstlin's major work, *Martin Luther: Sein Leben und seine Schriften*, 2 vols., 1875 (re-edited by Georg Kawerau, 2 vols., 1903), guided Luther research for several decades. Special mention, as perhaps the most significant Luther study of the nineteenth century, must be accorded Theodosius Harnack's work, *Luthers Theologie mit besonderer Beziehung auf seine Versöhnungs- und Erlösungslehre*, Vol. I, 1862; Vol. II, 1886 (2nd ed., 1927). In the preface to the second volume, Harnack directly attacked Ritschl's Luther interpretation for its neglect of basic motifs in Luther's theology, e.g., the wrath and hiddenness of God, the vicarious satisfaction of Christ, Luther's relationship to mysticism, etc. Yet in its own age this important work remained largely without effect on the theological controversy over the "real Luther." Harnack primarily concerned himself with the mature Luther (or with what he called the "total" Luther). Ritschl in effect conceded the partial validity of Harnack's interpretation insofar as he turned completely to the "young Luther" for support of his program. Thus Ritschl's recourse to the early Luther was in part polemically motivated and led him to posit a severe discontinuity between the early and the later Luther. One should also take note of Harnack's assertion that Ritschl's *Lutherdeutung* tended to distort and debase Luther's theology by annexing it to a questionable Kantian moralism. Cf. *Luthers Theologie*, II, 22: "It is not at all permissible, as Ritschl has attempted to do, to effect a theological union between Luther—who wishes to know nothing whatsoever of a 'merely moral wisdom'—and Kant, the foremost representative of moralism. Or one can do so only by comprehending Luther in a totally one-sided fashion, thus distorting and degrading him." This judgment has often been repeated (esp. since the advent of neo-Orthodoxy) in an increasingly stereotyped fashion and thus in such a way as to preclude debate. To my mind it is a charge which, if not without a certain warrant, can be made only upon careful qualification and only *after* due consideration for the positive accomplishments of Ritschl's Luther study. See below, p. 38, n. 34.

Ritschl, however, to attempt to bring these multifarious impulses to fruition in a masterful synthetic fashion, articulating Luther's leading themes with architectonic breadth in a system that was no less original for all its acknowledged dependence on the Reformer.

Ritschl, however, did not stop with the descriptive task, with a penetrating historical investigation. Rather, displaying characteristic sobriety, he undertook the far more demanding hermeneutical task of according Luther's insights continued relevance and vitality in a new historical context by allowing them to shape and inform his own constructive endeavors. Ritschl's Luther interpretation was accordingly an act of daring. To be sure this venture involved the possibility that Luther's theology would perhaps be too hastily assimilated to a new cultural situation and so abridged or distorted in the interests of a new apologetic task; that it would be invoked in support of a program whose presuppositions might be alien to its own original intentions or perspectives; in short, that Luther's powerful utterances might lose something of their own primal resonance and vitality and thus forfeit their own compelling accents. But a theology which is truly historical, which is fully cognizant that present interpretation is always *re*-interpretation, must ever run such risks. And the measure of Ritschl's theological greatness is that he sought to take such risks responsibly by a painstaking, long-term confrontation with the "historical Luther" predicated on a careful study of the original sources.

Ritschl especially showed himself a pioneer of modern Luther research by his expert handling of the available sources, in particular by his intense concentration on the works of the young Luther: the 1515-19 writings contained in the *Vollständige Reformationsacta und Documenta* edited by Valentin Ernst Löscher (3 vols., 1720 ff.). He expressed a decided preference for the early sermons and tracts dating from the period prior to the outbreak of the indulgence controversy (1515-17).[10] In these writings Luther gave felicitous expression to his new practical-religious interpretation of justification, doing so apart from any pressure to counter the arguments of his opponents (a pressure which could subtly alter both the original religious intent of his interpretation and its systematic form of presentation). In addition to Löscher's collection, Ritschl's primary source was the so-called Halle edition of Luther's works issued in twenty-four volumes by J. G. Walch (1740-53). He also employed the available

---

[10] J. & R. I, 134: "The preference I give to these last above all other writings of Luther, I found upon the fact that he suffered himself to be led by the attacks of his adversaries to a change of form in his position that is not immaterial to the proper apprehension of the question."

volumes of the newer Erlangen edition (1826 ff.) as well as de Wette's critical edition of Luther's correspondence (6 vols., 1825 ff.). Among Luther's writings his favorite, most frequently cited were the great Reformation treatises of 1520, especially the classic *On Christian Liberty*, and the two catechisms. Among the Lutheran Confessions (besides the catechisms) he accorded pride of place to the Augsburg Confession and its Apology.

Within the larger context of nineteenth-century Protestant theology, Ritschl's virtually lifelong concentration on the doctrine of justification, particularly that of Luther, has the overarching significance that thereby the *articulus fundamentalissimus* of Evangelical theology was once more brought to the fore. Ritschl like Luther was fully persuaded that justification is the vital heartbeat, the *sine qua non* of Christian thought, as the introductory sentence to J. & R. I clearly shows: "The Christian doctrine of justification and reconciliation, which I propose to unfold in a scientific manner, constitutes the real center of the theological system." [11] Protestant theology was in all seriousness again asking, or at least intending to ask, Luther's decisive question: How does man appear in the divine estimate? What is his posture *coram Deo?* Christian faith, so Ritschl maintained, does not have to do in the first place with man's own subjective autonomy, his vaunted sense of unlimited self-potential (as in the Enlightenment perspective), nor even with the pious God-consciousness as that manifests itself in the feeling of utter dependence (as in Schleiermacher's view of religion). It inquires above all after the religious relationship which obtains between a righteous God and sinful men, especially as that relationship is expressed in the historical appearance of Jesus of Nazareth, the Son of God and the Church's Lord.

The fundamental human predicament, held Ritschl, is one of alienation: sinful man lives in a state of separation from God and hence, in terms Ritschl appropriated from the Augsburg Confession, he is "without fear of God, without trust in God." [12] The inescapable reality of man's moral turpitude cannot be evaded by authentically Christian thinkers any more than the scrupulous Kant could gloss over the radical evil latent within the heart of "enlightened" man. Christian theology must therefore accord pride of place to the question of the restoration of fellowship with God, the perennial question of divine pardon and faith's response to that

---

[11] *Ibid.*, p. 1. In the German editions of J. & R. I, justification bears the traditional designation: "der Hauptartikel der stehenden und fallenden Kirche." Cf. J. & R. III, 141: forgiveness is "the foundationstone of the Christian religion."

[12] J. & R. III, 170, 333, 341. Cf. Augsburg Confession, II, 1, in BC, p. 29.

pardon. It must attend to the decisive issues of justification and reconciliation. The very fact that Ritschl's attention was riveted on this one cardinal problem—and that the problem was posed in this fashion: as the quest for the nature of the religious relationship between God and men—meant that, by intention at least, Luther's own profound *Heilsfrage* had once more entered the field and that his epoch-making insights might yet again fructify Protestant theology. Whatever one's final evaluation of the adequacy of Ritschl's actual performance to his stated intentions, the fact of those intentions remains and demands full recognition.

3. RITSCHL'S CRITICAL APPROPRIATION OF LUTHER'S MAJOR MOTIFS

Ritschl's prevalent attitude toward Luther was a combination of great respect, indeed reverence for the religious thinker and serious reservations about the theologian. Hence his appropriation of Luther's fundamental motifs displays a self-confessed indebtedness to the transforming insights of the young Luther along with a critical independence of specific doctrinal formulations advanced by the older Luther. On Ritschl's view the Luther of the Reformation's formative years (*ca.* 1515-20) had initially recovered the loftiest piety of the Medieval Church and then gave it new currency by directly opposing it to the prevailing ecclesiastical praxis of his day (especially Rome's penitential system). Luther's creative appropriation and renewal of medieval *sola gratia* piety, in conjunction with his biblical study and nominalist training, provided the further impetus to a penetrating critique of his theological inheritance from Scholasticism. In the process of attacking scholastic theology and defending his own newly achieved perspective, Luther articulated a series of profound insights into the authentic religious meaning of the Church's age-old teaching—insights which had the potential of completely transforming the received doctrinal tradition. Luther loosed the bonds of medieval intellectualism, sacramentalism, and clericalism. Above all, he engineered a radical break with the monastic *contemptus mundi*. In short, he recalled men to a Christianity once more construed as a religion—a new relationship with God based on God's own faithfulness to his redemptive purpose—rather than a system of doctrine and morals handed down by a hierarchical institution.

In all these respects Luther proved himself to be the Reformer of the Church. But when it came to systematizing his insights, reformulating traditional doctrines, moving beyond criticism to construction, Luther lacked both opportunity and the requisite scientific talent to consolidate his gains. Especially because he was ever obliged to defend his position against various counterproposals advanced from within as well as without the Protestant camp, he forfeited that recollection in tranquillity which is the presupposition of any unified exposition of a totality. His own doctrinal formulations, therefore, were frequently marred by inconsistency if not incoherence. He fell back into outworn and alien patterns of thought which only abetted the overthrow of his special religious interests. In the final analysis Luther could not safeguard those profound sentiments for which he had so passionately contended. In light of these considerations, Ritschl envisioned his primary duty as that of recovering Luther's original Reformation motifs and then recasting them in a new theological system which would actually be controlled by these motifs in both its form and its content. In what follows I propose to indicate briefly how this twofold dynamic of recovery and reformulation undergirds Ritschl's theological enterprise.

The Experiential Focus of Justification

Ritschl used the available sources to undertake a genetic analysis of Luther's view on justification, thereby achieving a basis for criticizing the Reformer's subsequent deflection from his original standpoint.[13] In the earlier works, so Ritschl maintained, Luther's practical comprehension of justification had achieved clearest expression. In the controversy over penance, which prompted him to assert and defend his new insights into justification, Luther did not ask how the sinner becomes saint, the unregenerate man regenerate, but specifically how the earnest believer can be certain of God's good favor and pardon in spite of the relative imperfection of his works. Here justification was set forth strictly as the personal experience of forgiveness within the Church, inducing the believer to look away from his good works to Christ's perfect satisfaction alone, it being assumed that he would in fact continue to perform such works. But in his later treatises, written under the partial influence of Melanchthon and especially owing to polemical considerations, Luther increasingly conformed his doctrinal statements on justification to the model of his Roman opponents. He was now compelled to consider the *idea* of justification per se (*justum facere*), a thought which his adversaries construed strictly under the rubric of efficient grace, that is, in terms of the causal relation of grace to works.

[13] For this entire section, see J. & R. I, 121-95 (Chapter IV: "The Reformation Principle of Justification by Faith in Christ").

In the main Luther acceded to this new formulation of the problem, insisting of course that faith is the sole foundation and value of works. He now placed justifying faith as the transition point between the state of sin and the state of grace, making such faith appear to be the climax of a conversion process rather than, as in the earliest position, the religious principle whereby the believer regulates his entire active life within the Church (renouncing all claims to merit, falling back on God's grace to cover his shortcomings, etc.).[14] This formal similarity in doctrinal structure only obscured the far different intentions of the Roman and Evangelical teachings. In the Roman doctrine justification is equivalent to sanctification or regeneration; in the Reformation position justification and sanctification are correlated (by the doctrine of the Holy Spirit) but not equated. The Roman doctrine addresses itself to the actual moral transformation of the sinner, viewing grace as the divine coefficient of man's own ethical activity (*gratia cooperans*). The Reformation interpretation comprehends justification as forgiveness, as the answer to the believer's imperfect attainments in sanctification, assuring him of God's full and free pardon in spite of his continuing consciousness of guilt (*gratuitas favor Dei*). Thus the Roman doctrine centers on moral-ethical considerations while the Evangelical teaching is religious throughout.[15]

The conceptual device which facilitated Luther's fateful change in form of doctrinal presentation was the distinction between law and gospel.[16] By means of this scheme Luther attempted to answer the theoretical question of how the unrighteous man in fact becomes righteous and capable of good works. He sought to show how under a chronological order of conditions the subject of justification passes from consciousness of sin to consciousness of grace through the twofold proclamation of law and gospel. Melanchthon systematically presented this transition in the form of *loci* such as *de lege, de evangelio, de fidei efficacia,* etc. Ritschl's basic objection to this procedure was that it implicitly surrendered the standpoint of the believing community. In the Church the consciousness of grace always determines from the very outset the believer's sense of sin, rather than being posited as a goal toward which the sinner is directed through preaching and the sacraments. Justifying grace is the believer's *present* possession, not the climax of a conversion experience. Particular-

[14] See J. & R. I, 168-70.

[15] See J. & R. I, 122-23; J. & R. III, 35-37; and esp. *Instruction,* p. 213, n. 1 (#36).

[16] Ritschl's critique of the law-gospel formula is treated at length in J. & R. I, 167-84. See also J. & R. III, 159-67.

ly in the sermons of 1515-17 Ritschl found that "Luther constantly bears in mind the fact that he is speaking to the Christian Church, and not to a miscellaneous number of sinners who require first to be converted." [17] But as a result of the law-gospel distinction there transpired a "dislocation of the various elements of the idea of the Church," inasmuch as the Wittenberg Reformers "abandoned the thought that the congregations before them were Christian." [18] The law-gospel scheme, as Ritschl interpreted it, always treats the Christian as if he were still unregenerate and requiring conversion. Further, because of this same law-gospel dialectic, Luther and Melanchthon were led to view repentance as evoked by dread of judgment and by self-contemplation in the mirror of the law, thus leading to the characteristic penitential struggle (*Busskampf*) of Pietism.[19] Consequently Ritschl asserted that he was actually following the young Luther by locating justification strictly within the context of regenerate life within the Church rather than attempting to correlate it with the temporal process of conversion.

For Ritschl, therefore, Luther's original idea of justification related immediately to *the believer's new understanding of himself* (as a reconciled child of God) *and of his place in the world* (as "lord" over the entire natural realm). Justification is an eminently practical teaching, directly treating the anthropological correlate of God's salvific action in Christ. It is concerned with neither an extrinsic analysis of the effects of Christ's redeeming work on the Father nor a theoretical account of the conversion process. According to Ritschl, Luther had thereby wrought a decisive change in the form of the medieval teaching on justification. The Scholastics had treated the doctrine of Christ's satisfaction in a purely objective way, with a view to its effects on God. Only then did they proceed to consider "the influence of the work upon man . . . in

[17] J. & R. I, 135.

[18] *Ibid.*, pp. 183-84. The rationale underlying Ritschl's polemic against the law-gospel distinction is multifaceted. He believed this distinction facilitated a legalistic regulation of the religious self-understanding (as in the "pietistic methodism of Halle"); that in effect it subordinated grace to legal standards (whereby the gospel was interpreted on juristic premises); that it also made the Church, which possesses the *ministerium verbi*, into a mechanism designed for the conversion of sinners; and that it gave room to natural theology by virtue of the very notion that there is a condemning law which at least in rudiment is already known to men, and which prepares for the proper reception of the gospel of Christ. See Paul Jersild, "Judgment of God in Albrecht Ritschl and Karl Barth," *The Lutheran Quarterly* 14 (1962): 328-46.

[19] This pietistic *Busskampf* was basically a continuation of the "monkish method of self-abasement" which Luther allowed to continue in Evangelical circles by conceding to the law a determinative role in bringing about repentance. See J. & R. I, 163; III, 161 ff.; also R. u. V. I, 2nd ed., 180-81.

an entirely different part of the system," namely, in the doctrine of justification proper (or inner renewal). Luther, however, coordinated and held in a tensive unity the two thoughts of Christ's satisfaction (objective) and the sinner's justification (subjective). He employed the former thought to underscore the utterly gracious and christocentric character of justification to the exclusion of merit; nevertheless he concentrated primarily on the latter. Indeed, said Ritschl, Luther's teaching on Christ's satisfaction seemingly assumed "the position of a subsidiary doctrine." [20]

This change in form of presentation signaled a far more significant change in the nature and content of the teaching on justification. It expressed Luther's central conviction that the fundamental bearing or focus of justification is precisely the believer's own continuous experience of forgiveness and acceptance by God. Certainly this experience is grounded on God's sentence of pardon and Christ's mediatorial office, but *what is decisive is that the believer represents the divine pardon as immediately present and efficacious for himself.* Justification, therefore, is "the religious regulating principle of the entire life of the believer in its subjective phases." [21] It moves him to renounce all claims to personal merit and consoles him for the imperfect, fragmentary nature of his good works. Even so, as a personal experience, it must not be confused with either a teaching "about" this experience or an analysis of some supposed "change" transpiring within the divine nature itself. As an operation of God oriented toward man it can be correctly explicated only in terms of its actual effects on man, and, while God certainly remains the subject of justification, the reality of forgiveness can be known only by attending to the practical difference it makes in the believer's self- and Church and world understanding. [22]

In summary, on Ritschl's reading, the early Luther devoted primary attention not to a doctrine of justification but to the personal religious experience and assurance of God's reconciling love. Luther thus inquired into the actual modifications of self-consciousness occasioned by the divine work of justification, setting forth its specifically *pro me* dimension in contrast to the arid objectivism of scholastic theology and later Lutheran neo-Scholasticism. [23] Ritschl maintained that Luther's religious

[20] J. & R. I, 121.
[21] J. & R. I, 135.
[22] See J. & R. III, 173-75.
[23] In Scholasticism Ritschl saw the Church transformed into a school, where religious values are subordinated to the acceptance of doctrinal formulas; whereas in Pietism the subjective praxis of justification is recovered, but apart from the churchly

recovery of this doctrine—the subjective certainty that God for Christ's sake graciously maintains fellowship with the faithful in spite of their continuing sin and sense of guilt—lay at the root of the Reformation and was accordingly the Reformation principle par excellence.[24] Nor was this a sectarian assessment of Luther's achievement. By virtue of his painstaking researches over many years into the New Testament, patristic and medieval expositions of this doctrine, Ritschl maintained that Luther had both recovered the original apostolic gospel and simultaneously preserved continuity with the highest piety of Western Catholicism.[25]

Ritschl also contended, of course, that Luther himself did not consistently abide by his reformatory insights. He found traces in Luther's later writings of that tendency, represented by Calvin and Gerhard as well as Melanchthon, to ground faith on a definite, clear knowledge of the articles of belief. This developing doctrinalism served to undermine the dynamic of Luther's original practical-experiential position and of the Reformation itself, issuing in Lutheran Orthodoxy.[26] Therefore Ritschl envisioned his paramount task as the recovery of the Reformation's specifically religious comprehension of justification. On the one hand, through critical-historical analysis he would demonstrate the magnitude of Protestant theology's discontinuity with its Reformation base. On the other, through his own constructive formulations he would recoup past losses and vindicate the abiding significance of Protestantism's root principle. Only by such a procedure, such a return to, and revalidation of, Luther's original practical viewpoint, could contemporary Protestantism overcome the explicit rationalism of speculative (Hegelian) theology, the implicit rationalism of intellectualistic Orthodoxy, and the sectarian, nonchurchly bias of both Pietism and Enlightenment individualism.

---

spirit of the Reformation, with the result that the sect supplants the Church. See J. & R. I, 123-26.

[24] See J. & R. I, 155, 157-58.

[25] *Ibid.*, pp. 164-67.

[26] Ritschl's charge of growing intellectualism in the theology of Luther and especially of Melanchthon is set forth most fully in his 1876 treatise, "Die Entstehung der lutherischen Kirche," *Gesammelte Aufsätze* (Leipzig, 1893), pp. 170-217. Briefly stated, this development took the form of an increased emphasis on the *pura doctrina evangelii* (doctrinal confession and theological formulations)—rather than on the *evangelium Dei* (God's gracious will disclosed in Christ's redemptive deeds)—as the basis of the true Church and the essential criterion for determining the presence of the true Church. While Ritschl considered Melanchthon to be the founder of the fully developed Lutheran Church and the author of scholastic Lutheranism, he also repeatedly pointed out that Melanchthon's ecclesiastical and theological labors found their relative justification in sixteenth-century historical circumstances.

The Correlation of Justification and Reconciliation

In the first instance, then, justification preeminently involves a personal experience of forgiveness. But what precisely is it in its form as a *divine operation?* Reflecting clear dependence on Luther, Ritschl defined justification as the free resolve on God's part to pardon sin without regard for the sinner's own moral rectitude. Through forgiveness God renders human sin and guilt inoperative with respect to himself and thus opens the way for reconciliation. For Ritschl as for Luther justification is manifestly forensic in nature, a *Gerechtsprechung* on the model of "the pronouncing of one as righteous by the sentence of a judge." [27] Justification entails a "creative act of God's will" whereby the merciful Father freely accepts the penitent into fellowship without the latter's actual sin and attendant sense of guilt forming a barrier thereto. It is specifically a synthetic judgment which attributes to the sinner a new standing before God solely on the ground of divine grace. Hence it is not an analytic judgment predicated on the subjective value of faith or the believer's good works.[28] And this gracious judgment is appropriated and rendered efficacious solely by religious faith, by complete trust and confidence in the unmerited goodness of God. It is indisputable that Ritschl clearly wished to underscore the Reformation insistence on *sola gratia* and *sola fides.*

In addition, this divine act of justification is no mere negative judgment which exhausts itself in the declaration of forgiveness or pardon. Ritschl, as also Luther, did not hold to a narrow one-sided concept of forensic justification. Justification is above all a telic judgment, leading to, and experimentally verified in, the believer's reconciliation, namely, his actual personal entrance into communion with God (or the surrender of enmity toward God) and into cooperation with the final purpose of God (or joint activity in the kingdom of God). Reconciliation is the subjective proof or individualizing of justification, evidenced in both the religious virtues of faith in providence, humility, patience, and prayer (or, in sum, dominion over the world) and in the moral virtues of fidelity in one's worldly calling and love for the neighbor (or, in sum, participation in the Kingdom). Reconciliation, therefore, is justification carried into effect, its divinely intended practical result. While the two elements are not wholly synonymous nor reducible one to the other, they belong inextricably

[27] *Instruction,* pp. 212-14; p. 213, n. 1 (#36). See J. & R. I, 145-46; III, 79-85.
[28] J. & R. III, 35; 80.

together. Justification is the purpose of God; reconciliation is the result purposed.[29]

Ritschl's warrant for his repeated emphasis on justification's telic referent was the theological position of the early Luther and Melanchthon. Both maintained the effective (*justum efficere*) as well as the imputative (*justum reputare*) dimensions of justification; both equated justification with reconciliation and regeneration no less than with forgiveness of sins.[30] In this way the Reformers sought to answer the charge that imputation involves merely the predication of an imaginary attribute. Of course the change which justification works in the believer is not, as in the Roman doctrine, a transformation of a *directly moral* kind. It has a thoroughly religious nature, leading the believer to render spontaneous reverence and trust to God. As the goal of justification, reconciliation is simply "the trustful apprehension of the divine compassion," and is not to be compared with the Roman concept of faith formed by love. The Christian's good deeds are to be understood as practical instances of his new relationship with God, not as meritorious works which lead to a final divine approbation.[31] In other words, as Ritschl expressed the matter, the immediate goal of justification is not good works but blessedness (*Seligkeit*): the believer's exercise of positive world rule through trust in the God who has created and redeemed men for just such spiritual dominion.[32] At the same time the recipient of divine forgiveness is *already* a member of the community which has appropriated as its final end God's own self-end revealed in Christ, namely, the kingdom of God or "moral organization of humanity through love-prompted action." [33] Therefore the believer continually verifies the restoration of his religious relationship with God through his moral activity in the Kingdom as a co-worker with God. But such activity must be considered the indirect rather than the direct result of forgiveness, since it is directly related to Christ's *revelation* of the divine will to the religious community of which he is Founder and Head. [34]

---

[29] *Instruction*, pp. 214-15 (#37). See also J. & R. III, 77-79; 173-74.

[30] J. & R. III, 72-73; 176-77; 600-601.

[31] *Ibid.*, pp. 144-45, n. 2; also pp. 35-38 and esp. pp. 494-95.

[32] *Ibid.*, p. 279.

[33] *Ibid.*, p. 13.

[34] J. & R. III, 35 ff.; 79, and 517-18. Ritschl has frequently, and all too facilely, been accused of "Kantian moralism" on the assumption that he granted primacy to the moral tasks of the regenerate life, and thus related justification to reconciliation merely as cause to effect or as means to end. This criticism is questionable for at least three reasons: it virtually assimilates Ritschl's position to what he describes as the Roman Catholic doctrine of justification; it obscures his careful distinction between the re-

Luther himself clearly indicated the path to be followed in the proper religious comprehension of the believer's renewal. The practical significance of justifying faith is not exhausted through the denial of work righteousness; rather, faith in God's goodness expands itself into confidence toward God and his guidance in every situation of worldly life. Spiritual lordship over the world is the practical purpose of justification, as Luther taught in his great treatise *On Christian Liberty.* In this work Luther gave timeless expression to the Christian ideal of life as the living faith which overcomes the world through childlike trust in divine providence based on reconciliation through Christ.[35] Through such faith the believer becomes a king over the entire natural order, freed from the world's destructive pressures and thereby freed for genuine service in the world. Ritschl, following Luther, understood Christian freedom to signify this unity of freedom from the world and for the world, the unity of *Gabe* and *Aufgabe.* Trust in God not only exercises itself in humility, patience, and prayer but also in faithful service toward God and men in one's worldly calling. In opposition to Pietism's "ideal of abstract self-negation" and Orthodoxy's "negatively ascetic conception of morality," Ritschl intended to revalidate Luther's concept of the *Beruf* or loving action in one's civic vocation.[36] Thus justification—the restoration of the sinner to his religious relationship with God—is not directly related to good works or moral transformation, but certainly does have immediate bearing on the way the believer understands his total life's work in the world.

Unfortunately the mature Luther failed to preserve his epoch-making insights into the connection between justification and the religious and

---

ligious and the moral activities of the Christian life; and it flies directly in the face of his oft-repeated statements that the believer's moral activity is only indirectly or remotely related to justification. Cf. J. & R. III, 79: "Justification or forgiveness, conceived as effective, thus is identical with reconciliation as expressive of mutual fellowship between God and man. If this denotes the basis of Christianity as a religion, the subjective functions of reconciliation will be directly religious. On the other hand, the functions of a moral kind, which spring from the independence of the will that is in harmony with God, must stand in a more remote relation to reconciliation with God, for they cannot be deduced without taking into account still other points of view." Elsewhere Ritschl states that justification, understood on the Evangelical view as "the restoration of the religious relation to God which the sinner neither has nor of himself can attain, . . . would stand related to moral activity towards men only as a *conditio sine qua non*" (III, 35). In other words, such moral activity presupposes forgiveness since vocational fidelity and love for the neighbor cannot be forthcoming or productive so long as the believer is enervated by his continuing sense of guilt over the manifest imperfection of all his works.

[35] See R. u. V. I, 2nd ed., 182 ff. Cf. *Instruction*, p. 233 (#51): "Faith in the fatherly providence of God is the Christian view of the world in an abbreviated form."

[36] J. & R. III, 665.

moral functions of the new life. Subsequently, for example, Luther limited the idea of Christian freedom "to its negative sense of freedom from the law and sin," and so lost hold on its all-important worldly components.[37] Little wonder that in Orthodoxy the idea of blessedness or eternal life (*Seligkeit*) was projected almost entirely into the next world and emptied of meaningful relation to present experience.[38] Furthermore, Luther became increasingly preoccupied with the issue of individual salvation, in effect making his private monastic quest for a gracious God into the central problematic of justification in every instance.[39] By employing the law-gospel formula he gave the impression that justification has to do purely with the repeated process of personal conversion from sinner to saint. The believer is led to think of himself as being simultaneously a lost and condemned sinner under the law and a completely forgiven child of God under the gospel, or as being at once outside the community of the redeemed and yet somehow still within it. The result is that the Christian's assurance of God's pardon must ever be won anew in the agonies of conscience—just as Luther constantly oscillated between despair and hope—and to that extent his certainty of salvation is actually undermined.

In sum, Ritschl asserted that the mature Luther dissolved the original secular and social context of justification, i.e., he surrendered both its telic relation to life in the world and its anchorage in the community's transpersonal consciousness of God's ever-present grace. Certainly Ritschl did not accuse Luther of intentional distortions. He traced Luther's failings directly to his lack of synthetic and constructive power, while Melanchthon, presumably the systematician of the Lutheran Reformation, only made matters worse by reverting to an Aristotelian methodology and frame of thought. Ritschl, therefore, viewed his theological task as one of bringing the Reformation to completion and Protestantism to maturity. He believed that by virtue of his own homogeneous formulation of justification's teleological relation to reconciliation—God's free pardon and the believer's response of practical world rule, redemption through Jesus and moral activity in the Kingdom—he had in fact returned to the cardinal teaching of the Reformation in its pristine form.

The Centrality of Divine Love

In considering the so-called general relations of justification, Ritschl maintained that the God who justifies the sinner is to be conceived

[37] *Ibid.*, p. 181.
[38] *Ibid.*, pp. 496 ff.
[39] See J. & R. III, 159 ff.

solely under the attribute of Father, and not, as in the Anselmic tradition of Scholasticism and Orthodoxy, that of Lawgiver and Judge.[40] God qua Father is the subject of reconciliation, the active Reconciler, not the passive object of some expiatory work from below. The redemptive activity of Jesus Christ is not to be construed as a vicarious satisfaction, appeasing a wrathful God and so enabling him to pardon sinners, but as the concrete manifestation of the divine mercy. Thus it is man who is reconciled, not God. Ritschl believed that with such emphases he was linking up with the very heart of Luther's evangelical theology, with what he designated Luther's theological first principle, namely, "the abiding revelation of love as the essence of God in Christ." [41] Indeed Luther "surpassed all previous theology when he brought love into prominence as the character which exhaustively expresses the Christian idea of God." [42] God's self-revelation in Christ, according to Luther, demonstrates that God is pure love who wills only good for the sinner; hence even sinful man is not deprived of the divine favor. Ritschl especially valued Luther's grand scriptural insight that God justifies the sinner precisely in his character as the Righteous One, that God's righteousness is nothing other than his creative love. Ritschl maintained that this single thought, had it been consistently applied, would once and for all have banished legalism from the theology of the atonement.[43]

Yet Ritschl also found pre-Reformation elements in Luther's doctrine of God. The most significant scholastic remnant was his concept of divine wrath:

A plain contradiction is involved in the way in which Luther derives reconciliation from the love of God, but at the same time derives from the wrath of God the satisfaction which Christ has to work out through the vicarious endurance of punishment. For it is impossible to conceive sinners, at the same time and in the same respect, as objects both of God's love and God's wrath.[44]

Thus even Luther himself, in spite of his own evangelical experience, could not finally break free from the idea of God's retributive justice. In the end he subordinated the order of grace to the order of law, for he taught that before God can forgive sinful men, his penal justice must be satisfied through Christ's vicarious fulfilling of the law and endurance of punish-

[40] *Ibid.*, pp. 93-99.
[41] J. & R. I, 159.
[42] *Ibid.*, p. 201.
[43] *Ibid.*, p. 202.
[44] J. & R. III, 263-64.

ment on behalf of sinners. Of course Luther also articulated a "purely dramatic" theory of God's reconciling activity to the effect that in Christ's suffering and death God himself had vanquished sin, death, devil, hell, even his own law. For his part, however, Ritschl dismissed this *Christus victor* motif as a patristic myth: it may have been nonlegal but was still thoroughly nonethical in its bearing, since it presumably left out of consideration the relation of Christ's personal victory to the corresponding activity of the human will.[45] Hence Luther overcame neither the juristic nor the mythic features of the traditional atonement doctrine, and so marked no lasting advance on the viewpoints expounded in medieval and patristic thought. Yet his original comprehension of God's value-creating and faith-evoking love contained suggestions which would materially have transformed such viewpoints. Here again Ritschl viewed his duty as that of sorting out the permanently valid from the merely time-bound elements in Luther's position, together with the systematic unfolding of the latent resources in Luther's profound insight that God is properly to be spoken of only as *eitel Liebe*.

The Centrality of Christ

The God who justifies is the God of pure mercy and thus the God who discloses his fatherly heart in Jesus Christ. Following in Luther's steps, Ritschl held that all genuine knowledge of God is based solely on his self-revelation in Christ. "In Christianity revelation through God's Son is the *punctum stans* of all knowledge and religious conduct." [46] Ritschl's starting point (reminiscent of Barth's approach!) is a biblical theology of the Name, i.e., as employed in Scripture "the name ['the God and Father of our Lord Jesus Christ'] denotes God insofar as he reveals himself, while the Holy Spirit is the power of God which enables the community to appropriate his self-revelation as Father through his Son." [47] Hence revelation as a trans-subjective, historical datum, not the religious consciousness, is the proper object of theological cognition. "In Dogmatics," said Ritschl, "Christ's person must be regarded as the ground of knowledge to be used in the definition of every doctrine." [48] To be sure, this revelation is completed only when the community acknowledges as Lord the Mediator who reveals God as Father. Thus the full significance of this gracious self-disclosure becomes intelligible only as reflected in the con-

[45] See J. & R. I, 4 ff.; 202-3. R. u. V. I, 2nd ed., 224.
[46] J. & R. III, 202.
[47] *Ibid.*, p. 273. See *Instruction*, pp. 182-86 (#11, 12, 13).
[48] J. & R. III, 331.

sciousness of the community (its awareness of being pardoned, etc.). Ritschl claimed that dogmatics requires the "alternating use of two principles," an objective (or dogmatic) and a subjective (or ethical) standpoint, setting forth the divine operations together with their reception by, and practical bearing for, the believing subject. Revelation necessarily includes the act of human reception.[49]

Ritschl viewed this revelation positivism as the extension of the Reformers' christocentrism and turned it to account in opposing all speculative metaphysics, natural theology, romanticism, and mysticism which threatened to obscure or undermine the historical and personal nature of revelation. He interpreted Luther's rejection of every theology of glory— all claims to knowledge of the divine essence via inference from the created realm—as wholly compatible, if not identical, with the Kantian critique of pure reason and its rejection of the metaphysical proofs for God's existence.[50] Ritschl believed that he had particularly allied himself with Luther's christocentric perspective when he based the Christian *Weltanschauung* exclusively on God's self-revealing and reconciling activity in Christ. Only that person who in the trust of his heart knows himself one with God's final purpose for the world manifest in Christ, and enjoys the *accessus ad patrem* granted by the Father to the community of the Son, can truly affirm that he is "free lord of all, subject to none" and so exercise genuine religious dominion over the world. When later Protestant theology, beginning already with Johann Gerhard (1582-1637), made faith in providence a part of natural theology, it not only paved the way for Deism but surrendered outright one of Luther's most practical motifs.[51]

At this juncture, however, Ritschl once again adopted a highly critical stance toward Luther himself. The deformation evident in later Protestant thought could actually be traced back to the great Reformer. Luther subverted his own Christ-centered theology when, in flat opposition to his

---

[49] *Ibid.*, pp. 34-35, 273. Cf. Ritschl's assertion: "If what is intended in Dogmatics is merely to describe objectively divine operations, that means the abandonment of the attempt to understand their practical bearing. For apart from voluntary activity, through which we receive and utilize for our own blessedness the operations of God, we have no means of understanding objective dogmas as religious truth" (III, 34). One should also take careful note that the so-called ethical viewpoint, following Schleiermacher's usage, has to do with the realm of *personal activity* or subjectivity. Such activity, however, may be religious (e.g., prayer) as well as moral (e.g., charitable works). When Ritschl says ethical, therefore, one must not simply take this as synonymous with moral. Undoubtedly this fundamental confusion has reinforced the judgment that Ritschl is purely a moralist.

[50] See J. & R. III, 211-26, and esp. *Theologie und Metaphysik* (Bonn, 1881).
[51] J. & R. III, 168-81.

oft-repeated strictures against seeking to fathom the Divine Majesty, he pursued a speculative doctrine of God. He posited a hidden God outside Christ, a God of wrath and implacable justice who in fact appeared wholly other than the merciful Father revealed in Christ. In the mature Luther, especially in the *Bondage of the Will* (1525), which he scored as an inferior work, Ritschl detected a regression into late scholastic categories of thought and an implicit surrendering of the results achieved in the earlier writings. "Luther's treatise against Erasmus," he asserted, "represents the peculiar spectacle of a theology broken in two, the one side being scholastic and in particular nominalistic, while the other is worked out by means of a knowledge of revelation." [52] This work contained irreconcilable tensions between Luther's nominalistic premises (the *Deus absconditus* is outside the law, as evidenced in predestination) and his new theology of grace (only the *Deus revelatus* is relevant for faith, whose saving will is identical with the contents of the moral law). Luther was thereby caught in a patent contradiction. He initially asserted that salvation is ultimately predicated on the secret will of the hidden God, subject to no law. At the same time he taught that in Christ God has revealed his gracious will to all men, as manifest in Christ's atoning work which is itself grounded on the moral law considered as God's immutable will. By retaining nominalistic ideas of God's absolute power and complete arbitrariness, therefore, Luther in effect undercut his christocentric doctrine of revelation, although he actually intended only to undercut the scholastic notions of free will and human merit through the concept of God's hidden will which alone works out man's salvation.[53]

The Centrality of the Church

In tandem with his christocentrism Ritschl asserted that the worth of Christ as the Revealer of God is certified only to the community of believers. To hold that the proper knowledge of God is possible only through Christ as Revealer is at the same time to hold that such knowledge transpires only within the believing community of which Christ is the Founder and Head. If theology is to be Christ-centered it must be no less Church-centered. Religion is inescapably social in nature, and the

[52] R. u. V. I, 2nd ed., 221. See I, 2nd ed., 218-24 for Ritschl's critique of Luther's inconsistent God concept.

[53] See J. & R. III, 440, and esp. Ritschl's "Geschichtliche Studien zur christlichen Lehre von Gott," *Gesammelte Aufsätze*, Neue Folge (Leipzig, 1896), pp. 25-176. Luther's position is treated in detail on pp. 66-89. Cf. John Dillenberger, *God Hidden and Revealed*, pp. 1-35.

Christian community is the fellowship of the redeemed who trace back their consciousness of forgiveness to the sacrificial obedience of Christ. As Ritschl argued: "We are able to know and understand God, sin, conversion, eternal life, in the Christian sense, only so far as we consciously and intentionally reckon ourselves members of the community which Christ has founded." [54] Access to the revelatory and soteriological significance of Jesus Christ, and so to the Jesus of history, comes only through conscious personal inclusion in the believing community, and that, in turn, means solely through the medium of the apostolic witness. The New Testament writings are the products of communal faith, providing the original and normative link to the revelatory-salvatory event of Jesus Christ. (Thus Ritschl also intended to appropriate the Reformation stress on *sola scriptura* together with the *solus Christus*.) [55] Such a position, bordering on fideism, enabled Ritschl to parry the thrusts of radical historical criticism. Only that individual who self-consciously stands within the believing community can rightly interpret the scriptural testimony and thus rightly comprehend the historical Jesus. A purportedly neutral biographical approach to this Jesus is a priori excluded. Apart from faith "the full compass of his historical actuality" remains hidden since faith alone sees that Jesus "belongs to a higher order than all other men." [56]

The paramount importance of the believing community is not limited, however, to the hermeneutical function of providing entry to the total revelatory event (the historical Jesus and the biblical witness to him). The Church is above all the locus of justification, the definite sphere within which the divine operation takes place.[57] On the one hand, Christ's redemptive work relates not to the individual as such but to

---

[54] J. & R. III, 4. Cf. III, 578: "The individual can experience the peculiar effect which proceeds from Christ only in connection with the community founded by Him, and on the presupposition of its existence. The assurance of Divine grace is bound up with this economy, and with nothing else. . . . For religion is always social."

[55] Cf. *Instruction*, p. 172 (#3): "It stands as the foundation principle of the Evangelical Church that Christian doctrine is to be obtained from the Bible alone," in support of which Ritschl cites Luther's Smalcald Articles, II, 2. Ritschl's commitment to the Reformation *sola scriptura* is evident in the original format of J. & R. Initially he planned only two volumes, a historical survey together with a biblical-systematic exposition. Owing to the bulk of the material to be treated, Ritschl separated the biblical from the systematic section but continued to maintain the centrality of the biblical material. Otto Ritschl, in his biography of his father, asserted that Ritschl's "theological system rested completely on his biblical theology." Indeed the biblical section was for Ritschl of constitutive significance for dogmatics, while the historical section was only of regulative value. See *Leben*, II, 165.

[56] J. & R. III, 3. Cf. *Instruction*, pp. 200-201 (#25).

[57] See J. & R. III, 108-14.

the community as a whole, in which the gospel of reconciliation is proclaimed and personally appropriated. The whole is always prior to its parts. On the other hand, the community not only mediates justification as the possessor of the ministry of the Word, but is also itself the direct object of God's declaration of pardon for Christ's sake. Ritschl interpreted the synthetic nature of God's justifying judgment as "the imputation of Christ's righteousness in such a way that the position, given to him and maintained by him, as Son of God and original object of God's love, is also imputed to those sinners who belong to the community of Christ by faith, and thus they are accorded the *accessus ad patrem.*" [58] Thus it is the standing of Christ relative to the Father which is imputed to the entire community of which he is Lord. Justification is not the transfer of personal moral worth or active righteousness from one individual to another, as Orthodoxy taught, but the taking up of Christ's community into the effective love with which the Father embraces the Son owing to his sacrificial obedience.[59]

Ritschl legitimated his comprehensive ecclesiocentrism by an appeal to Luther's theology, in particular to certain "striking statements" of the Reformer.[60] In the Large Catechism, for example, Luther held that "the Church, as a mother, bears and nurtures every individual through the Word," and maintained in the Small Catechism that "within the fold of the Christian Church God daily and richly forgives me, the individual, all my sins." It was axiomatic for Luther, therefore, that the community is the sole sphere for the proclamation and realization of God's will-to-forgive. In the treatise *On Christian Liberty* he depicted the Church as the Bride of Christ and, on the analogy of connubial union, spoke of the exchange of benefits between Bridegroom and Bride, Christ assuming the sin and guilt of the believers and in turn bestowing his own righteousness upon them. Accordingly Luther clearly indicated that "the blessings which accrue to the individual are only imparted to him in common with all the others with whom he is bound up, through the same salvation, in the unity of the Church." One must recall, however, that Ritschl accused Luther of ultimately neglecting or displacing this Church-centered locus of justification by attempting to expound the latter teaching on the basis of the ill-advised law-gospel formula. And by recovering and re-emphasizing the centrality of the covenant community for faith and life, Ritschl believed

[58] *Ibid.*, p. 167.
[59] *Ibid.*, pp. 64-72.
[60] For what follows, see J. & R. III, 110-11. Cf. *Instruction*, pp. 215-16 (#38).

he was joining up once more with the original determinative impulses of Luther's Reformation.

It should also be noted that Ritschl's heightened emphasis on the centrality of the religious community was not only of apologetic value and soteriological import for him but was of fundamental *methodological* significance. "Theology is bound to take up this view, and only so is there any hope of constructing a theological system which deserves the name." [61] The traditional method of Protestant dogmatics until Schleiermacher, modeled on Melanchthon's *Loci*, was nothing less than rationalistic throughout, lacking homogeneity of perspective. At one point it treated of man as originally created in the state of integrity (with the correlate of an original covenant of works and a natural knowledge of God); at another of fallen man in the state of corruption (with the correlate of universally inherited sin, requiring universal redemption on the premise of God's retributive justice); and only at a third stage did it take up the believing community's knowledge of Christ as Redeemer in the state of grace (even here conforming the interpretation of redemption to alien juristic premises). These conflicting standpoints apropos of the basic theological data could only result in a confusion or dislocation of the entire system, affording entry to all manner of rationalistic argumentation and speculative impulses and terminating in a typically scholastic bifurcation of "natural" and "revealed" truths.

Ritschl repudiated this Melanchthonian heritage in the name of Luther's new principle for theological construction, according to which "every part of theological knowledge is construed from the standpoint of the Christian community, since only so can the worth of Christ as Revealer be employed throughout as the basis of knowledge in solving all problems of theology." [62] In practice this new principle meant that theology as a science should attend to its objects, especially the Christian experience of forgiveness, with a view to unfolding their present value and meaning for the community. Theology must necessarily adopt the standpoint of the redeemed community in order rightly to comprehend this data, working back as it were from effect to cause, from the community's present consciousness of reconciliation to its original ground in the past revelatory event of Jesus Christ, a process of inquiry which pre-

[61] For what follows, see J. & R. III, 4-5. Ritschl says of the traditional method: "A method which is so predominantly inspired by purely rational ideas of God and sin and redemption is not the positive theology we need, and which can be defended against the objections of general rationalism" (p. 5).

[62] *Ibid.*, p. 6.

supposes faith at all points. If once this starting point were surrendered, then the possibility of a positive theology would go by the board, for Christian theology is necessarily the handmaid of faith. Theological method, therefore, inescapably circular in nature, taking up into itself the community's faith-acts in its examination of the community's faith-data in order to serve the community's present faith-needs. As Luther so clearly perceived, the inner dynamic of all rightly ordered theology is precisely this movement "from faith for faith." And so Ritschl felt himself impelled to a reconstruction of Protestant dogmatics under the aegis of Luther. "That task I essay," he confided, "in the full consciousness that my action is justified and rendered imperative by the standard writings of the Reformation." [63] In short, Ritschl claimed to have recovered and renewed the underlying intention of Luther's theology: to break with all speculative metaphysics, natural theology, mysticism, etc., through a theological system at once Christ-centered and community-oriented, a system rooted by conscious design in Christian faith as an event *sui generis,* i.e., as the correlate of God's objective self-revelation in Jesus Christ.[64]

The Correlation of Revelation and Faith

Genuine knowledge of God, then, is exclusively bound up with the revelation in Christ and with the standpoint of the redeemed community which Christ founded. And such knowledge in turn takes solely the form of *unconditional trust* in the God who discloses himself as pure love. This correlation of revelation with faith points to a concluding, all-important feature of Ritschl's theology as informed by Luther: the cardinal motif that owing to the very nature of religion there can be no merely "disinterested" knowledge of God, or, positively stated, that "religious knowledge consists of value-judgments." [65] For Ritschl knowledge of God is distinctly religious, as opposed to theoretical or philosophical, only insofar as God is conceived as the solution to the existential predicament in which man qua finite spirit finds himself vis-à-vis a hostile, indifferent world. The *Heilsfrage* is the necessary precondition and correlate of the *Gottesfrage* (even as Luther's doctrine of God was soteriologically informed). God is truly known only in the form of the believer's value-judgment to the effect that it is God alone who "secures to [him] such

---

[63] *Ibid.,* p. 7.

[64] Cf. *Theologie und Metaphysik* (Bonn, 1881), p. 62: "The epistemological method which I follow in theology corresponds to the authentic intention of Luther, in particular his resolve to break with scholastic theology."

[65] J. & R. III, 211.

a position in the world as more than counter-balances its restrictions." [66]

Faith, therefore, must not be confused with an abstract knowledge which poses as a preliminary to faith, purporting to comprehend God and Christ in their essential nature *before* pronouncing on their value or worth for the believer. The truth is that only *in and with* the explicit personal affirmation of their immediate worth for us do we in fact comprehend their true nature. Nor is religious knowledge to be confused with scientific judgments which appraise objects in respect of their causes, the nature of such causes and their relation to other causes, since in religious cognition the self judges all sensations according to their value for the ego in terms of the feeling of pleasure or pain which they evoke.[67] Accordingly, in order to express adequately who God *is*, it is imperative to say who God is *for me*. My own self-understanding is inseparably bound up with my knowledge of God, for all God-talk is at one and the same time talk about my place before worldly reality as a whole, i.e., whether I feel the pleasure which accompanies the dominion over the world vouchsafed by God, or feel pain owing to the lack of God's help to that end.[68] God, therefore, is not an object of theoretical cognition but the direct correlate of faith, given in and with a religious value judgment. As Ritschl said: "A judgment concerning God that is not effected by complete trust in him has no cognitive value, and half-knowledge is not worthy of the name." [69]

Throughout his writings Ritschl consistently buttressed this rejection of all disinterested knowledge of God by recourse to Luther's celebrated explanation of the First Commandment. There Luther unambiguously asserted that God and faith are inextricably conjoined, that to know who God is one must have God in the trust of the heart:

> To have a god is nothing else than to trust and believe him with our whole heart. As I have often said, the trust and faith of the heart alone make both God and an idol. If your faith and trust is right, then your God is the true God. On the other hand, if your trust is false and wrong, then you have not the true God. For these two belong together, faith and God. That to which your heart clings and entrusts itself is, I say, really your God. [70]

Certainly neither Ritschl nor Luther intended to suggest that true saving faith autonomously produces its own special object of religious devotion.

[66] *Ibid.*, p. 212.
[67] *Ibid.*, pp. 203-4.
[68] *Ibid.*, p. 205.
[69] R. u. V. I, 2nd ed., 219.
[70] Large Catechism, I, 2-3, in BC, p. 365. Cf. J. & R. III, 211 ff.

For both theologians, as previously noted, the concept of God is given in a determinate fashion as precisely *that* God who discloses himself in Jesus Christ by the power of the Holy Spirit through the testimony of Holy Scripture. As Ritschl himself noted, Luther's explanation is totally christo-centric: "For the 'goodness and power' of God, on which faith casts itself, is in Luther's view revealed in the work of Christ alone." To say "no disinterested knowledge of God" is to say nothing other than "no knowledge of God save in Christ alone." Religious knowledge, therefore, cannot be reduced to "the arbitrary feeling of the subject," so that "a man's God varies as his faith," for Luther clearly distinguished between a true and an illusory faith. "Faith which is genuine and sincere can be exercised only in response to the true revelation of God," and so religious knowledge is permanently bound to God's self-disclosure in Christ.[71]

The central point in such considerations is that Ritschl, like Luther, wished to lay bare the preeminently personal dimensions of faith, as expressed in the believer's ongoing conviction—predicated on his appropriation of the gospel of forgiveness—that in Christ God is decisively *pro me.* "Loving will," said Ritschl, "is the being or essence of God himself; thus God in his revelation through Christ is assuredly present for us, and accordingly can be had by the man who through Christ is awakened to complete trust in him." [72] Saving faith, therefore, must be distinguished not only from every form of illusory wish-fulfillment but also from every *fides historica, fides auctoritatis, fides implicita,* etc., which submerge the personal dynamics of faith beneath the accumulated weight of tradition or the Church's teaching office. Following Luther, Ritschl defined faith simply as *fiducia* or personal trust and confidence in the Father of mercies before whom believers stand in the posture of beloved children. Or, more formally stated, "faith which, as related to the promise attached to the work of Christ, appropriates forgiveness, is to be understood as trust in God and Christ, characterized by peace of mind, inward satisfaction and comfort." [73] This unconditional trust which apprehends the God who in Jesus Christ declares himself unreservedly for the sinner thus brings with it those consolations of religion which constitute the solution to man's predicament in the world and his attendant sense of guilt before God.

It is evident, then, that Ritschl certainly intended to do justice to the

---

[71] J. & R. III, 212-13.
[72] R. u. V. I, 2nd ed., 219.
[73] J. & R. III, 142.

historical fact of revelation as God's once-for-all disclosure in Christ. At the same time he sought to verify the present reality of such revelation precisely by adjudging it of profoundly personal worth in all the changing circumstances of temporal existence. And he called on Luther to support him in this enterprise, confident that Luther's statements on the intimate oneness of God and faith "expressed various truths of which the theology of the schools both earlier and later has taken no account, and which its modern successors combat even yet." [74] The aptness of this latter contention is supported by W. von Loewenich's striking remark that "Luther's endeavor to understand all biblical proclamation of redemption as pronounced *pro me* has found here in Ritschl's thought a reverberation which, to my knowledge, exceeds that in any earlier theologian." [75]

4. THE SIGNIFICANCE OF RITSCHL'S ENCOUNTER WITH LUTHER'S THEOLOGY

It should now be evident that to a paramount degree Ritschl took his theological bearings from his encounter with Reformation thought. He self-consciously sought to reform Evangelical theology by a penetrating investigation of the Reformation's "practical root ideas" (*praktische Grundgedanken*). He undertook such an endeavor in constant dialogue with Luther and the other Reformers, as well as with the various confessional writings and the later dogmaticians. It is particularly noteworthy that at each major juncture of his theology he took pains to legitimate his position by recourse to Luther. He appropriated Luther's formative ideas and found in them his own impetus to theological reform. As a devoted student of the young Luther he discovered in the 1515-1520 writings the sharpest, most internally consistent expression of Luther's reformatory insights and then endeavored to take them up into his constructive labors.

Following Luther's lead, he concentrated on justification as the central doctrine of Christian theology. He construed such justification as God's forensic and synthetic judgment, proceeding from his sheer unmerited mercy, mediated by Christ's sacrificial atonement and appropriated by faith alone. As God's act justification is necessarily effective, really transforming the pardoned one by bestowing upon him a new self-understand-

---

[74] *Ibid.*, p. 212. Thus the distinction between religion and theory, between practical and theoretical cognition, is rooted for Ritschl specifically in the Reformation distinction between *fiducia* and *fides historica*, not simply in a general concept of religion.

[75] *Luther und der Neuprotestantismus*, p. 96.

ing and calling him to love's labor in the world, so that Christian existence in its totality is both *Gabe* and *Aufgabe*, both gift and task. Further, justification is an event which is indissolubly bound up with the Christian community, the fellowship of the reconciled, through which that event is ever rendered continuous and contemporaneous. And, finally, the God who justifies is known as merciful Father solely through his self-disclosure in the historical appearance, the person and work, of Jesus of Nazareth, a revelation certified only to the community of believers and realized solely under the form of unconditional personal trust.

Taken as a whole these insights operated as a transforming leaven in Ritschl's vocational self-awareness, challenging him to a reconstruction of Protestant theology in the name of the Reformation. Just as Luther himself returned *ad fontes* in order to effect reform by recovery, so also Ritschl appropriated his biblical and Reformation heritage in the interest of continuing reform. And even as Luther's "conservatism" necessitated a severe discontinuity with his immediate theological past, so Ritschl also understood his labors as marking a serious but requisite breach with many generations of Protestant theological tradition. In a certain sense the task of the reformer is ever one of critical conservatism: conservation without criticism leads to fundamentalism, criticism without conservation to iconoclasm. And while Ritschl patently was no iconoclast, neither was he a repristinationist. As has been repeatedly noted, his approach to Reformation theology was one of selective appropriation. He was sharply critical of the mature Luther for his presumed regression into a nominalistic doctrine of God, a juridical or Anselmic view of the atonement, an intellectualistic distortion of faith, in short, for his surrender of the believing community's standpoint and the weakening of his original practical-religious comprehension of justification. Thus Ritschl's Luther interpretation provides a case study in what it means to stand self-consciously within a tradition while rejecting traditionalism.

By returning to the young Luther of the Reformation's formative period, Ritschl believed he was recapturing the real Luther, that he was at last setting forth an authentic *Lutherbild*. And so his Luther interpretation was not only an act of historical recovery but an invitation to continuous polemics. He felt himself called to oppose and correct the distorted, party-oriented interpretations of Luther which had perennially bedeviled Protestant theology in its various inter- and intra-confessional struggles.[76]

---

[76] Cf. J. Pelikan's remark in *Luther the Expositor* (St. Louis, 1959), pp. 39-40: "During the past century the interpretation of Luther and of his theology has suc-

Hence he also envisioned himself as standing above party strife in a kind of splendid isolation, exposed to painful misunderstanding and harsh antagonism from every side.[77] In particular, he excoriated the ecclesiasticized Luther of the neo-Lutherans, the "Melanchthonized" Luther of Orthodoxy and repristinating Confessionalism, the individualistic Luther of the Enlightenment, and the sectarian Luther of Pietism. Inasmuch as Protestantism had persistently failed, in both its theological system and churchly praxis, to apprehend and validate the genuine practical-religious impulses of Reformation theology, it had no less failed to attain maturity.[78] Thus it could not, in its contemporary state of debility, effectively counter the prevailing positivistic and materialistic forces of the times. Eroded by neo-Scholasticism and sectarianism, it could scarcely convince its cultured despisers that the Christian religion moves in the realm of personal value judgments rather than disinterested knowledge, and presupposes conscious personal inclusion in the universal religious society of believers who confess a common Lord.

In Ritschl's estimate, therefore, contemporary Protestant theology was frittering away its precious Reformation heritage. It was doing so, on the one hand, by arid metaphysical speculations predicated on a rationalistic natural theology and, on the other, by a narrow doctrinalism and recrudescence of scholastic *Autoritätsglaube*. And even the so-called mediating theology was bogged down in a subjectivist analysis and explication of the pious consciousness, a procedure which threatened to undercut faith's historical moorings and neglected Christianity's powerful telic impulse to the moral reconstruction of society through love-prompted action in the kingdom of God. Hence Ritschl's critical dialogue with Luther and the other Reformers was not rooted in mere antiquarianism. Nor was it even a filial act of *pietas* toward the faith of the fathers. Far more, rather, it was the dynamic expression of his own reformatory consciousness vis-à-vis contemporary Protestantism and of his apologetic needs in the face of a world view based on mechanistic natural science. Perhaps it may be said without undue exaggeration that his was a prophetic reappropriation of the past, a profoundly personal involvement with the tradition

---

ceeded in disengaging itself from the older type of confessional polemics. This was partly because so many of the theologians and historians who took the lead in Reformation scholarship were the theological descendants of Albrecht Ritschl."

[77] See the prefaces to the 2nd and 3rd editions of J. & R. III, vii-viii, and esp. Ritschl's pointed rejoinder to his critics in the *Theologie und Metaphysik*.

[78] This emphasis on the "immaturity" of contemporary Protestantism comes to particularly clear expression in the Luther *Festrede* of 1883.

deriving from that most fundamental of prophetic convictions: *ecclesia semper reformanda.*

Precisely this dynamic encounter with Luther's theology—an involvement at once critical and constructive, conserving and yet reforming, rooted in history and yet oriented toward contemporary polemics and apologetics—provided a decisive impetus to the formation of a Ritschlian school. It was evident to Ritschl's contemporaries, and particularly to a rising generation of young Protestant theologians, that he was opening new vistas to them by his creative reappropriation of their Reformation heritage. He demonstrated that Evangelical theology could be both kerygmatic and answering, living out of its biblical and Reformation resources in order to speak responsibly to its present situation. In his own unique way the sober Ritschl conveyed to his young hearers and readers a sense of excitement, a vision of new possibilities for a theology grounded on the classic statements of Reformation faith. It is not surprising, therefore, that Ritschl's leading disciples invariably traced the power with which his theology gripped them to his proposed renewal of Luther's fundamental teachings. Indeed they viewed Ritschl's creative adherence to Luther as the distinguishing mark of his theology in contrast to other current theological options. Julius Kaftan, for example, maintained:

Albrecht Ritschl was the first to raise the fundamental demand to take up and set about the theological task in the way Luther had originally proposed, in that he bestowed pride of place upon the faith-principle as the only possible way to knowledge of God. Due to this he has become a leader and teacher for me and others. [79]

Perhaps the clearest expression of such indebtedness to Ritschl as a Luther interpreter was the warm testimony given by Martin Rade, the well-known editor of *Die christliche Welt:*

To occupy oneself with Ritschl and to be acquainted with Luther were one and the same thing. I had completed my total course of studies at Leipzig, hence at a high Lutheran faculty. No one there . . . had the talent to compel us to the study of Luther. But with Ritschl one immediately breathed the spirit of the Reformation. . . . This study seized and thrilled our entire being; it so inspired us that out of it we received a mission for our own day.[80]

[79] As quoted in Wolff, *Die Haupttypen*, p. 139.
[80] As quoted in Stephan, *Luther in den Wandlungen seiner Kirche*, p. 80. Cf. also Rade's essay, "Unkonfessionalistisches Luthertum: Erinnerung an die Lutherfreude in der Ritschlschen Theologie," *Zeitschrift für Theologie und Kirche* 45, Neue Folge 18 (1937): 131-51.

As might be expected, however, it was Adolf von Harnack who most pointedly linked the dynamics of Ritschl's theological program with Luther's precedent:

> Ritschl's uniqueness, following Luther, consisted solely in this: that he looked upon religion, and above all the Christian religion, as a powerful reality in and for itself, distinguishing it from every philosophy; further, that he strongly emphasized its historical-positive nature and thereby repudiated speculations over the so-called "natural religion and theology"; that he also held together faith and ethics in closest union; and, finally, that he employed the specific characterization of the Christian religion in the chief confessional traditions as the most important key for a more profound understanding of Christianity. This originality of his theological thinking dominated both the major works and all the individual essays which he composed during the height of his powers.[81]

Even a cursory glance at the scholarly productions of the Ritschlians shows that Ritschl's impetus to Luther study bore abundant fruit.[82] The very existence of this school provides weighty extrinsic evidence for the centrality of Luther scholarship in Ritschl's own theological endeavors, and underscores the enduring indebtedness of modern Luther research to so-called Ritschlianism. From such a consideration it is clear why no less a

---

[81] "Albrecht Ritschl: Rede zum hundertsten Geburtstag am 30. April 1922 in Bonn gehalten," *Erforschtes und Erlebtes* (*Reden und Aufsätze*, Neue Folge, Vierter Band, Giessen, 1923), pp. 335-36.

[82] The breadth of "Ritschlian" Luther scholarship is indicated by the following authors and titles: W. Herrmann, *Der Verkehr des Christen mit Gott, im Anschluss an Luther dargestellt* (1886; 7th ed., 1921). F. Kattenbusch, *Luthers Lehre vom unfreien Willen und von der Prädestination nach ihren Entstehungsgründen untersucht* (1875); *Luthers Stellung zu den oecumenischen Symbolen* (1883); *Die Doppelschichtigkeit in Luthers Kirchenbegriff* (1928). P. Drews, ed., *Disputationen Dr. Martin Luthers in d. J. 1535-1545 an der Universität Wittenberg gehalten* (1895). K. Thieme, *Die sittliche Triebkraft des Glaubens: Eine Untersuchung zu Luthers Theologie* (1895). J. Gottschick, *Luthers Anschauungen vom christlichen Gottesdienst und seine thatsächliche Reform desselben* (1887); *Die Heilsgewissheit des evangelischen Christen, im Anschluss an Luther dargestellt* (1903); *Luthers Theologie* (1914). M. Rade, *Doktor Martin Luthers Leben, Thaten und Meinungen, auf Grund reichlicher Mitteilungen aus seinen Briefen und Schriften dem Volke erzählt*, 3 vols. (1887). K. Müller, *Luther und Karlstadt* (1907); *Kirche, Gemeinde und Obrigkeit nach Luther* (1910). K. Benrath, *Luther im Kloster 1505-1525: Zum Verständigung und zur Abwehr* (1905). Th. Brieger, *Die Reformation* (rev. ed., 1914); *Martin Luther und Wir: Das reformatorische Christenthum Luthers seinen Kernpunkten nach dargestellt* (2nd ed., 1918). In addition, see the treatment accorded Luther in A. v. Harnack's *Lehrbuch der Dogmengeschichte*, III (1889; 5th ed., 1932); F. Loof's *Leitfaden zum Studium der Dogmengeschichte* (1889; 4th ed., 1906); and O. Ritschl's *Dogmengeschichte des Protestantismus*, 4 vols. (1908 ff.).

leader of the Luther renaissance than Gustav Aulén should assert: It is to the lasting credit of the Ritschlian theology that it "called into being an intensive Luther research" and "could scarcely have undertaken any other work which in the existing situation could possess more decisive significance for theology." [83]

[83] As quoted in Wolff, *Die Haupttypen*, pp. 127-28. Wolff also cites the following statement by Aulén: "The Ritschlian theological school gave itself wholeheartedly [*mit Lust und Liebe*] to Luther research. One might well claim that its greatest theological contribution lay in this, that it brought new impetus to this investigation" (p. 215).

11 REFORMATION AND CONTINUING REFORMATION

1. THE REFORMATION PRINCIPLE AND THE FORMATION OF PROTESTANTISM

Thus far I have treated Luther's place in Ritschl's theology in a somewhat expansive fashion, sketching in broad strokes the leading features and underlying rationale of Ritschl's Luther interpretation. This initial survey clearly shows that Ritschl's relationship to Luther is neither casual nor incidental, but bears directly on the innermost substance of Ritschl's total theological enterprise. Yet the full richness and significance of this encounter have by no means been exhausted. It is certainly correct, but nonetheless insufficient, to maintain simply that Luther's fundamental motifs, such as the practical-experiential idea of justification, the primacy of divine love, the existential character of faith, etc., inform Ritschl's systematic theology. Nor does it suffice to note that Ritschl was an important Luther scholar owing to his careful attention to the seminal writings of the young Luther and his impetus to Luther studies among his disciples. It is much more the case that Luther's theology takes on *normative* status and import for Ritschl inasmuch as, on Ritschl's view, Luther gave definitive expression to the authentic, original Christian understanding of self and world in the light of God's grace.

In his notable academic address delivered in 1883 at Göttingen, commemorating the four-hundredth anniversary of Luther's birth, Ritschl remarked:

As the Reformer of the Church [Luther] has become the signpost to that interpretation of redemption and its effects which not only shines forth in the New Testament documents, but can also be shown to be the sound basic concept of Western Catholicism.[1]

From 1857 onward, Ritschl had devoted considerable time and energy to a probing investigation of Luther's classic interpretation of redemption and its effects. The results of this investigation are set forth most concisely in the two editions of volume one of *Justification and Reconciliation* under the general rubric: "The Reformation principle" (*das Princip der Refor-*

[1] *Festrede*, p. 7.

57

mation). It is my contention that in the period of his major works (from 1870) Ritschl employed this Reformation principle—which he found most clearly articulated in the writings of the young Luther—as his overarching hermeneutical and axiological category, and that specifically as follows:

(1) As the key to his interpretation and assessment of the Reformation and the rise of Protestantism;

(2) As the basis for his critical reading of the entire history of Protestant theology; and

(3) As the determinative factor in his vocational consciousness and comprehensive theological undertaking.

Ritschl could label this all-important category simply the *Reformation* principle since he held it to be Zwingli's and Calvin's as well as Luther's fundamental thought. In section 26 of the first edition (1870) of J. & R. I, he carefully delineated the so-called lever (*Hebel*) by which Luther and Zwingli first effected actual Church reform in the sixteenth century and gave rise to the historical phenomenon of Protestantism. Ritschl briefly summarized this leading principle of the Reformation as follows:

The assurance of justification by faith through Christ, as it is laid hold of by the believer who already has a standing in the Church and is striving to do the will of God, is to both men alike the common lever by means of which they seek to achieve the Reformation of the Church; for the Reformers coupled with that subjective assurance of salvation the fundamental view of the Church as being the fellowship of believers who have been sanctified by God, and, as a consequence from this view, repudiated the importance for the salvation of the individual traditionally ascribed to the Church's legally constituted organs, as well as the authority conceded to them.[2]

It is thus evident that for Ritschl the Reformation principle was a combination of two mutually conditioned and inseparable components: the *religious self-understanding* or personal assurance of salvation for Christ's sake through faith alone, and the *religious Church understanding* or personal certainty of belonging to the universal community of Christ foreordained by God. To be more precise, the Reformation of the sixteenth

[2] J. & R. I, 155. Section 26 (pp. 152-67) bears the title: "The Reformation Principle." In the second, revised edition of this work (= R. u. V. I, 2nd ed., 1882), section 26 (pp. 174-85) is entitled, "The Practical Religious Reference of Justification by Faith." This change is only Ritschl's way of indicating more precisely the central, decisive feature of the Reformation principle.

century was the historical expression of new perspectives on the way the believer relates himself to God's grace in Christ and to the entire community of faith, with a view to the way in which he understands his total religious and moral life within the Church. In Ritschl's terms, the moving principle of the Reformation took the form of a "practical experience of the living member of the Church of Christ." [3] Ritschl insisted that, apart from the requisite sensitivity to the subtle reciprocity obtaining between these two forms of religious sensibility, the Reformation would remain unintelligible, especially to those "partisans of a radical school-theology" who comprehend it as simply a change in objective doctrinal formulations.[4]

Having once isolated this principle in the Reformers' writings, especially in the 1515-20 works of the young Luther, Ritschl took it up into his historical and systematic labors in sweeping fashion. In fact the underlying intention of his works remains obscure if the authoritative presence and force of this principle are overlooked. This category enabled him to interpret and evaluate the original *formation* of Protestantism and to account for its subsequent *deformation*, serving also as the impetus to his avowed work of *re-formation*. By such a procedure he validated his commitment to classical Protestantism, the sixteenth-century Reformation becoming for him the impulse to continuing Church reform. The remainder of this chapter will be devoted to the explication and support of this far-reaching contention. It is first necessary to examine more closely the various component parts of the "Reformation principle" and to discuss their specific role in the original formation of Protestantism.

The Religious Self-Understanding

The Reformation had its inception in Luther's attack on indulgences. Soon this attack was broadened into a general assault on the whole penitential praxis of the Roman Church.[5] According to Ritschl, the practical import of Luther's leading principle of justification by faith comes into focus only when contrasted with Rome's sacrament of penance, *not* its doctrine of justification. For both Luther's idea of justification and Rome's penitential system relate to the believer's assurance of forgiveness in the face of his continuing sin and consciousness of guilt; thus both treat the religious regulation of his self-understanding, or the way in which he represents God's grace to himself.

[3] *Ibid.*, p. 140.
[4] *Ibid.*, p. 159.
[5] For what follows, see J. & R. I, 133-46.

The immediate point at issue between the two sides was the nature of the contrition which precedes absolution.[6] On the Roman view such contrition was in theory the result of prevenient grace; in practice, however, it was a work of the penitent himself as regulated by the law, by the demand for a scrupulous recounting of individual sins and the absolute detestation of all sin. Only then was contrition complete and the penitent predisposed to the reception of justifying grace. Luther, by contrast, refused to ground the assurance of forgiveness on the mechanical completeness of confession. Such a legalistic procedure actually threw the despairing penitent back on his own inner resources and made absolution conditional on a tortuous self-analysis, thereby occasioning even greater anxiety. Instead Luther based such assurance solely on Christ's promise of forgiveness, pronounced by the priest and appropriated or individualized by faith in that promise. On Luther's view, then, forgiveness had already been granted in Christ's own sentence of absolution, to be mediated through the priest as the representative of the Church's power of the keys, and to be laid hold of in personal trust and confidence. It is such faith which alone justifies, not any feeling of self-detestation that is to be deliberately worked up. Accordingly, as Ritschl summarized the matter, to speak of justification by faith is really to point to the believer's personal certainty that his standing before God is predicated not on his own work or merit but on God's antecedent grace, and that he has free access to God in spite of his continuing sense of guilt since God for Christ's sake freely pardons him.

What was it, then, that actually came to expression in the Reformation? For Ritschl the decisive factor at work here was precisely this personal experience of ongoing divine forgiveness, this new self-understanding rooted in "grace alone" and "faith alone." The Reformation as an "outer" or historical event was the multifaceted working out *in concreto* of this "inner" (one might say "psychic") event, especially insofar as this new awareness of unconditional grace effected a dramatic change in the way Christians understood the Church as the bearer of grace. In any case, contrary to the prevailing Orthodox view, the Reformation was not in the first instance a reform of doctrine, as if it were simply a confrontation between two opposing sets of dogmatic formulas and so at root a scholastic dispute. It marked nothing less than an epochal transformation of the religious self-consciousness, of which every particular doctrine was only

[6] *Ibid.*, pp. 139 ff.

the subsequent expression and effect.[7] Accordingly justification by faith is no mere dogmatic *locus* objectively construed in a comprehensive theological system. Instead it denotes "the believer's dominant verdict passed upon himself from a religious point of view," for in spite of the continuing imperfection of his good works he knows himself forgiven through his appropriation of God's pardoning love disclosed in Jesus Christ and mediated to him by the Church (in its form as the fellowship of all believers).[8]

Ritschl steadfastly maintained, therefore, that Luther's "practical" understanding of justification signaled an ultimate break with every form of theological intellectualism or doctrinalism:

When Luther at once places [the thought of justification] in a position of central importance, and emphasizes his own view of it as the decisive and indispensable truth, he means by justification through faith a subjective religious experience of the believer within the Church, and not an objective theological *dictum* in the Church's system of doctrinal beliefs.[9]

Whereas Orthodoxy characteristically turns justification into a dogmatic proposition to be accepted on the authority of Scripture, and thereby makes the gospel of forgiveness into a new law, namely, the demand for right belief, Luther himself originally viewed justification strictly as a personal religious experience, complete in itself and continuous and realized solely on condition of trust in God's unmerited goodness pronounced in the Church's message of reconciliation. Hence, on Ritschl's reading of the early Luther, the Reformation arose out of, and gave expression to, a "practical root idea," or, as we would perhaps now say, it was grounded on a profoundly existential understanding by the believer of his relationship with God. On the one side stands the free grace of God actualized in Christ's work of reconciliation, on the basis of which the sinner may rightly think of himself as the object of God's declaration of forgiveness.

---

[7] Cf. J. & R. I, 146-47: "Systems of doctrine are not causes, but rather effects, of Church reformation, since the reformation of the Church arose rather out of a definitely expressed practical religious consciousness on the part of its leaders, whereby a change was wrought in the attitude of Christian communities or bodies of men towards the thing which up till then had been understood by the name of Church. . . ." In this statement the reciprocity between the "personal" and the "social" factors in the experience of justification is clearly expressed: the new religious self-understanding transforms the religious Church-consciousness (and is continually reinforced within this communal context). Ritschl's interpretation of Reformation history and theology conforms to his basic historiographical axiom: "every change in theology presupposes changes in the religious and Church consciousness" (*ibid.*, p. 18).

[8] J. & R. I, 147.

[9] *Ibid.*, p. 121.

On the other side is personal faith whereby the believer altogether disregards the value of his works and relies solely on the divine pardon. By such faith he attains to a religious self-estimate in which he is ever conscious that grace is really his, that owing to Christ's mediatorial work on behalf of his community God is truly God for him.[10] This coordination of *grace and faith* determines the character of justification in Evangelical theology, in contrast to the conjunction of *grace and merit* in the Roman doctrine.

In the first place, then, the Reformation principle denotes a thoroughly religious self-understanding on the part of the believer whereby he constantly refers every aspect of his life in the Church to the ever-present grace of God revealed in Jesus Christ. Thus justification by faith operated in Luther's theology as "the religious regulating principle of the practical life" or, in another formula, as "the religious principle that regulates the moral life of the regenerate." [11] This perspective means that justification applies solely to the person who "already has a standing in the Church and is striving to do the will of God," namely, the regenerate person who is actively engaged in bringing forth good works. Luther always assumed that the believer "continues in the love of God and of goodness even when he falls into sin," that "only that repentance is genuine which proceeds from love of righteousness and of God." [12] Justification by faith is no carte blanche for either antinomianism or libertinism. It is the answer to the "comparative imperfection of the works of believers," or, similarly stated, it evidences "God's grace as the counterpoise of imperfect works." [13] The believer is always *in via*, ever moving toward the goal of victory over sin but nonetheless ever falling short of this desideratum. Hence justification, at least in the early Luther, has to do completely with the removal of the believer's consciousness of guilt stemming from the inchoate nature of his progress in sanctification. It presupposes that "dissatisfaction with self which is the indispensable prerequisite of all religious reformation." [14] Such self-dissatisfaction, to be contrasted with self-detestation, is truly liberating and far removed from despair because the believer, by virtue of his certainty of forgiveness *sola gratia*, is under no compulsion to look to his own work righteousness or personal merit. He

---

[10] *Ibid.*, p. 145.
[11] *Ibid.*, p. 144, and the title heading of Section 23: "Luthers Gedanke von der Rechtfertigung der religiöse Regulator des sittlichen Lebens des Wiedergeborenen."
[12] J. & R. I, 143-44.
[13] *Ibid.*, pp. 137-38.
[14] *Ibid.*, p. 137.

cheerfully renounces all claims to worthiness and relies wholly on the divine benevolence. In brief, then, the young Luther expounded a true religious self-estimate in the light of grace alone, a mode of piety which militates against both self-righteousness and excessive moral scrupulosity, thereby safeguarding the spontaneity of good works and freeing the believer for his moral vocation in the world.

Luther thus developed his doctrine of justification within the context of, and in opposition to, the Roman sacrament of penance. The indulgence controversy had led him to a deeper questioning of the entire penitential system of the Roman Church. As a result of his fundamental principle of justification by faith, he was constrained to condemn this system as legalistic throughout. He was persuaded that "the penitence which flows from contemplation of particular sins, from legal fears, and from apprehension of future woe, only makes men hypocrites and greater sinners than before." In place of such "mechanical unspirituality or aimless self-torture" he substituted, as we have seen, "a purely religious regulation of the consciousness of salvation." [15] The Roman penitential praxis, therefore, regardless of its doctrine of prevenient grace, clearly exhibited a deficient soteriology, making of Christ a new Law-giver rather than the Revealer of God's unbounded mercy for the despairing sinner. This defective soteriology served to disclose contemporary Catholicism's discontinuity with the purest piety of Western Catholicism. In practice, if not in theory, it had become a debased Catholicism, giving expression to a moralism and legalism that had plagued the Church ever since the Pauline struggle with Pharisaism.

The Religious Church Understanding

Together with the personal dimension of the Reformation principle, there also comes into play a no less important ecclesiological or social dimension. For the religious estimate of self is possible only within the larger context of the believing community. That perfect righteousness which is the Christian's by faith alone is the righteousness of him who is the Founder and Lord of the Church. Thus God's sentence of pardon relates immediately to the total community, not to the solitary individual. For just as Christ the Head is prior to his Body the Church, so the latter is prior to the individual believer. Furthermore, since justification is the governing principle of the entire life of the regenerate person, the latter's relationship to the community is obviously presupposed.

[15] *Ibid.*, pp. 144, 142.

For it is only within the community of the faithful that the good news of divine pardon is proclaimed and can be personally appropriated. And so what actually transpired in the Reformation, or, more accurately, what actually *occasioned* the Reformation as a historical phenomenon, was that the Reformers "so brought their followers to a correct position on the subjective certainty of salvation that the value of the original idea of the Church at once achieved determinative influence on their sensibilities." [16] In sum, the Reformation was truly a *Church* reformation, a specific stage in the history of the Church and not merely a scholastic controversy or sectarian movement, because it recovered and revalidated the true nature of the Church as the *communio sanctorum*, the universal priesthood of believers. The subjective consciousness of salvation is grounded on the Church's gospel of reconciliation. But this proclamation of divine pardon is the instrumentality of the *entire* community, for the power of the keys has been given by Christ to all believers, not to a special class within the community which has assumed for itself the plenitude of divine authority. The forgiveness of sins or absolution, therefore, is "lodged with the Church as the abiding fruit of Christ's obedience" and is applied to individuals by their ministers (qua servants of Christ) or by any single Christian whatsoever (qua priest among priests).[17]

Of course the Roman Church also taught that the Church is essentially the *communio sanctorum*, since such was the doctrine of the Apostles' Creed. But its actual polity undermined its age-old teaching and gave room to the distorting influences of sacerdotalism and institutionalism:

> The peculiar shape which the polity of the Church had, as a matter of fact, taken, had led to an impression that the congregation of the faithful existed only as a result of the clerical functions of government and of administration of the sacraments, so that men were at that time accustomed to understand by the Church (apart from which salvation was impossible) that aggregate of constitutional rights and sacramental privileges which is lodged in certain representatives through whose instrumentality alone every saving privilege must be held and all assurance of salvation regulated.[18]

Thus the Roman Church's current ecclesiology was no less deficient than its soteriology. On its view the Church is really a type of "causal mechanism" directed to the conversion of sinners; in other words, the community of believers first comes into existence only as a product of the hier-

[16] *Ibid.*, p. 156. (Revised translation my own.)
[17] *Ibid.*, p. 142.
[18] *Ibid.*, p. 156.

archical clergy, as the creation of the so-called *ecclesia repraesentans.* On the Evangelical view, however, the community is "the *end* of everything that goes by the name of Church." Indeed it is the very *ground* of the Church since the ministry of the Word belongs to the whole community as its own instrumentality and is not merely wielded by the clergy.[19] And so the ancient claim that "outside the Church there is no salvation" rightly means that there is no salvation apart from the total religious society of believers; it does not entail that salvation is impossible apart from the magisterium and priestly hierarchy. In the Reformation, then, Christians again came to understand the Church in its proper sense as the divinely founded community of believers constituted by Word and Sacraments rather than by legal ordinances and a privileged class.[20]

When Ritschl, therefore, came to speak specifically of "the leading principle of the Reformation and of that entire phenomenon within the Church itself which arose from it, namely, Protestantism," he was most emphatic that only the indissoluble union of these two cardinal elements —the religious self-understanding and the religious Church understanding, the personal and the social dimensions of justifying faith—could account for the revolution in religious sensibility which engendered the actual reformation of the Church:

It is not at all sufficient to describe [this principle] with any such vague and bald formula as that it consisted in assigning value to the religious disposition, above every outward expression of it, and above every outward means of producing it. For justifying faith, as the Reformers understood it, is a frame of mind that is essentially determined by regard to the historical (and thus objective) appearance of Christ. The peculiarity, however, of the *Church*-reformation achieved by Luther and Zwingli, is by no means at once expressed in that subjective consciousness of justification through Christ by faith, however perfectly and truly apprehended. We cannot hold it up as the principle of the Reformation and of Protestantism at all, unless we take it in its close reciprocal connection with that objective conception of the Church which regards it as being before everything, and before all legal ordinances, the divinely-founded community of believers. In order to express accurately the one principle of the Church-reformation, we must take both these together in their inseparable connection and reciprocal influence: on the one hand, the thought of the certainty of salvation in the individual believer—a certainty which is independent of and rises above all mentionable instrumentalities; and on the other hand, the thought of the community of believers under Christ—a community appointed and foreordained by God.[21]

[19] *Ibid.*, pp. 183-84.
[20] *Ibid.*, p. 129.
[21] *Ibid.*, pp. 157-58.

In a much briefer yet equivalent formula Ritschl stated that "the subjective consciousness of salvation was maintained in the Reformers in reciprocal connection with their idea of the Church as the fellowship of believers." [22] These two organically interrelated factors were operative as the dynamic of Church reform in the sixteenth century and account for the rise of Protestantism. Together they constitute the "Protestant principle" for Ritschl, and apart from their reciprocity Evangelical Christianity cannot rightly be understood or preserved. The health of Protestantism must always be gauged by its fidelity to this animating principle, by the maintenance of its unique religious consciousness (the *sola gratia* piety of the Reformers)—a consciousness itself founded on a positive christocentricity (recognition of the historical Jesus as the divinely appointed agent of reconciliation)—and its no less unique Church consciousness (recognition of the community as the divinely foreordained object of justification, the bearer of the gospel of reconciliation, and the universal priesthood of believers). Protestantism becomes debilitated whenever it in any way obscures this twofold recognition of a special piety and a special community, both of which are grounded on a special revelation.[23]

The Religious World Understanding and Its Theological Significance

On March 20, 1873, Ritschl sent his friend Ludwig Diestel a letter whose contents have a most significant bearing on the present investigation. In the process of carrying through the systematic exposition of his recently completed historical and biblical studies, Ritschl had become increasingly aware of the decisive importance of a particular concept which he had previously considered only in connection with ethics and which he found wholly lacking in the traditional dogmatics.[24] He saw that this concept—which we may label the "world correlate" of reconciliation—was absolutely essential to the proper structuring of a doctrinal system centered on the Christian experience of justification. It is surely legitimate to consider this new insight an eventful "discovery" since it led to a dramatic reorientation of Ritschl's reflection on the nature of the Christian religion, and was to loom large in the Ritschlian system as one of its most characteristic and compelling motifs.

[22] *Ibid.*, p. 156.
[23] Cf. *Instruction*, pp. 171-73 (#1, 2, 3).
[24] Vol. I of J. & R. had already been published in October of 1870; by the autumn of 1872 Ritschl had completed the biblical section (to be published separately as Vol. II in 1874); at the time of this letter to Diestel he was making steady progress on the systematic portion (to be published also in 1874 as Vol. III).

"I have become convinced," he wrote, "that a certain consequence of reconciliation which heretofore I have always located within the province of ethics—namely, sonship to God, freedom from and over the world—must form as leading a point of view for dogmatics as the idea of the kingdom of God. These are surely the two chief aims of Christianity in a practical religious and moral reference. Both are lacking not only in the traditional dogmatics, but also in the presentation of the Protestant Confessions. With the idea of the kingdom of God one cannot get further than that Christianity is a doctrine of morality; its nature as a religion can be upheld only through the other idea." [25]

We shall have ample occasion to consider the overarching importance of this distinction for the whole of Ritschl's theology, but it may be remarked at once that he certainly intended to avoid that wholesale "moralization" of Christianity of which his critics have not infrequently accused him. He wished to emphasize the unique religious goal of Christianity—freedom from guilt and over the world (achieved by the historical Founder of Christianity and mediated to his disciples)—no less than its unique moral end in the kingdom of God (established on earth by Jesus and to be progressively realized among and by his disciples). And while Ritschl argued for the mutual reciprocity and harmonious balance of these two chief aims, he always contended against any indiscriminate fusion of religion and morality.[26] Whether he was always able to maintain this equilibrium is another question.

It was early in 1873, therefore, when Ritschl apparently first comprehended the full theological significance of reconciliation's world correlate, attempting thereafter to give it adequate expression in his dogmatics. "If justification by faith is the basal conception of Evangelical Christianity," he wrote in J. & R. III, "it is impossible that it can express the relation of men to God and Christ without at the same time including a peculiar *attitude of the believer to the world* founded upon that relation." [27] God, self, and world: these are the three points necessary "to determine the circle by which a religion is completely represented." [28] Ritschl especially scored Protestant theology for its neglect of reconciliation's world reference, as evidenced both in Orthodoxy's narrow individualism (focus-

[25] *Leben*, II, 148. Subsequently Ritschl modified his judgment about the presumed omission of this motif in the Protestant Confessions; he repeatedly cited Melanchthon's idea of "Christian perfection" found in the Augsburg Confession and the Apology.

[26] See J. & R. III, 490 ff., for Ritschl's attack on the moralistic distortion of justification in "the schools of Bengel and Schleiermacher" (which represented what Ritschl calls " 'sanctification' pietism").

[27] J. & R. III, 168 (italics in original).

[28] *Ibid.*, p. 29.

ing primarily on the believing soul's intercourse with God) and in Schleiermacher's subjectivism (locating the essence of religion in the feeling of utter dependence, with dogmatics limited to the unfolding of the contents of the pious God-consciousness), as well as in Pietism's ascetic ideal of life. But while the dogmatic tradition of Protestantism proved singularly sterile in this regard, Ritschl did find in the young Luther a clearly expressed, fully positive appreciation of the believer's new relationship to the world resulting from justifying faith. In the second edition of J. & R. I (1882) he included a new five-page section (pp. 181-85) directed primarily to Luther's *On Christian Liberty* as the classic statement of the believer's religious dominion over the world. Ritschl's discovery of 1873 had thus worked itself back into his continuing historical investigations and in Luther he found weighty support for the validity of this new insight. Once again it was the Luther of the Reformation's formative years whom Ritschl introduced as his star witness in the prosecution of his case against a derelict Protestantism. Again it was a "practical root idea" of the young Luther which he took up as an index to the essence of Christianity as a religion of reconciliation, and as a norm for measuring theology's fidelity to this essence.

For present purposes the significant passages from the second edition of J. & R. I are the following:

The practical significance of justifying faith in Luther's sense is by no means exhausted through the denial of work-righteousness and by the religious regulation of the active life. For this connection [of faith and praxis] itself follows from the thought of justification and reconciliation through Christ only insofar as faith in this grace expands itself into trust in God and his guidance in all situations of life in the world. Luther has instructively articulated this combination in his 1520 treatise, *de libertate christiana*. The "freedom of a Christian man"—that he is lord over all things—was introduced by Luther as a concept correlative with the righteousness which the soul makes its own by faith in the Word of God, i.e., the proclamation of liberation through Christ. . . .

The freedom of the Christian is not a passive predicate of believers. On the contrary, because the believer broadens his trust in the promise of grace or justification into a submission to God's providence in the midst of all his trials, he does not pretend merely to be independent of or indifferent to the bewildering and restrictive influences of the world, but in his fellowship with Christ actually governs all things which distress him and cast him into uncertainty. He exercises his positive freedom as nothing less than a sovereign authority, because in his reconciliation with God he has achieved the maintenance of his own spiritual personhood. . . .

Lordship over the world through trust in God, especially over the evil arising out of it, is the practical telic-correlate [*Zweckbeziehung*] of justification, which Luther discovered in the footsteps of Paul and which Melanchthon was able to formulate in the classic documents of the Reformation. For whoever is reconciled with God is also [reconciled] with the course of the world, which is conducted by God in one's best interests.[29]

Christian freedom or religious dominion over the world—what I have called the world correlate of reconciliation—is thus, in Ritschl's interpretation of Luther, the practical goal of justification by faith. These findings again afforded Ritschl proof positive that Luther's original idea of justification was oriented completely toward personal experience and praxis. It specifically treated a religious state of mind (evoked, to be sure, by a historical perception) and so was in no case an abstract, theoretical, disinterested, propositional *Hauptartikel* in a doctrinal system to be believed solely on scriptural or ecclesiastical authority.

It is not my intention at this point to consider the adequacy of Ritschl's exegesis of the Reformation's classic documents, but simply to comment on the specific meaning which he in fact attached to them. In the first edition of J. & R. I, as has been noted in the previous sections, he explained the Reformation *Ansatz* and the concomitant rise of Protestantism by reference to profound changes worked by the Reformers in the contemporary religious self- and Church understanding. As is apparent from the revised edition of J. & R. I, he subsequently went on to sound a distinctly new note. He broadened the scope of the Reformation principle to include the *religious world understanding* as the immediate practical result of justifying faith. In addition to stressing the personal and social dimensions of justification, Ritschl now highlighted its secular facets. Not only does the believer surrender every pretension to personal merit, regulating his advance in sanctification solely by the thought of grace alone; he also experiences a genuinely liberating, confident attitude toward the world because he knows it to be God's world, subject to the Creator's benevolent rule on behalf of his spiritual creation. As finite spirit he is at the mercy of nature's hostile forces, but through his experience of divine acceptance his unique spiritual dignity, far superior to that of the natural realm, is wholly vindicated, and he is enabled to exercise a religious lordship over the world. As a result he no longer looks upon worldly misfortunes as divine punishments for sin but affirms them as educative instruments within the providential economy of God. Because he knows himself a forgiven child of God, enjoying free and complete access to God in prayer, he confidently entrusts himself to his heavenly Father's

[29] R. u. V. I, 2nd ed., 181, 182-83, 184-85.

guidance of the world. In the words of the Augsburg Confession frequently cited by Ritschl: "Whoever knows that he has a Father reconciled to him through Christ truly knows God, knows that God cares for him. . . ." [30] In brief, being reconciled to God the believer is no less reconciled to the course of the world, not in passive resignation but with the irrepressible joy and boldness born of faith. Ritschl's key term *Versöhnung*, in its wider context, is best explicated in terms of this reciprocity obtaining between the believer's acceptance by God and his attendant acceptance of God's world rule displayed in his own spiritual dominion over the world. As a description of the religious consciousness, reconciliation means that the sinner's mistrust of God and dependence on the world have given way to positive trust in God and independence of the world.

Ritschl's characteristic and best-known designation for this world correlate of justification is the Christian life ideal (*das christliche Lebensideal*, sometimes also referred to as the Christian *Lebensanschauung, Lebensführung, Lebensordnung, Lebensleitung,* or *Lebensmotive*).[31] While it might be possible to trace the immediate genesis of this construct to sources other than Luther's theology (e.g., to Kant's Second Critique or Lotze's *Microcosmus*), Ritschl himself persistently maintained that he was simply renewing one of Luther's seminal but long-neglected insights. He singled out the writings of the young Luther as the definitive, authoritative source for the proper comprehension of the self-world correlation in Evangelical theology. In his *Festrede,* for example, he claimed that Luther had placed all subsequent theology in his debt because he had "pointed out the way to the original world- and lifeview of Christianity (*Welt- und Lebensanschauung des Christenthums*)." [32] He conceded, of course, that this *Lebensideal* was not unique to the Lutheran Reformation but was in fact the common content of both the New Testament and historic Western Catholicism (insofar as the latter was not wholly dominated by the world-denying tendencies of monasticism).[33] Luther's reforms were basically conservative in nature, a return to the ancient roots and a recovery of that piety which in varying degrees had continually

---

[30] Augsburg Confession, XX, 24, in BC, p. 44. Cf. J. & R. III, 6 (n. 3).

[31] See J. & R. III, 168-92; *Instruction*, pp. 226-64 (#46-77 on "The Christian Life"); and esp. *Pietismus*, I, 36-61.

[32] *Festrede*, p. 7.

[33] See J. & R. III, 613, where Ritschl distinguishes between oriental and occidental species of monasticism, the former comparable to Buddhism in its world negation, but the latter retaining "a general value in history . . . because, while resting on a basis of certain world-negating motives, it applied itself to ordered labor in many forms, i.e., to the task of world-mastery in the sense of technical and intellectual culture."

animated the Christian community since its founding. Yet in actual practice the Christian life ideal was for Ritschl always best conveyed in its distinctively Reformation guise. Besides relying on the tract *On Christian Liberty* he repeatedly cited the famous sentence from the Small Catechism—"Where there is forgiveness of sins, there also is life and blessedness"—as epitomizing Protestantism's religious world consciousness.[34] For by *Seligkeit* or eternal life Luther did not mean a wholly transmundane mode of existence but precisely that present lordship over the world springing out of justifying faith.[35]

In addition to appropriating Luther's celebrated motif of Christian freedom, Ritschl also adapted to his purposes the less familiar Melanchthonian concept of Christian perfection. For when Ritschl delineated the content of the Christian life ideal under the title of Christian perfection (*die christliche Vollkommenheit*), he had in mind that combination of religious and moral virtues—faith in divine providence exercised in humility, patience, prayer, and faithfulness in one's calling—which Melanchthon had masterfully set forth in various articles of the Augsburg Confession and the Apology.[36] Such perfection, it is to be noted, has nothing to do with the idea of personal sinlessness or completeness of good works, as if it were merely an external quantitative notion, but strictly pertains to "the qualitative judgment of the religious-ethical life as something complete in its kind." [37] In other words, in spite of the abiding imperfection of his good works the Christian does attain perfection or completeness through accomplishing his total ethical lifework in labor for the Kingdom and developing his religious character in the exercise of faith in providence. "In this coherence of the spiritual life," said Ritschl, "the individual attains to the value of a whole which is superior to the worth of all the world as the order of a partial and naturally conditioned existence." [38] Individual life, therefore, is to be valued as an incomparable good in its

---

[34] Small Catechism, VI, 6, in BC, p. 352. See *Festrede*, p. 14.

[35] See J. & R. III, 98-99, 496 ff. Ritschl frequently calls attention to the fact that in the tract *On Christian Liberty* Luther virtually equated *justitia*, *vita*, and *salus*.

[36] Augsburg Confession, XVI; XX, 24-25; XXVII, 49-50 (BC, pp. 37-38; 44-45; 78-79). Apology II, *passim* (BC, pp. 100-107). The *locus classicus* is A.C. XXVII, 49-50 (Latin text): "For this is Christian perfection: honestly to fear God and at the same time to have great faith and to trust that for Christ's sake we have a gracious God; to ask of God, and assuredly to expect from him, help in all things which are to be borne in connection with our callings; meanwhile to be diligent in the performance of good works for others and to attend to our calling. True perfection and true service of God consist of these things and not of celibacy, mendicancy, or humble attire." See J. & R. III, 169 ff.

[37] *Instruction*, p. 229 (#48).

[38] *Ibid.*, p. 232 (#50).

71

own right, far superior to the value of the whole world, because God has in fact created men to exercise earthly dominion and through Christ has called them to a participation in his own sovereign lordship over the world. When the believer makes himself one with Christ and his community through faith, he at the same time makes himself one with God's own transcendent, supramundane self-end, and therewith attains perfection.

The primary theological significance of the *Lebensideal*—in its status as the "practical telic-correlate of justification"—is its function as the principle of verification or experiential proof of justification. We have previously observed that a major problematic which occupied Luther, impelling him to reform, was the believer's subjective certainty of forgiveness. Because of the Roman Church's widespread failure to console anguished consciences burdened with guilt, owing to its legalistic sacrament of penance and its institutionalization of the office of the keys, Luther was led to ground the assurance of salvation solely on the believing perception and appropriation of God's unmerited grace disclosed in Christ. In this way Luther also restored the original view of the Church as the universal community of those who, having been so graced, maintain their standing before God by faith alone, apart from the mediation of any special class of believers supposedly possessing superior graces, acknowledging as their Lord none but the one Mediator between God and men, and themselves constituting the priesthood of all believers. In the final analysis, however, Luther anchored the believer's full assurance of salvation on his new relationship to the world, on what Ritschl called the believer's life task.

If justification by faith is really the *sine qua non* of Christian thought and life, it must make some practical difference: As an operation of God on the believer it necessarily effects a change in the person concerned. And this change is evidenced in the Christian *Lebensführung*, the religious and moral activity of the new life, which provides the decisive means for verifying the present reality of justification. For Luther, therefore, the certainty of forgiveness is brought into being through that selfsame dominion over the world which characterized the total life course of the Church's Lord: complete trust in God's providential care, patience amid trials and sufferings, humility and prayer. Whereas the sinner once showed his mistrust of God by being dependent on the world, he now proves the real transformation worked by divine forgiveness insofar as his trust in God "is combined [with] a new lordship over the world due to confidence in God's all-embracing care." [39]

[39] J. & R. III, 174.

Thus the category of the *Lebensideal* treats the mode of existence in the world of the person who knows he is justified through faith alone. It purports to define a particular structure or ordering of Christian life within the Church. Justification always entails a new relation of the self to the world as well as to God; indeed the new self-God correlation becomes intelligible only in light of the new self-world correlation. Owing to the divine pardon the believer becomes, in Luther's formula, both priest and king. He is made a priest specifically through adoption by God; he has access to the Father as shown in the privilege of prayer. At the same time he is made a king through his "trust in God who governs all things for the best, and will help the believer to surmount all obstacles." [40] Thus the *Lebensideal* points especially to the direction of the will to a certain end, namely, religious world rule. Hence it also involves the development of the Christian's character in conformity to his Lord, who is the Exemplar of such spiritual dominion.

Ritschl repeatedly appealed to Luther and Melanchthon in support of this position:

Reverent trust in God's protection and providence in every situation in life, the invocation of God in prayer, and patience under the sufferings which he ordains, constitute, according to the teaching of Luther and Melanchthon . . . , the content of the religious freedom over the world in which the believer experiences his justification; they constitute the activity which is called forth by the pardoning grace of God, when it moves one who was formerly a sinner to lay aside the mistrust of God which goes along with the unrelieved sense of guilt. This religious change, which establishes the believer's independence of the world, in addition makes it possible for him to attain to moral independence of character. [41]

Along with this specifically religious goal of world dominion through faith in providence, the *Lebensideal* includes a particular moral end as well:

The Christian ideal of life . . . includes two different kinds of functions, the religious and the moral—trust in God, by which we rise superior to the world, and action prompted by love towards our neighbor and tending to produce that fellowship which, as the *summum bonum*, represents at the same time the perfect good. When we make it our personal end—as far as time and place and calling demand or permit—to second and assist all others in respect of their true destiny, we act from a good will and according to the law of God. [42]

[40] *Ibid.*, p. 169.
[41] *Ibid.*, p. 177.
[42] *Ibid.*, p. 333. Cf. *Instruction*, p. 232 (# 50): "The Christian perfection which corresponds to the personal example of Christ himself separates itself into the re-

This moral function of the *Lebensideal* is the believer's active participation in the kingdom of God, characterized by faithfulness in his worldly calling and loving action toward his fellowmen. Freedom over the world and activity in the Kingdom: these functions of the Christian life are the two chief aims of Christianity which Ritschl noted in his letter to Diestel. And precisely this "double character of the Christian life" proved for Ritschl that Christianity is indeed the perfected spiritual and moral religion.[43]

As developed by Ritschl in Luther's name, therefore, the concept of the Christian *Lebensideal* was meant to express a carefully articulated balance between the divine action and the human response, between God's antecedent grace and the believer's consequent life conduct. This life ideal certainly presupposes the religious self-consciousness which refers the believer's total life activity in the Church to grace alone. Ritschl by no means wanted the religious world consciousness to threaten its soteriological base, while at the same time he could not allow the emphasis on *sola gratia* to cut the nerve of responsible action in the world. Otherwise the *justum reputare* and the *justum efficere*, the declaring just and the making just, would fall asunder. The inner connection between grace (*Gabe*) and worldly action (*Aufgabe*) must be construed in this way: grace qua forgiveness is the indispensable presupposition of dominion over the world and moral activity in the Kingdom; such religious and moral action is the practical goal of grace. For Ritschl the measure of any theology was the degree to which it maintained this balance, giving full scope to both factors and holding both in organic conjunction. The authentic structure of Christian existence would be imperiled if one or the other factor were accorded preeminence.

Lastly, it should also be noted that Luther's teaching on Christian freedom was formulated in direct opposition to the prevailing Roman Catholic *Lebensideal*. Catholicism's principle of worldly praxis was equally as defective as its soteriological and ecclesiological principles. Whereas Luther interpreted the evangelical world understanding or life goal as dominion over the world through joyful trust in God's providential guidance, the Catholic ideal of life was flight from the world as exemplified

---

ligious functions of sonship with God and dominion over the world, i.e., trust in the fatherly providence of God, humility, patience, prayer, and into the ethical functions of dutiful action in one's calling and the development of the ethical virtues." It is apparent that "*das christliche Lebensideal*" and "*die christliche Vollkommenheit*" are interchangeable terms.

[43] Cf. J. & R. III, 13.

in monasticism.[44] "The evangelical Christian is called on to exercise the freedom arising from justification amid the trials and hardships of life; the monk has no occasion for anything of the kind, for he has withdrawn himself from them." [45] This Catholic structuring of the active life actually helped undermine the religious self- and Church understanding, for all three factors are so closely connected that alterations in one inevitably set up repercussions in the others. As formulated by Luther, the evangelical self-consciousness is grounded wholly on childlike trust in God's fatherly benevolence; it "looks to the divinely guaranteed certainty that guilt has been blotted out, and the recurring sense of guilt deprived of its power to separate us from God." The Catholic mode of religious feeling is based on childlike fear of God (*timor filialis*); it "looks exclusively to the ever-threatening possibility of offending God." [46] Positive dominion over the world is incompatible with such a self-awareness in which one is constantly fearful in all life situations of transgressing against the moral order, since the subject of this consciousness would fail to attain both independence of character and the certainty of his spiritual superiority to the natural realm. In addition, the evangelical Christian consciously allies himself with the entire fellowship of believers in order there to apprehend for himself the community's "public standing in the pardoning grace of God." [47] But the monk attempts to mark himself off from others by his superior attainments in sanctification and thereby to enjoy a private intercourse with God based on merit. When Luther, therefore, proclaimed the freedom of the Christian as both priest and king, this was truly a reformatory action of the most far-reaching consequences. It radically called into question the Church's current understanding of the Christian's religious relationship to God, to the whole community of believers, and to the world at large. Little wonder that Ritschl constantly returned with such fondness to Luther's great 1520 treatise, for in this work the essence of Protestantism and of the Christian gospel had achieved consummate expression.

[44] Cf. *Festrede*, p. 15: "Luther's interpretation of Christianity, directed to the end of spiritual lordship over the world, surpasses [Catholicism's] primary outlook in which flight from the world [*Weltflucht*] is posited as the goal of life [*Lebensideal*]." In addition, continues Ritschl, Luther's "interpretation of the Church as the religious community, in which legal ordinances are only subordinate expedients, invalidates the Catholic assumption that the Church is in the first place precisely such a legal order, a type of state, namely, the spiritual universal-state."

[45] J. & R. III, 180.

[46] *Ibid.*, p. 178.

[47] *Ibid.*, p. 180.

2. THE DEFORMATION OF PROTESTANTISM

The foregoing considerations clearly show that the Christian *Lebensideal* or religious world consciousness is the third integral component or constituent element of the Reformation principle. By his patient, scholarly exposition of these three determinative factors (the religious self-, Church, and world understanding), each of which expresses a specific dimension of justification by faith (the personal, the social, and the secular), Ritschl believed he had uncovered the motive force of the Reformation. Reform came about because of the believer's dramatically new self- and world understanding within the Church. The Reformation was the result neither of some marked improvement in ecclesiastical morals nor of orthodoxy's final triumph over heterodoxy. The transformation of the religious consciousness, not the elaboration of new doctrines, is the key to this momentous event. As has also been shown, Ritschl regarded the young Luther as the ultimate source and authoritative exponent of this Reformation principle, identifying the latter as "the practical root idea of Luther's Reformation." [48] And precisely therein resides the overarching significance of Luther's theology for Ritschl's total program. For not only did Ritschl employ this principle as his interpretive category in explicating the onset of the Reformation and the rise of Protestantism; he also accorded it priority as his axiological category in assessing the continuity-discontinuity between original Reformation Christianity per se and its subsequent historical forms. *Das Princip der Reformation* now opened up to Ritschl the inner dynamics of Protestantism *in toto*.[49] Having located the formation of Protestantism in the three forms of religious sensibility rooted in justification, he attributed its deformation to its subsequent failure to maintain these leading ideas, and so came to view his own vocational task as the re-formation of Protestantism through a creative reappropriation of Luther's original insights. In this way the theological stance of the young Luther became Ritschl's index to Protestantism's theological vitality and his impetus to reform.

Trained as a critical historian in the Tübingen school of F. C. Baur, Ritschl was especially sensitive to subtle nuances and modifications within basic theological concepts, along with their reciprocal alterations in the

[48] *Festrede*, p. 27.

[49] This axiological category was also employed to work backward from the Reformation in order to assess the latter's continuity-discontinuity with New Testament, patristic, and medieval forms of Christianity. Cf. Ritschl's "Festrede über Reformation in der lateinischen Kirche des Mittelalters, zur akademischen Preisvertheilung 8 Juni 1887," *Drei akademische Reden* (Bonn, 1887), pp. 30-46.

sphere of practice.[50] His critical studies of Protestant theological history, with particular reference to the doctrine of justification, led to the conclusion that Luther's reformatory ideas never achieved complete expression in Evangelical thought or practice. For that reason a truly reformed Protestantism remained much more an ideal than an accomplished fact. This deformation began already in the Reformation era, indeed in the theological labors of the mature Luther and Melanchthon. "The most practical ideas of the Reformation," wrote Ritschl, "disappeared from later Lutheran theology. And this defect made its appearance even in the writings of the Reformers themselves." [51]

In his important *Festrede* of 1883 Ritschl provided his most succinct and direct critique of the Wittenberg Reformers. Of Luther he claimed:

Although one could grant that Luther himself did not articulate all the possible implications of the Christian freedom pointed out by him, one would certainly expect that the norm of original Christianity discovered by the Reformer would always have been clearly present in his mind and could be exhibited as the thought which permeates all his writings. This, however, is not the case. . . . A mass of theological reflections is deposited in Luther's writings wherein the practical apex or the new Reformation ideal of life is left out of consideration.[52]

Ritschl's appraisal of Melanchthon was much more critical, since he held Luther's humanist colleague to be chiefly responsible for the theological failure to safeguard the original Reformation piety:

He achieved a penetrating expression of Luther's leading ideas in the Augsburg Confession and its Apology, but he never exhaustively investigated the value of reconciliation with God for life in the Church. In his theological textbook he was at no time able to formulate the practical proof of reconciliation or justification as he had successfully done in the Apology to the Augsburg Confession. To be sure, in a general way Melanchthon understood and repeated Luther's significant suggestions for a new, positive form of theology which would surpass its medieval stage; yet he failed to pursue that course. Instead he allowed the whole of theology to remain in that form which lay at the root of medieval Scholasticism. In this Melanchthonian theology—whose design and scope have been considered normative up to the present day— Luther's reformatory series of thoughts has found no place, and his fundamental assertions relative to theological method no application.[53]

---

[50] Cf. Ritschl's critical remarks on the historical method employed in the works of Baur and I. A. Dorner, J. & R. I, 10-19.

[51] J. & R. III, 181.

[52] *Festrede*, p. 17.

[53] *Ibid.*, pp. 17-18.

In the light of Luther's systematic deficiencies and Melanchthon's reintroduction of a scholastic metaphysics and methodology, Ritschl felt justified in pronouncing this remarkable condemnatory verdict: "The genuine ideas of the Reformation were more concealed than disclosed in the theological works of Luther and Melanchthon." [54] If Protestantism, therefore, is to recover its original integrity, Luther must be opposed to Luther, and Melanchthon to Melanchthon. Repristination is out of the question. History must be overcome by history, i.e., by means of critical historical analysis the kernel must be removed from the husk and this "essence" of Reformation Christianity must then be unfolded in a new dogmatic system. Ritschl viewed his own life's work as the carrying out of these twin tasks.

Deformation in Luther and Melanchthon

The specific points at which Ritschl took serious exception to the mature Luther and Melanchthon have already been outlined in Chapter I. In general their theological failures were largely the result of their immediate historical situation. The internal development of Lutheran theology was primarily determined by the requirements of ongoing confessional controversy, especially by the pressing need to respond to polemical attacks from the side of both Roman Catholicism and left-wing radicalism within the Protestant camp. "Hemmed in by this attack from both sides, and concerned to maintain the legal ground of the Roman Empire upon which the Reformation put itself in motion and sought to secure its permanence, the Reformers brought their cause under the roof of a theology which must necessarily overshadow the practical motifs and implications of Luther's ideas." [55] This *Streitlage* meant, in the first instance, that Luther and Melanchthon had to respond to Romanist countercharges by adopting, for apologetic and polemical purposes, the prevailing Catholic ways of formulating the issues. Catholic questions shaped Protestant answers. As Ritschl said, "Whoever is required to defend his position against opponents who cannot attain to his newly inaugurated mental horizon runs the risk of abridging and dislocating it." [56] Thus the decisive issue of justification became centered more on the problem of relating grace to good works (a moral issue) than on the believer's consciousness of reconciliation with God (a religious issue). This change in focus re-

[54] *Ibid.*, p. 18.
[55] *Ibid.*, p. 19.
[56] *Ibid.*, p. 18.

sulted in a shift away from the practical sphere (justification verified in religious and moral activity) to the realm of the theoretical (how the *injustus* becomes *justus*), from subjective self-understanding within the Church to objective dogmatic propositions setting forth the conversion process in detail and tacitly abandoning the standpoint of the believing community. Similarly, in order to maintain their catholicity over against the sectarian *Schwärmer* and their legal footing in the Empire, the Reformers endeavored to prove their doctrinal continuity with the ancient Church, as displayed, for example, in their retention of the ecumenical creeds, their liturgical conservatism, and their persecution of anti-trinitarian heretics. While such a procedure was historically imperative, since the Reformers denied any intention of founding a new Church, it meant that the Church tended to be identified by its doctrinal purity rather than its religious comprehension of divine grace. Ritschl concluded, therefore, that "the scholastic curtailment of the understanding of salvation in the Lutheran Church is to be explained through the limitations imposed upon the German Reformation by its theological opponents and by the political demands of the Holy Roman Empire." [57]

This trend toward doctrinalism and intellectualism was further reinforced by abrasive relations with fellow Evangelicals (the sacramentarian controversy with the Swiss Reformers) and culminated in Lutheranism's bitter internal controversies in mid-century (the Gnesio-Lutherans *versus* the Philippists). "From the outset," said Ritschl, "nothing deformed the Reformation more than the contentious spirit which was exercised in its very midst among the various groups." [58] In every instance it was doctrine which came to prevail over life, or over that religious experience of *sola gratia* which underlay all doctrine, at which preconceptual level there was genuine unity among all the mainline Protestant Reformers regardless of a certain diversity in theological formulations. It is scarcely surprising, then, that Ritschl should invoke his most pejorative epithet against this deformation of the Reformation principle: "*Schulmässigkeit,*" i.e., scholasticism, party spirit. The Church had been made into a school where the acceptance of dogmatic formulas is superordinated to the actual experience of justification. In his critique of Roman Catholicism Ritschl had previously pointed out that, "on account of the machinery declared to be necessary—the sacraments and active fulfilment of the laws of God

[57] *Pietismus,* I, 85-86. Cf. J. & R. I, 126-33.
[58] *Festrede,* p. 21.

and the Church," justification could "never possibly pass as a simple experience into the soul of the believer." [59] He now concluded that Evangelical Christianity, through its own degradation of justification into a dogmatic proposition, had in effect reverted to Catholic "externalism" and surrendered its "simple experience" of forgiveness. Justification was no longer a practical principle, but increasingly involved merely "disinterested knowledge." [60] The gospel of free grace had become a *regula fidei*. The Lutheran Reformation had become Lutheran Orthodoxy. "When, accordingly, school-tradition raised itself to a position of supreme power in the Lutheran Church, the imperfectly expounded thought of justification by faith came to be unintelligible just in proportion as men treated it, in the first instance, as an objective doctrine, and made its religious value to depend upon acceptance of the formula." [61]

In addition to leveling the general charge of incipient doctrinalism and lack of systematic rigor, Ritschl indicated the precise manner in which Luther and Melanchthon unwittingly undermined their basic principle in each of its dimensions. They distorted the religious self-understanding by introducing the law-gospel distinction, regulating the believer's repentance by inducing terrors of conscience before the divine law (which he has failed to fulfill) rather than by confirming his present faith in the gracious promise of forgiveness (for in spite of his imperfect sanctification the true believer continues to love God and yearn for the good). Hence the Christian must repeatedly undergo a conversion, passing from a state of sin to one of grace in a potentially violent oscillation of conflicting emotions. By granting the law a regulative function in effecting repentance, Luther had in fact reverted to his monkish method of self-abasement.[62] And since the believer must forthwith account himself one of a larger body of sinners requiring conversion, his religious Church understanding is also undercut. The *communio sanctorum* becomes a *corpus mixtum*, composed of saints and sinners in varying degrees of sanctity, where the private need of conversion completely overshadows the corporate consciousness of reconciliation. Further, the religious world understanding is no less distorted because Christian freedom is now defined in a wholly negative fashion as freedom from sin rather than as positive world dominion. So also the idea of the kingdom of God is given a purely personal, quasi-mystical meaning as the inward union of

[59] J. & R. I, 122.
[60] Cf. J. & R. III, 34-35.
[61] J. & R. I, 123.
[62] Cf. J. & R. III, 160 ff.

Christ with believers (*unio mystica; regnum Christi est spirituale*), rather than being set forth as the fellowship of moral action prompted by love.[63] Hence both the religious and the moral components of the Christian *Lebensideal* go by the board and the believer's certainty of salvation, vouchsafed in his total life's work, again becomes problematic.

Deformation in Orthodoxy, Pietism, and Schleiermacher

Lutheran Orthodoxy continued and heightened these fateful developments.[64] Its comprehension of the self-God relationship was at root thoroughly legalistic, predicated on the theory of a divine world order characterized by God's retributive justice. It posited the moral law as the original dispensation determining all religious intercourse between God and men, and "thereupon grace retired into the position of a divine dispensation which is merely relative." [65] The believer is related to God the Lawgiver and Judge as the citizen is to the state or civil government, his actions being recompensed by either rewards or punishments. On such a model grace is merely an accident, serving only to uphold the priority and immutability of the law, since forgiveness becomes merely the remission of those penalties which according to divine justice necessarily follow sins. This legal framework likewise determines the specific nature of redemption. The latter must be carried out in such wise that God's honor or penal justice is preserved. By his vicarious satisfaction Christ must voluntarily endure the punishments rightly due the sinner and so avert the divine wrath evoked by the breach of law, in the process vindicating the law's just claims. All along the line the gospel subserves the law. Further, by interpreting sin primarily in terms of the breach of law and the penal sentence imposed by a judge, Orthodoxy also failed to determine its subjective nature as consciousness of guilt. In brief, it *legalized* and *objectified* the religious self-consciousness. We have noted how it also transformed the Church into a school or party, requiring acceptance of dogma as the precondition of religious fellowship.

In addition to its objectivism and legalism, Orthodoxy manifested an acute *individualism*. Owing to its preoccupation with personal salvation it neglected the believer's new position anent the world. By making the chief point in justification the transfer or imputation of Christ's active righteousness to the believer, thus representing the latter as passive, it "cast un-

[63] *Ibid.*, pp. 287-88. See also pp. 10-14; 98-99.
[64] See J. & R. I, 234-89; III, 245-62.
[65] J. & R. III, 40. Cf. *Instruction*, pp. 220-21, n. 3 (#42).

certainty upon the task of life." [66] The telic relation of justification to reconciliation with the course of the world (as well as with God) was obscured, *Seligkeit* becoming a wholly otherworldly goal instead of a present possession. Perhaps Orthodoxy's most serious defect was its transformation (as in Johann Gerhard) of special faith in divine providence into an article of natural theology. The natural man himself, apart from the Christian experience of reconciliation in the Church, can attain to the truth that God in his goodness guides the world for the sake of his spiritual creation.[67] As a result Orthodoxy prepared the soil for the growth of rationalistic Deism, as is shown precisely in the scholastic nature of both.

Pietism rightly rejected Orthodoxy's depreciation of justification's subjective determinants and attempted, on Luther's authority, to recover the personal praxis of the regenerate life. Yet it actually reappropriated the alien features in Luther's theology rather than his original reformatory ideas. Indeed Pietism was for Ritschl basically a throwback to sixteenth-century Anabaptism and, through the latter, to medieval modes of ascetic piety (especially Spiritual Franciscanism).[68] It preserved and even sharpened Luther's monastic *Busskampf*, inculcating in the believer a tendency to morbid fancies. The subjective assurance of salvation was rendered uncertain by making it depend upon an acute conversion experience rooted in meditation upon sin in general and insistence on creaturely nothingness before God. "The uselessness of these methods," held Ritschl, "is plain from the fact that they really render uncertain the attainment of joyous trust in God as the mark of being pardoned, and that if it is attained at all it is not continuous." [69] While the religious self-understanding was thus perverted by revivalistic legalism, the Church consciousness became sectarian. The society of the truly converted, distinguished by special attainments in piety, was separated from the empirical Church. The true Church is really the pious conventicle, the *ecclesiola in ecclesia*.[70] And in the realm of the life ideal, Pietism represented but a variant on Catholicism's *Weltflucht* and *contemptus mundi*.[71] It was pervasively ascetic in character, locating the goal of life in self-abnegation and otherworldliness and thereby deprecating the religious value of one's worldly

[66] J. & R. III, 72.
[67] *Ibid.*, pp. 181 ff.; 624-25. Cf. *Pietismus*, I, 86.
[68] See *Pietismus*, I, 3-98 ("Prolegomena"); J. & R. I, 513-77 (Chapter X).
[69] J. & R. III, 162.
[70] *Ibid.*, pp. 156-57. Cf. J. & R. I, 123-24.   [71] *Instruction*, p. 240, n. 1 (#56).

vocation. Ritschl's aversion to Pietism, therefore, represented much more than an idiosyncratic bias against personal Christianity or methodistic practices. It proceeded from the delineation and normative application of what he took to be the Reformation's original self- and world under- standing in the Church. He was prepared to show on historical-critical grounds that Pietism, like Orthodoxy, had abandoned the heritage of the Reformation.

Space does not permit a detailed exposition of Ritschl's assessment of all the manifold configurations of Protestant life and thought. My in- tention has been to demonstrate by several illustrations that *in each instance Ritschl measured the varieties of religious belief and practice by their degree of conformity to the "Reformation principle."* His critique of Schleiermacher may be cited as a final illustration of this procedure.[72] Ritschl's attitude toward the father of modern theology was always some- what ambivalent. He had to show himself a legitimate heir of Schleier- macher's achievements without suggesting that he was merely an epigon or imitator. He had to acknowledge indebtedness but, as befits a reformer of theology, also to point out fateful deficiencies. When he penned the following indictment of nineteenth-century German theology, he did not exempt Schleiermacher from its purview:

German theology, in its reaction from Rationalism, has almost entirely failed to appropriate in a comprehensive way that whole circle of thought which so unfolds into the doctrine of justification by faith as to become the basis of religious independence of the world through trust in the Father of Jesus Christ. [73]

Thus his approach to Schleiermacher mirrored that to Luther: it was at one and the same time critical and conserving.

Ritschl readily conceded that Schleiermacher had indeed inaugurated a new epoch in Protestant theology. Although Schleiermacher founded no school he distinguished himself as a "law-giver" for subsequent theolog- ical study. In opposition to Orthodox scholasticism and Enlightenment moralism he recovered the Reformation emphasis on the *subjective* quality of religion as a special form of self-consciousness deriving from redemption through Christ. As Ritschl put it, in Schleiermacher "redemption has

[72] For Ritschl's critique of Schleiermacher, see J. & R. I, 440-93; J. & R. III, 9-12; and esp. *Schleiermachers Reden über die Religion und ihre Nachwirkungen auf die evangelische Kirche Deutschlands* (Bonn, 1874).
[73] J. & R. III, 188-89.

become operative as a principle for the moulding of the devout self-consciousness, which does not take its shape from a legally enjoined doctrine and constitution, but from the never-ending value of the Redeemer for the society founded by him." [74] His preeminent contribution, however, was his recovery of the *social* dimension of Christianity, namely, the religious Church understanding of the Reformers. Reconciliation with God cannot be conceived outside the fellowship brought into being by the historical Founder of Christianity. It is to the believing community as a whole that the Redeemer imparts his uninterrupted God consciousness. Schleiermacher's particular greatness was that he elevated this understanding of Christianity's social nature to the plane of theological methodology, deriving theological assertions from the religious consciousness of the redeemed community. He thus overcame the *locus* method of the Melanchthonian tradition, with its explicit objectivism and individualism.

Yet Schleiermacher's revitalization of Protestantism fell short in one all-important respect. Although he specifically designated Christianity a teleological religion, he directed such massive attention to the redemption wrought by Jesus that he neglected the divine final end embodied in the kingdom of God. He neutralized the believer's new relation to the world by interpreting redemption as the removal of the obstructions to the God consciousness posed by the world consciousness. This is a strictly negative view of forgiveness, obscuring the positive freedom over the world brought into being through reconciliation with God. Ritschl particularly traced this defect to Schleiermacher's failure to appropriate Kant's leading thought: "the specific distinction of the powers of the will from all powers of nature." [75] By virtue of his own relative freedom as a moral agent, the believer's relationship to God is not merely one of utter dependence. He is no less equipped to operate as God's willing co-worker in the realization of God's final purpose for the world, the moral society of nations. Although Schleiermacher was truly a Moravian of a higher order, Ritschl found that he still bore traces of Pietism's otherworldly or acosmic tendencies.

[74] J. & R. I, 449.
[75] *Ibid.*, p. 444. Ritschl also attributed Schleiermacher's failure to treat adequately the teleological nature of Christianity to his "underestimate of the religion of the Old Testament" in which "the concrete conception of the one, supernatural, omnipotent God is bound up with the final end of the Kingdom of God, and with the idea of a redemption" (J. & R. III, 9).

3. THE RE-FORMATION OF PROTESTANTISM: RITSCHL'S VOCATIONAL SELF-UNDERSTANDING

The upshot of Ritschl's far-ranging critique of Protestant theology is patent. Writing four centuries after Luther's birth, he was constrained to render the melancholy verdict that Luther's Church reform, precisely in its most vital features, had consistently failed of final realization:

Until now the practical root idea of Luther's Reformation has not been employed in all clarity and vigor for the regulation [*Normierung*] of Protestantism's many tasks, i.e., it has still not been directed to the ordering of theology and its demarcation from all useless forms.[76]

Consequently Protestantism was still languishing in its infancy, adding point and pathos to the Ultramontane contention that the Protestant schismatics should return to the bosom of Holy Mother Church. Yet Ritschl also entertained hope, and articulated concrete plans, for a revitalized Protestantism through a comprehensive reappropriation and revalidation of Luther's practical insights:

I should like to advance the thesis that to date Protestantism has not yet emerged from its age of teething problems, but that its independent course will begin when—on the basis of a thoroughgoing comprehension of its practical root ideas—it reforms theology, fructifies churchly instruction, shores up the moral sense of community and achieves political resoluteness for the actualization of those spiritual riches which one of her greatest sons once acquired for our nation.[77]

Ritschl's own vocational awareness was completely permeated and controlled by his resolve to bring Protestantism to maturity, to a *selbständiger Gang*, by making Luther's Reformation the ground of continuing

---

[76] *Festrede*, p. 27.

[77] *Ibid.*, pp. 27-28. Ritschl continues: "To this end we do not have recourse to any instruments of coercion, but we may and must have confidence in the power of the truth we have come to know and in the divine assistance which has been promised to the upright. Or is there perchance in this matter some form of support more certain than God's help? We are inspired to trust [in this divine aid] and to conduct ourselves accordingly precisely by Luther's own personal conduct. Throughout his entire public life there runs a characteristic trait which coincides with that practical proof of Christianity expounded by him: confidence in God for the legitimacy and durability of his affair, in defiance of appearances and political probabilities." Ritschl then goes on to cite Luther's famous letter to Melanchthon (June 29, 1530) on the occasion of the presentation of the Augsburg Confession, in which Luther admonished his apprehensive colleague to bring the whole affair under the rubric of faith.

reform. In Luther's name he aimed to purge theology of all alien forms —Orthodox intellectualism, pietistic sectarianism, Enlightenment individualism, natural theology, mysticism, speculative metaphysics—which debased the Reformation principle and impeded the progress of Protestantism. His left-wing critics (e.g., Pfleiderer) charged him with irrationalism and obscurantism because he denied the necessity of articulating Christian faith within a larger philosophic framework. His right-wing critics (e.g., Frank, Luthardt) took him to task for his frontal attacks on the confessional writings and the Reformers themselves, and especially because he in turn scorned these critics as theologians of repristination. Ritschl for his part accused both sides of an anti-churchly, partisan, scholastic spirit and, in the midst of controversy, reposed in the confidence that he had Luther on his side and so stood in the mainstream of Reformation theology.[78]

Only at his peril can the student of Ritschl's theology neglect or minimize the diverse facets of this remarkable vocational consciousness: its fixation on Luther as religious thinker par excellence and exemplar of ongoing reform; its critical intensity leading to sweeping judgments of great severity; its acute sobriety heightened by a sense of the magnitude of the task at hand; its pugnacity and tenacity in the face of adverse criticism. Throughout this study I have argued that this theological self-awareness at once grew out of and authenticated Ritschl's abiding commitment to the Reformation and to Luther's theology in particular. I have assumed that his accomplishments as well as failures can be fairly appraised only if the underlying intention of his labors has first been brought to light and accorded sympathetic reception. To that end ample evidence has been brought forward showing that his avowed purpose was nothing less than to reclaim and systematically unfold Luther's practical comprehension of justification in all its pristine power and fullness. It is his single-minded pursuit of this goal which imparts to Ritschl's works their peculiar symmetry and architectonic quality. He viewed his massive historical, biblical, and systematic labors as fundamentally of one piece: the comprehensive attempt to explicate, clarify, and defend the Reformation principle as the essence of the apostolic kerygma, Western Catholicism, and authentic Protestantism, and therewith to rid this great tradition of all foreign growths. Yet Ritschl's modern readers have persistently tended to overlook this unifying dynamic, and to fragment this structural whole, by directing their critical attention to a limited number of his key

---

[78] See J. & R. III, 191, and esp. 660.

concepts (theory of value judgments, idea of the Kingdom, the *Lebens-ideal*, etc.). What one gains in depth by such a procedure, however, is paid for in a loss of breadth and a blurring of perspective. In view, then, of Ritschl's specific goals and positive achievements, Adolf von Harnack was not far wrong in styling him "the last of the Lutheran Church fathers." Indeed, as W. von Loewenich has aptly remarked, "according to his own self-understanding one could assay to designate him the 'first Lutheran Church father.' " [79]

[79] *Luther und der Neuprotestantismus*, p. 111.

III RITSCHL'S INTERPRETATION OF THE YOUNG LUTHER

In the previous sections of this study I have unfolded and endeavored to substantiate the basic contention that Ritschl's interpretation
of Luther's theology is of fundamental significance for Ritschl's comprehensive theological enterprise, to such an extent that the latter cannot be
fairly or fully appraised without careful scrutiny of the former. I have
argued that Ritschl's Luther study substantially informed his theology
in both a systematic respect and a historical-critical dimension. In his
dogmatics Ritschl selectively appropriated what he considered to be
Luther's leading motifs. While he lamented the failings of Luther the
theologian, he lauded the seminal insights and profound spirituality of
Luther the religious genius. He claimed to have recovered Luther's practical ideas in their original form and to have given them new currency in
his own homogeneous system. Simultaneously, in his historical investigations, he employed the so-called Reformation principle, drawn from a
close reading of the young Luther, as his primary hermeneutico-axiologi-
cal category. He interpreted and evaluated the entire history of Protestantism in light of its fidelity to its Reformation heritage, concluding that
the Evangelical Church had not yet come of age because it had not yet
assumed full responsibility for its first principles.

Ritschl's multifaceted encounter with Luther's theology has been previously described as an act of critical appropriation, in contradistinction
to mere repristination or traditionalism. Indeed it should be evident that
such repristination was wholly out of the question owing to Ritschl's
actual scholarly findings. On his view Luther's theology was not in fact
a coherent, consistent whole which could be taken over in its totality.
Upon examination it was seen to be a fragmented, "broken" theology,
marred by lack of internal consistency and systematic precision. Luther
himself had failed to order and preserve his original religious insights;
little wonder they failed of realization in subsequent generations. As for
Melanchthon, he only succeeded in casting these ideas into an alien neo-
scholastic mold. In a very real sense, then, the Lutheran Reformation

as a *theological* event was stillborn, although it certainly marked a decisively new stage in the history of the Church. Precisely this grave theological deficiency gave shape to Ritschl's dominant vocational self-understanding and task: the contemporary re-formation of Protestantism in the name of the unfulfilled Reformation of the sixteenth century.

Having explicated and analyzed the major features of Ritschl's Luther interpretation, I now propose to assess its general validity. The characteristic feature of this interpretation has been shown to be the dynamic of *return* to the "real" or young Luther and concomitant *rejection* of the "deformed" or mature Luther, all with a view to the contemporary systematic *reformulation* of Luther's original religious motifs. Pursuant to the dominant historical concern of this essay, I shall forego any substantive investigation of Ritschl's actual reconstruction of Luther's theology in order to focus critical attention on the underlying, all-important process of "return" and "rejection." This dual procedure immediately poses several relevant questions. What is the relation of Ritchl's "authentic" Luther to the "historical" Luther of the primary sources, as well as to the modern *Lutherbild* which has emerged during the past five decades of intensive research? Can Ritschl's specific criticisms of the later Luther be sustained? Has he correctly pinpointed Luther's central insights? What important elements in Luther's theology has he perhaps minimized or obscured? How accurate is his delineation of the young Luther's theological development, particularly his genetic analysis of the Reformer's doctrine of justification? Taking a cue from such questions, I shall concentrate in this chapter and the next on a number of serious defects or noteworthy shortcomings in Ritschl's total perspective, without attempting to appraise both his failings and positive achievements in the light of his own historical situation. Such a final evaluation, intent on taking "the measure of the man," will be reserved for the conclusion. In the present chapter attention will be directed primarily to Ritschl's interpretation of the young Luther.

1. SUMMARY OF RITSCHL'S FINDINGS

In order to facilitate a critical estimate of Ritschl's interpretation, it may first prove helpful to summarize his primary findings. Ritschl, as we have seen, focused on Luther's "practical fundamental principle of justification by faith" together with the correlative *praktische Grundgedanken* which cluster round this center of the theological system.[1] Young

[1] J. & R. I, 139.

Luther's concept of justification was specifically practical for Ritschl in the following closely related senses:

(*a*) It was directed to the pastoral consolation of the believer who is distraught by the continuing imperfection of his regenerate life. The young Luther articulated his views on justification within the broader context of the controversy over penance, which had been evoked in turn by the indulgence controversy. Repudiating Rome's legalistic penitential system, Luther construed justification as the religious means of pacifying the anxious conscience, directing the penitent to "that free gift of forgiveness of sins, or of absolution, which is lodged with the Church as the abiding fruit of Christ's obedience." [2] Thus justification primarily treats of the believer's dominant self-estimate based on God's unconditional pardon for Christ's sake mediated by the community of the faithful. For Luther, therefore, justification was no abstract doctrine or theoretical proposition but a "practical experience of the living member of the Church of Christ." [3] At the same time this experience of free forgiveness operates as the religious regulator of the believer's active life in the Church, prompting him to renounce all claims to merit and releasing him from the aimless self-torture of a mechanical contrition. In addition, Luther's original viewpoint clearly expressed the mutual reciprocity between this religious self-estimate and life in the Church, inasmuch as the believing community is itself the locus of this experience, the bearer of the gospel of forgiveness, and in fact the direct object of God's will-to-forgive. For Luther justification was thus both personal (experiential) and social (churchly), or, in Ritschl's language, practical. In Chapter II these dimensions of justification were discussed under the dual rubric of the religious self-understanding and the religious Church understanding.

(*b*) It was opposed to the theoretical question, characteristic of the Roman teaching, of "how and by what means an actually righteous person, who can be judged as such in consistence with truth even by God, is produced out of a sinner." [4] Justification on the Roman view was theoretical or abstract because it could "never possibly pass as a simple experience into the soul of the believer" owing to "the machinery declared to be necessary—the sacraments and active fulfilment of the laws of God and the Church." [5] For Luther, however, justification originally had nothing to do with any conversion process but solely with the "simple experience"

[2] *Ibid.*, p. 142.
[3] *Ibid.*, p. 140.
[4] *Ibid.*, p. 122.
[5] *Ibid.*

of divine forgiveness. Because this experience pertains only to the regenerate person who is already performing good works within the sphere of the redeemed community, it relates strictly to the believer's assurance of salvation in spite of the abiding imperfection of his works. In brief, justification answers to the profoundly personal problem of religious certainty, not to the abstract problem of how the sinner makes the transition from sinner to saint under the tutelage of an ecclesiastical institution operating as a conversion mechanism.

(c) It was preeminently directed to "praxis," namely, the total religious and moral life of the believer in the world. For Luther justifying faith not only regulates the Christian's religious self-understanding and his active life in the Church; it also broadens into trust in God and his guidance of the world in all life situations. Such faith is not simply a "receptive organ" but is simultaneously the "active instrument of all Christian life and action."[6] Thus the "practical telic-correlate" of justification by faith is Christian freedom or spiritual lordship over the world, displayed in faith in providence, patience, humility, and prayer. And having become one with God through forgiveness, the believer also becomes one with God's ultimate purpose for the world or universal final end revealed by Christ: the kingdom of God. As a result justifying faith is indirectly the motive power for one's love-prompted moral conduct in the Kingdom and fidelity in his civic vocation. Through such religious and moral activity the believer attains Christian perfection. He is thereby raised above the natural order and "the ideal of spiritual personality as a whole in its own order is reached."[7] Furthermore, precisely through carrying out his total life's work (as distinct from specifiable good works) in the Kingdom, he is assured of salvation because he is in fact *already* experiencing such blessedness in exercising world dominion and loving conduct toward his fellowmen. In Chapter II this secular dimension of justification was treated under the rubric of the religious world understanding—the *Lebensideal-Lebensführung*—or reconciliation in its broadest sense.

For Ritschl himself these practical ideas constituted the essence of catholic Christianity throughout the ages and of Protestantism in particular. It was Luther's recovery of these first principles which justly warrants his honorific title of Church Reformer. Yet Ritschl the conscientious Protestant historian, precisely out of loyalty to his Reformation heritage, must concede that Luther's reformatory work lacked both pre-

---

[6] *Ibid.*, p. 138.
[7] J. & R. III, 668.

cision and completeness, with dire consequences for the subsequent course of Evangelical Christianity. Ritschl's critique centered on the following paramount defects:

(*a*) Luther subverted his original insights by adopting certain alien conceptual categories and regressing into medieval (especially nominalistic) patterns of thought. Above all the law-gospel distinction, adopted for polemical and apologetic purposes, distorted the idea of the Church by treating the believer as basically unregenerate and as the repeated subject of a pietistic conversion experience (*Busskampf*). Repentance now involved a religious self-estimate based on legal standards rather than abiding confidence in God's goodness and faith in the gospel. In short, the law-gospel scheme threatened Luther's Church-centered *sola gratia* piety. This scheme also deformed Luther's early idea of justification by making it appear to be his answer to the Catholic question of how the sinner becomes saint. The Evangelical and the Roman concepts of justification, regardless of their vastly different intentions and practical functions, now seemed identical in form: presumably both were theoretical descriptions treating the idea of justification itself (*justum facere* or *Gerechtmachung*); presumably both pertained to the causal relation between grace and good works (moral transformation rather than religious self-comprehension). Luther further undermined his evangelical theology by opposing God's wrath over sin to his love, in the event reverting to Anselm's juristic theory of vicarious satisfaction and Occam's notion of the hidden, arbitrary God.

(*b*) Luther's original position was especially distorted by his lack of systematic proficiency, in part the result of historical pressures as well as personal limitations. (Unfortunately Luther's successors perpetuated this same incapacity for genuine "scientific" theology.) Both Luther and Melanchthon failed to transcend their purely religious apprehension of justification and so could not frame an adequate "teleological" *doctrine* oriented to religious-moral activity in the world. That is to say, on the level of church instruction and constructive theology they were unable to systematize the integral relation between faith and ethics, between justification and sanctification, although they asserted such a connection on the ground of personal religious experience and scriptural exegesis. To be sure, Luther did attempt to formulate the organic connection between justification and renewal through a type of Christ mysticism that actually anticipated Andreas Osiander's mistaken position. Hence, while his religious ideas remained truly seminal for Ritschl, Luther's doctrinal formulations were incomplete to say the least.

(*c*) Ritschl's critique particularly concentrated on the damage done to the original Reformation principle by the developments outlined above. The religious self-understanding was weakened by a growing legalism and objectivism; the religious Church understanding by a sectarian preoccupation with individual salvation and personal sanctity (traceable to the law-gospel distinction); and the religious world understanding by neglect of the supra-personal, world-oriented facets of the kingdom of God concept and the attendant restriction of Christian freedom to its essentially negative features (forgiveness of sins rather than positive world rule). The history of Protestantism is largely the record of such distortions in both theory and practice, a story which can be traced back to Luther's lamentable inability to systematize and safeguard the subtle reciprocity between justification by faith and the Christian's life in the Church and in the world.

Inasmuch, then, as Luther's practical root ideas had been repeatedly obscured if not surrendered, the re-formation of Protestantism was imperative. In his capacity as a co-founder (with F. C. Baur) of modern *Dogmengeschichte*, Ritschl both discerned this challenge in its historical lineaments and confronted Protestant theology with it. In his role as a systematic theologian he made this reformatory task his own, thereby becoming in his own eyes and those of his adherents a veritable *Lutherus redivivus*.

2. THE PROBLEM OF THE YOUNG LUTHER

Ritschl's Luther is primarily the young Luther of the Reformation's formative years, a period of literary activity stretching from the highly esteemed sermons of 1515-17 to the memorable *On Christian Liberty* of 1520. Ritschl attached special importance to the years antedating the indulgence controversy, 1515-17, a time during which Luther penned various sermons and tracts expounding his practical concept of justification in its pristine form.[8] Already by 1517 Luther's evangelical

---

[8] In addition to a number of sermons and letters from the years 1515-17, Ritschl cites the following works of the young Luther: *Disputation vom freien Willen*, 1516; *Disputatio pro declaratione virtutis indulgentiarum*, 1517 (Ninety-five Theses); *Sermo de poenitentia*, 1518; *Erklärung an den Cardinal Cajetan*, 1518; *Auslegung der Zehn Gebote*, 1518; *Resolutionen über die dreizehn Sätze gegen Eck*, 1519; *Auslegung der 22 ersten Psalmen*, 1519; *Kürzere Auslegung des Briefes an die Galater*, 1519; *De captivitate ecclesiae Babylonica*, 1520; *De libertate christiana*, 1520; *Enarratio epist. et evang.*, 1521; *Sermon von dreierlei gutem Leben*, 1521; *Vorrede zum Römerbrief*, 1522; *Vermahnung sich vor Aufruhr zu hüten*, 1522.

theology had achieved clarity in all essential points. Indeed the ensuing controversy with Rome proved detrimental to Luther's original position by engendering his misguided polemical concern with the issue of conversion. His reformatory struggles with his opponents actually abetted the distortion of his reformatory insights. The ultimate validity of Ritschl's Luther scholarship obviously depends greatly on the accuracy of his portrait of the young Luther. Error at this crucial point would adversely affect the whole. Critical attention, therefore, must initially be directed to the problematic features of this portrait.

The overriding limitation of Ritschl's Luther interpretation is that he erected it on such an extremely narrow base, both in respect of chronology and primary sources. He found the authentic Luther in but a handful of writings dating from a brief span of years. His avowed preference for the Luther of the years of "calm"—his antipathy toward the "polemical" Luther—virtually excluded from the outset any thorough investigation or sympathetic appraisal of the "total" Luther, since Luther's comprehensive theology was literally forged in the fires of lifelong controversy (with Romanists, Humanists, Enthusiasts, Sacramentarians, Antinomians, etc.). The excessively restricted scope of Ritschl's *Lutherbild* also derives from his thesis of severe discontinuity between Luther's original piety of grace alone and his subsequent doctrinal formulations. Ritschl repeatedly asserts, without demonstrating in detail, that Luther's attempts at doctrinal statement betrayed his religious sensibilities. What renders this discontinuity thesis especially questionable, besides its inherent tendentiousness, is Ritschl's failure to survey in depth Luther's later writings. Apart from numerous references to the catechisms, Ritschl pays scant attention to the "mature" Luther. Particularly noteworthy is his virtual neglect of a major work of the later Luther, the *Galatians Lectures* of 1531/1535.[9]

[9] Ritschl was insufficiently aware that Luther, throughout his career, devoted massive attention to the precise articulation of his teaching on justification. Cf. Paul Althaus, *The Theology of Martin Luther* (Philadelphia, 1966), p. 225: "With the single exception of the doctrine of the Lord's Supper, Luther throughout his life devoted more theological work, strength, and passion to this doctrine than to any other." It was especially during the years 1530-1532—the period of the presentation of the Augsburg Confession, of the "Roman Confutation" and Melanchthon's "Apology," and of Luther's lectures on Galatians—that the doctrine of justification was accorded concentrated attention. In 1530 Luther announced his intention to write a special treatise, "De justificatione." In fact by August of that year he had sketched out a so-called *Rapsodia seu conceptus in Librum de loco justificatione.* Unfortunately this projected work was never brought to fruition. However, the lectures on Galatians, begun on July 3, 1531, and completed on December 12 of that year (but first published in 1535), contain the substance of the mature Luther's formulation of his *caput doctrinae.* For details of Luther's (and Melanchthon's) work on this doctrine during

Ritschl in fact never did specify the exact period or occasion when Luther's "deviation" supposedly commenced or revealed itself most clearly. He could point to a number of dates: the years 1520-22, when Luther presumably began to take up the idea of *Gerechtmachung*; or 1525, the time of the controversy with Erasmus, when Luther published the unsatisfactory *On the Bondage of the Will*; or 1528, when Melanchthon's *Visitation Articles* accommodated Luther's notion of justification to the religious sensibilities of "theologically and religiously uneducated persons" through the explicit use of the law-gospel formula, a procedure which Luther himself sanctioned in spite of the subsequent objections of Johann Agricola.[10] This lack of specificity on Ritschl's part suggests either that he remained uncertain in his own mind about the date and precise nature of Luther's defection—in which case he should have more rigorously analyzed the development in Luther's thought, with a view to continuity no less than discontinuity; or that he was committed a priori to the discontinuity hypothesis—in which case chronological exactitude and cautious inquiry would largely be superfluous.[11]

The scope of Ritschl's interpretation was also limited by a most significant factor over which he had little direct control: he was compelled to work with incomplete sources. Within twenty years of Ritschl's death, research into the young Luther had been revolutionized by manuscript discoveries of Luther's earliest biblical lectures (1513-18). The lectures on the Psalms (1513-15), Romans (1515-16), Galatians (1516-17), and Hebrews (1517-18) already display ideas and themes which Ritschl was to

---

these years, see Robert Stupperich, "Die Rechtfertigungslehre bei Luther und Melanchthon, 1530-1536," in *Luther and Melanchthon*, ed. Vilmos Vajta (Philadelphia, 1961), pp. 73-88. See also Martin Greschat, *Melanchthon neben Luther: Studien zur Gestalt der Rechtfertigungslehre zwischen 1528 und 1537* (Witten, 1965).

[10] J. & R. I, 182.

[11] I have previously suggested that Ritschl was committed to this discontinuity hypothesis for primarily polemical reasons, inasmuch as Theodosius Harnack had invoked and presumably substantiated Luther's support for an orthodoxist view on substitutionary atonement, vicarious satisfaction, law and gospel, the wrath of God, etc. Harnack, however, had simply assumed unbroken continuity in Luther's theology from first to last. He undertook no genetic investigation of specific doctrines but remained content with a synthetic and "systematic" presentation. Ritschl, by contrast, claimed the young Luther for the liberal (anti-orthodoxist) camp and, by a genetic analysis of the doctrine of justification, sought to legitimate this claim. Thus Ritschl had no real quarrel with the supposition that the "mature Luther" and later Lutheran Orthodoxy were in basic agreement; but he was wholly intent on demonstrating that the young Luther—namely, the "authentic" and "original" Luther, in short, the Reformation Luther—had articulated entirely different viewpoints which Protestantism had in fact never fully assimilated to the present day. See above, p. 28, n. 9.

attribute only to the later (post 1520) Luther, and they provide a far more comprehensive context within which to interpret Luther's early thought than was available to Ritschl. I propose to test Ritschl's findings vis-à-vis the young Luther by concentrating on two major issues:

(a) His contention that Luther's original concept of justification functioned strictly as the practical solution to the believer's inchoate righteousness; and

(b) His rejection of the law-gospel distinction as a late, polemically motivated development.

Justification in the Young Luther

Ritschl maintained that Luther's original idea of justification pertains solely to the believer who, striving to fulfill God's will, remains constantly aware of the relative imperfection of his works. The context of justification is this Christian concern with self-renewal [*Lebenserneuerung*]; its function is the pacification of consciences troubled by imperfect attainments in sanctification.[12] In brief, justification by faith—or the personal appropriation of forgiveness for Christ's sake—is the solution to the inchoate righteousness of the regenerate. It involves the pastoral consolation of earnest believers, not the conversion of sinners. In addition to being the answer to the Christian's consciousness of guilt, this practical experience of forgiveness regulates his entire active life within the Church, to the end that he attributes all moral achievements to grace alone and not to merit. Thus for the believer justification has the immediate value of a covering for sins and an antidote to self-righteousness.

In spite of numerous felicitous observations and insightful analyses, Ritschl's understanding of the young Luther on justification is open to serious doubts. Perhaps the fairest judgment that can be rendered is that he "domesticated" Luther's theology of sin and grace. In the first place, he saw the basic issue as that of inchoate righteousness (*justitia inchoata*). For Luther himself, however, the fundamental problem was always that of the righteousness which holds good before God (*justitia coram Deo*). In effect Ritschl heard Luther asking: "How can I, in spite of my moral failings, be certain of God's favor?" In fact Luther's own decisive question was: "How can I, radical sinner that I am, stand in God's presence?" God's righteousness and human unrighteousness, not the believer's moral

12 See J. & R. I, 133-39.

imperfection and sense of guilt, hold sway in the matter of justification. Indeed the real meaning of imperfection and guilt—the true nature of the human predicament, including the grave situation of *homo religiosus* —can be comprehended only when one sees that God's own righteousness forms the standard whereby the human quality is judged, that it alone is the norm of all justice.

What Luther understood by God's righteousness is inextricably bound up with his concept of God's very "Godness," that inescapable living presence in virtue of which he is the Creator and Sustainer of all reality, exercising lordship throughout heaven and earth. Luther's position on justification (as indeed his total theology) is completely informed by his confession of faith in "God the Father, Almighty, Creator of heaven and earth." At the heart of his teaching there looms one all-important question: "How do matters stand between the Creator and his rebellious creatures, between the Righteous One and sinners?" The aged Luther related that in his early years the very thought of the *justitia Dei* cast him into despair, leading him to the edge of blasphemy, for at that time he understood it to mean that punitive justice whereby God pays to the sinner what is due him, namely, death and eternal damnation (a view which at first, on the basis of Rom. 1:17, Luther also believed to be the sum of the gospel).[13] While Luther's so-called evangelical breakthrough entailed a dramatically new interpretation of God's righteousness, he always understood justification as treating of God's verdict rendered on his creatures according to the standard of his own Godhood.

Ritschl, however, tended to distort the consistently theocentric orientation of Luther's thought when he related justification primarily to "the believer's dominant verdict passed upon himself from a religious point of view."[14] One cannot rightfully claim that Ritschl merely substituted a thoroughgoing anthropocentrism for Luther's supposed pure objectivity. It is indisputable that Luther also treated of justification in its immediate bearing on the believer's self-understanding, namely, in its "man-ward" dimension. But Luther's position is seriously compromised if one fails to consider the full range of his thoughts on justification's "God-ward" dimension, and in this latter respect Ritschl did not speak in Luther's own accents. Luther repeatedly explicated justification within the context of the First Commandment: the Creator God enters into relationship with his people by calling for their unceasing trust in his goodness and their

[13] Cf. "Preface to the Complete Edition of Luther's Latin Writings, 1545," LW 34, 327-38.
[14] J. & R. I, 147.

unfeigned love toward their fellowmen. God claims the whole person for himself and for the neighbor, and precisely in this total claim his own deity comes to expression. Behind this claim stands the weight of his glory. Hence only when a person understands that he ever lives before the God of majesty and power—that he is answerable to the Holy One who lays claim to his total being—does he actually comprehend the dreadful reality of his sin as an affront to the Divine Majesty, a denial of God's holy will, and so a refusal to let God be God. Then his self-estimate is truly radicalized: he perceives the depths of his turpitude; he knows and confesses himself to be man in revolt. Sin cannot adequately be measured by reference to the consciousness of imperfection or the pain experienced upon failing to attain one's own moral ideal. It is nothing less than robbery of God's glory, and God's judgment on this rejection of his deity expresses itself in his wrath. What is paramount in the matter of justification, then, is not, the believer's sense of guilt but God's response to rebellious, ungodly men.

Luther's perspective on justification, therefore, comes into focus only when this supreme question is first asked: "How does the righteous God regard the sinner? What is the sinner's posture *coram Deo?*" Luther gave a double-edged answer to this eminently "theo-logical" question: God regards the sinner according to both his strict judgment and his tender mercy.[15] Both appraisals hold good at one and the same time and both apply to the total person. Considered in himself, sinful man is the object of wrath and condemnation, having no claim whatever on the divine goodness. However splendid his virtues before others, he remains a radical sinner before God. How could he appear otherwise? For before the God who searches the heart, his life is stamped by a pervasive egocentricity and active opposition to the divine will. Turned in upon himself, he is powerless to love the Lord his God with all his heart or his neighbor as himself. Herein resides the enormity of the human predicament: man must obey God's commandment but cannot; nevertheless God ever holds him responsible even in the midst of his impotence. Therefore it is truly a fearful thing to fall into the hands of the living God. And yet precisely *this* man—unloving, undeserving, ungrateful, ungodly—is the recipient of

---

[15] See especially the treatise "Against Latomus" (1521), LW 32, 137-260: "You will therefore judge yourselves one way in accordance with the severity of God's judgment, and another in accordance with the kindness of his mercy. Do not separate these two perspectives in this life. According to one, all your works are polluted and unclean on account of that part of you which is God's adversary; according to the other, you are genuinely pure and righteous" (p. 213).

God's love and acceptance. "The love of God," said Luther, "does not find its object but rather creates it." [16] God in his righteousness is not at rest but ceaselessly active. In Christ, the supreme *opus Dei*, he shares his own righteousness with sinners: "For God does not want to save us by our own but by an extraneous righteousness which does not originate in ourselves but comes to us from beyond ourselves, which does not arise on our earth but comes from heaven." [17] The God who is abscondite in his unfathomable majesty, and no less hidden in his wrath over man's robbery of his glory, reveals himself in Christ as "nothing but burning love and a glowing oven full of love." [18] His wrath over sin is real, but is not the ultimate reality; it forms only the backdrop to his ineffable love. Wrath and love stand in tensive unity; both are expressions of God's Godhood. Because he is *holy* love, God condemns the sinner and hates his sin. Because he is holy *love*, God pardons the sinner and heals his sin. Where Ritschl, then, sees justification in the young Luther as the answer to imperfect attainments in sanctification, Luther himself ever and again announces it in the accents of the Pauline paradox (Rom. 4:5): the righteous and holy God freely pardons the unrighteous and ungodly. From first to last Luther's theology bears doxological witness to this "miracle of grace."

Not only did Ritschl erroneously limit justification to the problem of inchoate righteousness, he also obscured Luther's estimate of the nature of sin in the regenerate. Indeed one could argue that precisely at this point—in their respective appraisals of the universal human predicament (including the situation of the believer)—Ritschl and Luther part company most dramatically, and that here Ritschl's Luther interpretation is most vulnerable to attack. Where Ritschl speaks of the believer's "relative imperfection," Luther repeatedly speaks of his root sinfulness. In his *Heidelberg Disputation* (1518) Luther argued that "the works of the righteous would be mortal sins if they would not be feared as mortal sins by the righteous themselves out of pious fear of God." [19] For Luther

---

[16] LW 31, 41 ("Heidelberg Disputation," 1518, Thesis 28). Luther explains: "This is the love of the cross, born of the cross, which turns in the direction where it does not find good which it may enjoy, but where it may confer good upon the bad and needy person" (p. 57).

[17] *Romans Lectures* (1515-16), p. 4.

[18] WA 36, 425, 1 ("Predigten des Jahres 1532"). On the preceding page the famous utterance is found: "If I were to paint God I would so portray him that in the very depths of his divine nature there would be nothing else than a fire and passion which is called love for people. Correspondingly, love is precisely that thing which is neither human nor angelic but divine, yea, God himself."

[19] LW 31, 45-46 (Thesis 7). In his "Against Latomus," Luther defined sin as

even Christian man, considered according to his sinful nature, remains totally sinful. That concupiscence which remains after baptism is not, as in scholastic theology, merely the "tinder" to sin (*fomes peccati*) but radical sin subject to God's just condemnation. It does not merely cling to the carnal man but qualifies the total person as totally sinner.[20] In himself as sinner, therefore, even the believer remains in the same predicament as the unbeliever: he lives under the wrath of God. His sole refuge is Christ's alien righteousness which is his by faith alone. Indeed there is no more dangerous state than that of the religious man who remains blind to his true condition because of his claim to even relative goodness. Luther distrusted the *homo religiosus* far more than he did the honest pagan. "The world is at its best in men who are religious, wise, and learned," he concedes, "yet in them it is actually evil twice over." [21] Spiritual pride is the besetting temptation of the pious, and pride is the primal sin. Hence, *especially* in the regenerate, sin must be *magnified*. Because "we must come to know that righteousness which is utterly external and foreign to us, . . . our own personal righteousness must be uprooted." [22]

In discussing Luther's position on the sin of the regenerate, Ritschl pointed to that "dissatisfaction with self which is the indispensable prerequisite of all religious reformation." [23] Luther himself, by contrast, insisted on the need for self-accusation, self-condemnation, even self-hatred.

"the radical ferment which bears fruit in evil deeds and words" and spoke of "that deeply hidden root of sin which is the cause of men being pleased with, relying, and glorying in these things [virtues] which are not felt to be evil" (LW 32, 224; 226). Since Ritschl maintained that Luther spoke only of the believer's "relative imperfection," it comes as little surprise that he could not discern any fundamental difference between Luther's *sola gratia* piety and the purest piety of the Middle Ages, save that "Luther constantly [looked] at the comparative imperfection of the works of believers, while his medieval antecedents directed their attention chiefly to the relative perfection of such works wrought in the believer by grace, although bidding men disregard their meritorious value" (J. & R. I, 137).

[20] See LW 32, 228, for Luther's view to the effect that "wrath and grace have to do with persons" (or the whole man). In his "Preface to the Epistle of St. Paul to the Romans" (1522), Luther's *totus homo* motif is clearly stated: "Flesh and spirit you must not understand as though flesh is only that which has to do with unchastity and spirit is only that which has to do with what is inwardly in the heart. Rather, like Christ in John 3(:6), Paul calls everything 'flesh' that is born of the flesh—the whole man, with body and soul, mind and senses—because everything about him longs for the flesh. . . . Thus 'the flesh' is a man who lives and works, inwardly and outwardly, in the service of the flesh's gain and of this temporal life. 'The spirit' is the man who lives and works, inwardly and outwardly, in the service of the Spirit and of the future life" (LW 35, 372-73).

[21] LW 26, 40 ("Galatians Lectures," 1535).

[22] *Romans Lectures*, p. 4.

[23] J. & R. I, 137.

The person whom God justifies is the self-condemned sinner who upholds the justness of God's verdict on him even to the point of resigning himself to eternal condemnation. The young Luther's dominant theme is that only the utterly humbled person can stand before God. "Indeed, the entire Scripture teaches nothing else than humility." [24] To be sure, such humility and self-accusation are not a meritorious work of the believer himself; otherwise the whole framework of egocentric piety would not be overcome. It is God the Holy Spirit who is the agent of the believer's self-condemnation, effecting the mortification of sin through the instrument of Christian proclamation, the twofold message of law and gospel.[25] Through the spiritual use of the law, which uncovers sin even on

---

[24] *Romans Lectures*, p. 48.

[25] According to Thesis 95 of the "Disputation Against Scholastic Theology," 1517 (LW 31, 9-16), "to love God is at the same time to hate oneself and to know nothing but God" (p. 15). But, according to Thesis 84, precisely this *amor Dei*, which is simultaneously the *odium sui*, is the work of the Holy Spirit: "The good law and that in which one lives is the love of God, spread abroad in our hearts by the Holy Spirit" (*ibid.*). For a penetrating analysis of Luther's use of this Augustinian terminology outside, and in frequent opposition to, a strictly Augustinian framework of thought, see Regin Prenter, *Spiritus Creator* (Philadelphia, 1953), pp. 3-9. Prenter writes: "The subject of the act of self-condemnation is not the natural self of man, but God himself, who in the act of self-condemnation makes himself the master in man. . . . This is Luther's solution to the problem of the knowledge of sin. The Holy Spirit himself is the subject of the self-condemnatory act" (p. 7). Luther's position on this matter may profitably be contrasted with that of Ritschl in his dogmatics. Ritschl, of course, maintained that the full religious significance of sin qua separation from God and opposition to the divine will could only be acknowledged by the believer who measures himself against the standard of God's Kingdom (which is both the divine self-end and man's own highest good). At the same time, the self as *moral agent* experiences guilt as "the disturbance of the proper reciprocal relation between the moral law and freedom, which follows from the law-transgressing abuse of freedom" (J. & R. III, 57). Ritschl goes on to assert that "guilt can be the expression of such a contradiction only provided that, even subsequent to a transgression of the law, both the law and freedom continue to operate . . ." (p. 58). For Ritschl, then, sin and guilt in part evidence themselves as moral man's misuse of freedom vis-à-vis the moral law: they express the felt gap between the "ideal" and the "actual." For Luther, however, the depths of sin and guilt can only be comprehended through divine revelation, through the proclamation of God's word of judgment on the "person," whereby the latter understands himself as both answerable and inexcusable *coram Deo*. Further, sin for Luther entails a guilt of "being," not simply of "act." The *totus homo* is corrupt before he ever acts, and thus the notion of a "free will" before God is chimerical. Whereas Ritschl grants a certain autonomy to "moral man," Luther is absolutely insistent that only that person is justified whom the Holy Spirit has emptied of every claim to "morality" in God's sight. I suggest, therefore, that Ritschl's anthropology, predicated on the "spirit/nature" distinction derived from Kant, marked in part a reversion to that "idealistic" concept of man which undergirded much of medieval piety, i.e., man's own *amor summi boni*—understood as the judgment of the "higher self" (*spiritus*) on the "lower self" (*caro*)—is granted a determinative role in the comprehension of sin and guilt.

the heights of religious achievement (such as the monastic life), God himself empties the believer of pride, while through the gospel the Spirit brings Christ and his righteousness and bestows himself as the transforming power of Christian existence. Thus for Luther the believer's sin remains so deeply implanted that it must ever anew be *revealed* through God's word of judgment, with the result that the gospel then shines forth as the ever new revelation of God's boundless mercy. What Ritschl has so evidently failed to convey in his interpretation is Luther's sense of sheer awe and amazement that God in Christ daily justifies the ungodly through his living Word. As one studies Ritschl's Luther interpretation, *a single disturbing question repeatedly presents itself:* Are we really dealing here, as in Luther himself, with the righteous God's pardon and transformation of the unrighteous, or simply with the consolation of the disquieted, i.e., the justification of the religious man whose good works are incomplete, who strives after God's will but strives imperfectly, rather than the justification of the sinful man who even amid his best works remains man in revolt? [26]

By minimizing the gravity of sin in the regenerate, Ritschl also failed to comprehend adequately a further important dimension of justification in the young Luther. While it is true that God pardons the ungodly—indeed he acquits only the self-confessed sinner—he does not leave the sinner in his sin. Justification is no mere legal fiction, a purely juridical transaction in the heavenly court. Whom God justifies, them he also sanctifies: "The wisdom and power of God are the life according to the gospel and the very rule of the Christian life, by which he *makes and reputes* us wise and strong before himself—and this according to our inner being." [27] Precisely because sin is still such a force even within the believer, sanctification involves nothing less than new creation. Where Ritschl speaks of the "Christian's business of self-renewal" (as the counterpoise to his weakness and imperfection), Luther constantly speaks of God's *nova creatio*, indeed *creatio ex nihilo* (as the counterpoise to man's root sinfulness). The God who pronounces a person righteous for Christ's

[26] What H. R. Mackintosh once wrote concerning Ritschl's teaching on sin and grace, compared to that of the New Testament, might also be said *mutatis mutandis* with respect to his Luther interpretation: "What Ritschl teaches is sober in tone, but it is seldom tinged with the wonderful feeling of the New Testament; we do not easily think of it as stimulating the reader to joy unspeakable and full of glory. Yet if the gospel is a theme of wonder, the theology which ought to catch and absorb something of that glow but does not, fails even as theology. It has in part lost touch with the great realities" (*Types of Modern Theology: Schleiermacher to Barth*, pp. 173-74).

[27] *Romans Lectures*, p. 20; italics added.

sake through faith is the same God who is making him righteous through the gift of the Creator Spirit. Through baptism the Spirit of Christ dwells within the believer, progressively conforming him to his crucified and resurrected Lord. As Luther wrote in *The Babylonian Captivity of the Church* (1520):

[It is] indeed correct to say that baptism is a washing away of sins, but the expression is much too mild and weak to bring out the full significance of baptism, which is rather a symbol of death and resurrection. . . . The sinner does not so much need to be washed as he needs to die, in order to be renewed and made another creature, and to be conformed to the death and resurrection of Christ, with whom he dies and rises again through baptism.[28]

From his earliest lectures on the Psalms (1513-15) to his final lectures on Genesis (1535-45), Luther consistently viewed justification as a making righteous (*Gerechtmachung*) no less than a declaring righteous (*Gerechtsprechung*).[29] The young Luther was particularly fond of the parable of the Good Samaritan as illustrating, when interpreted tropologically, God's progressive healing of the sinner within the Church.[30] What Ritschl saw

[28] LW 36, 68.

[29] Cf. Paul Althaus, *The Theology of Martin Luther*, p. 226: "Luther uses the terms 'to justify' [*justificare*] and 'justification' [*justificatio*] in more than one sense. From the beginning, justification most often means the judgment of God with which he declares man to be righteous [*justum reputare* or *computare*]. In other places, however, this word stands for the entire event through which a man is essentially made righteous (a usage which Luther also finds in Paul, Romans 5), that is, for both the imputation of righteousness to man as well as man's actually becoming righteous. . . . This twofold use of the word cannot be correlated with Luther's early and later theology; he uses 'justification' in both senses at the same time, sometimes shortly after each other in the same text.'

[30] Cf. *Romans Lectures*, p. 130: "So, then, this life is a life of cure from sin; it is not a life of sinlessness, as if the cure were finished and health had been recovered. The church is an inn and an infirmary for the sick and for convalescents. Heaven, however, is the palace where the whole and righteous live." This sanative process, to be sure, is perfected only beyond the grave in the resurrection of the body. Therefore Luther, particularly from *ca.* 1518 onward, insisted that what God works in us must always be subsumed under what he has already freely and fully bestowed upon us, i.e., the "declaring righteous for Christ's sake" takes precedence over the "making righteous through the Creator Spirit." The believer can rightly claim "I am righteous" only on the ground of Christ's alien righteousness, not in view of the beginnings of the new creation within him. Thus the ultimate basis of religious certainty ever remains faith's recurrent appropriation of an "alien and passive" righteousness. Yet for Luther progress in sanctification is real because the Spirit of Christ dwells within the believer, conforming him to Christ. As a result the story of the Christian life between baptism and the resurrection is that of constant battle between "flesh" and "Spirit," between the "old

as a later deflection into Romanist modes of thought—Luther's concern with the "transformation" of the sinner into a saint, the transition from *injustus* to *justus*—was in fact a recurrent motif in Luther's theology from first to last.[31]

Adam" and the "new man." From what was said previously it might appear that, according to Luther, the believer ever remained in his sin, i.e., always a sinner, never a saint. Hence it must be stressed that for Luther the believer remains a sinner only under God's strict judgment. If God were to deal with him solely on the basis of his wrath, then even the believer must forego all hope in spite of his "newness." But because God regards him in mercy for Christ's sake and has bestowed on him his Spirit, the believer's works are truly God-pleasing and without blemish. In brief, the Christian man is at one and the same time both a righteous person and a sinner, owing to the duality of God's judgment on the total person and the believer's own concrete existence as at once "flesh" and "Spirit." Or, as Luther also expressed the matter, under the strict judgment of God sin in the believer is *peccatum regnans*. Under grace and the Spirit it is *peccatum regnatum*. What must be emphasized in this context is that Luther employed the *simul justus et peccator* formula, and thereby underscored the radicality of sin even in the believer, in order to safeguard the "for Christ's sake," not to discount the reality of sanctification. Indeed, the believer's continuance in sin makes sanctification all the more imperative, while the gift of the Spirit makes it an indubitable reality.

[31] Cf. *Romans Lectures*, p. 322: "For by repenting [the believer] becomes righteous from being unrighteous. Repentance is, therefore, the medium between unrighteousness and righteousness. And thus he is in sin as the *terminus a quo* and in righteousness as the *terminus ad quem*." It must be acknowledged that Ritschl would have been correct in charging Luther with a regression into Romanist modes of thought had Luther understood this "transformation" or sanative process as the progressive creation of a new and higher nature (*habitus*) within the believer, in view of which "newness" God would reckon him righteous. (Then justification would be understood as an analytic rather than a synthetic judgment.) But Luther in fact constantly polemicized against this physical understanding of justification. At no time does the believer possess any formal righteousness of his own, but he is ever being formed by Christ and the Holy Spirit. Thus for Luther justifying faith is properly a *fides Christo formata* in contrast to the scholastic notion of a *fides caritate formata*. For Luther transformation (or the new life, or progress) is not comprehended as a real progressive growth in one's own empirical righteousness whereby one could at last stand *coram Deo*, but, as Gordon Rupp points out, "a progress in faith, hope and love, a dwelling in the Righteousness of Christ through faith, in the power of the Holy Ghost" (*The Righteousness of God*, p. 183), or, in Prenter's words, "a constant flight away from one's empirical piety to Christ as the alien righteousness" (*Spiritus Creator*, pp. 98-99). Luther indicates the dynamic and progressive character of justification by describing the believer as *"semper peccator, semper penitens, semper justus"* (WA 56, 442, 17). At the same time justification is complete, because faith apprehends that perfect righteousness of Christ which renders the believer wholly acceptable and fully righteous before God. Luther traces this dual character of justification to the believer's simultaneous possession of both grace (pure mercy for Christ's sake) and gift (the real presence of the indwelling Spirit).—"A righteous and faithful man doubtless has both grace and gift. Grace makes him wholly pleasing so that his person is wholly accepted, and there is no place for wrath in him any more, but the gift heals from sin and from all his corruption of body and soul. . . . Everything is forgiven through grace, but as yet not everything is healed through the gift" (LW 32, 229).

In view of these varied considerations, Ritschl's interpretation of the young Luther on justification is not only dubious but patently defective. His reading of Luther seriously compromised the dominant theocentric context of Luther's thought (for God's very Godness is at stake in this matter of sin and grace); minimized Luther's estimate of the gravity of sin in the believer (for even amid his best works the Christian remains totally sinner, save for the gift of Christ's alien righteousness); and neglected the transformationist motif in Luther's position (for justification is not simply pardon or forgiveness but nothing less than new creation). On Ritschl's interpretation, justification for Luther had to do primarily with the removal of the believer's consciousness of guilt owing to his moral shortcomings. For Luther himself, as the primary sources (especially the *Romans Lectures*) bear out with virtually monotonous insistence, the paramount issue is the removal of God's verdict of condemnation which hangs over and threatens the sinner because of his root sinfulness.

Certainly Luther, no less than Ritschl, was directly concerned with the solution to the believer's consciousness of guilt, with what might be called the subjective concomitants of justification (the feeling of liberation in contrast to the feeling of guilt, etc.). In fact it was Luther's own profound awareness of guilt, his acute agonies of conscience (*Anfechtungen*), which impelled him on his momentous quest for a gracious God. But that awareness, those agonies, this spiritual quest: all derive their pathos and significance from their anchorage in Luther's overarching theocentric perspective, wherein the self is always comprehended *coram Deo*. One cannot claim, therefore, that Luther was more objective than Ritschl, that Luther had little interest in the affective states of the person who is justified. The point is that Luther, owing to his consistent theocentrism, *radicalized these affective states* in a way that Ritschl's interpretation has simply left out of account. In brief, Ritschl neglected to consider Luther's so-called *Urerlebnis*, his primal anguish of conscience—the overwhelming sense of being threatened by the consuming fire of the Divine Majesty, as a result of which one also feels "hemmed in" by the world—owing to the terrible corruption of the human heart.[32] Conspicuous by their absence are such authentic Lutheran motifs as the holiness and the wrath of God, the believer's "suffering" (*passio*) under God's word of judgment, the Spirit-wrought capitulation of "moral man," etc. When abstracted from these motifs, however, the young Luther's doctrine of justification not only

[32] For an insightful treatment of Luther's understanding of the human situation under the divine judgment, see Werner Elert, "Under the Wrath of God," in *The Structure of Lutheranism*, I (St. Louis, 1962), 15-58.

loses its inner power and distinctive character but becomes virtually unintelligible.

The Distinction Between Law and Gospel

The ability to distinguish between law and gospel was for Luther the highest theological art. "Whoever knows well how to distinguish the gospel from the law should give thanks and know that he is a real theologian." [33] Luther regarded this crucial distinction as the very heart and center of the doctrine of justification: "When this distinction is recognized, the true meaning of justification is recognized." [34] Luther's gravest charge against the Roman Church was that "the pope has not only confused the law and the gospel; but he has changed the gospel into mere laws, and ceremonial laws at that." [35] It is indisputable that Luther employed this distinction, in Gerhard Ebeling's words, "to designate the essential nerve of theological thinking: that which makes a theologian into a theologian because it provides the fundamental index to the content of Holy Scripture." [36] When Ritschl rejected this distinction as a foreign element in Luther's "practical" perspective on justification, he was in effect setting aside the cornerstone of Luther's biblical theology.

To be sure, Luther's own utterances cited in the preceding paragraph are all found in a single late work (1535). The decisive question is whether Luther, *prior* to the indulgence controversy and polemics with Rome, articulated his concept of justification in terms of the law-gospel formula. The answer is that already in its earliest form Luther's theology is shaped by this distinction. In the first series of lectures on the Psalms (1513-15) Luther announced: "In the Holy Scripture it is best to distinguish the spirit from the letter, for that truly makes one a theologian." [37] In subsequent lectures and treatises Luther increasingly moved away from this Augustinian letter/spirit contrast (in which "shadow" is opposed to "reality") to the customary law/gospel distinction (in which the law is

---

[33] LW 26, 115 ("Galatians Lectures," 1535).
[34] *Ibid.*, p. 313.
[35] *Ibid.*, p. 117.
[36] Gerhard Ebeling, *Luther: Einführung in sein Denken* (Tübingen, 1964), p. 121. See the following works for analyses of Ritschl's rejection of the law-gospel formula: Robert Schultz, *Gesetz und Evangelium in der lutherischen Theologie des 19. Jahrhunderts* (Berlin, 1958), pp. 168-78; Gerhard Forde, *The Law-Gospel Debate: An Interpretation of Its Historical Development* (Minneapolis, 1969), pp. 96-119; and Paul Jersild, "Judgment of God in Albrecht Ritschl and Karl Barth," *The Lutheran Quarterly* 14 (1962): 328-46.
[37] WA 3, 12, 2 ("Dictata super Psalterium").

God's "demanding" word and the gospel his "promising" or "giving" word). The precise development of Luther's thought on the law-gospel distinction is a highly complex matter, but from the earliest period forward there is a discernible continuity in his testimony to the supreme theological importance of this distinction. In 1521, for example, he asserts: "Virtually the entire Scripture and the whole of theological knowledge depend on the correct understanding of law and gospel." [38] Taken in itself, then, Ritschl's explicit repudiation of the law-gospel formula, in direct opposition to Luther's own oft-repeated testimony to its centrality, places a question mark over the whole of his interpretation and indicates a serious failure to hear Luther aright. I shall attempt to put this failure into context when, in the next chapter, I inquire into the basic defect of his exposition. Here it may be noted that the inadequacy of Ritschl's conclusions about the law-gospel formula was already conceded, at least in part, by Adolf von Harnack. Harnack gratefully yet critically appropriated the fruits of his mentor's Luther studies. In his *History of Dogma* he consciously moved away from Ritschl's position when he forthrightly stated: "Luther was also able to describe the whole of Christianity under the scheme of law and gospel; nay, at a very early date he embodied his new knowledge in this scheme." [39]

Ritschl, however, is also due a favorable word. Viewed from a certain qualified perspective, his dismissal of the law-gospel formula as "un-Lutheran" appears not only cogent and defensible but faithful to Luther's deepest intentions. What rendered this formula suspect in his eyes was his belief that it directly occasioned the pietistic insistence on a specifiable and repeatable conversion experience as the presupposition of personal salvation. In other words, this formula was supposedly the fruit of Luther's monkish training in Christianity, while Pietism simply con-

[38] WA 7, 502, 34 ("Postillen," 1521).

[39] Adolf von Harnack, *History of Dogma*, VII (New York, 1961; reprint of the Eng. trans. of 1900 from the 3rd German ed.), 204. In a footnote Harnack writes: "Lipsius has convinced me that in following Ritschl I have not done justice to Luther's doctrine of the law in its bearing on repentance. But I cannot agree with all that he sets forth, and chiefly for this reason, that—however clearly we can see what Luther himself ultimately wished with his distinction between law and gospel—the Reformer's expositions are not found when we go into detail to be harmonious" (n. 1, pp. 205-6). Harnack's reference to R. A. Lipsius is to the latter's monograph, "Luthers Lehre von der Busse," *Jahrbücher für protestantische Theologie* 18 (1892): 161-340. For a treatment of Harnack's Luther interpretation and its indebtedness to that of Ritschl, see Jaroslav Pelikan, "Adolf von Harnack on Luther," in *Interpreters of Luther: Essays in Honor of Wilhelm Pauck* (Philadelphia, 1968), pp. 253-74. See also Robert Kübel, "Ueber die Darstellung des Christentums und der Theologie Luthers in Harnacks Dogmengeschichte III," *Neue kirchliche Zeitschrift* 2 (1891): 13-57.

tinued and exaggerated Luther's monastic "terrors of conscience." In effect, contended Ritschl, Pietism regarded Luther's idiosyncratic experience in the cloister as the perpetually valid model of all Christian experience of God's grace. On this model the knowledge of sin comes strictly from the preaching of the law, which continually awakens despair over one's sins (past as well as present) and thus leads to true repentance; while the subsequent assurance of grace derives solely from the gospel-proclamation, which continually awakens the saving faith that appropriates forgiveness. First law and sin and death; then (and only then) gospel and grace and life. Ritschl considered such a *modus operandi* intolerable because it could only produce Christian schizophrenics. The believer would forfeit both his peace of mind and religious certainty by being forced repeatedly to consider himself at one and the same time a beloved child of God and a base slave of sin. On Ritschl's view only the gospel and faith, not any demand for conversion, can effect true repentance. Heartfelt contrition presupposes love of the good, the positive adhesion of the will to the moral ideal present in the New Testament picture of Christ's obedient suffering unto death. When Ritschl rejected the law-gospel formula as the theological precipitate of Luther's private monastic experience—which Pietism took over and transformed into a regulative feature of Christian existence—he actually intended to uphold what was Luther's own most dearly treasured perception: the transcendent superiority of the gospel to that legalistic manipulation of the anxious conscience which invariably leads either to moral scrupulosity or self-satisfied complacency. In Luther's name, and if need be against Luther, Ritschl intended to oppose all nomistic piety.

In his own way, therefore, Ritschl called welcome attention to the untenability of a purely external and mechanical correlation of law and gospel which might do service in revivalistic preaching. He erred, however, in attributing such a correlation to the mature Luther.[40] Throughout his career Luther maintained that law and gospel display an indissoluble unity in evangelical preaching. While sharply distinguished, they must

---

[40] Cf. J. & R. I, 180, where Ritschl rightly remarks that in 1516 Luther maintained that the gospel "alone interpets the law in its spiritual sense, and so attains to *mortificatio* or repentance." Ritschl was mistaken, however, in asserting that Luther subsequently broke with this original viewpoint, that Luther "entirely abandoned the view that such an apprehension of the law as leads to repentance is itself conditioned by a certain measure of saving faith" (p. 183). Cf. WA 39-I, 416, 8 ("Disputatio prima contra Antinomos," 1537): "The law and the gospel neither can nor ought to be separated, even as repentance and the forgiveness of sins [must not be separated]. For they are intimately bound together and involved in each other."

not be separated; theirs is an opposition in unity. Luther's formula, stated somewhat baldly, is law *and* gospel, not law *then* gospel. It is solely from the perspective of the gospel that the law can be comprehended and used aright: "The gospel makes of the law a disciplinarian that leads to Christ." [41] While the so-called "spiritual" function of the law (*usus legis theologicus*) is to awaken and convict of sin, such an operation would only engender hypocrisy and the other concomitants of nomistic piety if it were abstracted from the gospel and made into an independent, self-contained entity. Such legalistic preaching, held Luther, would burden consciences far more than all the papistic babble about works and merit. God's wrath revealed in the law would work nothing but unspeakable despair in the conscience if the consolations of the gospel were not immediately conjoined. Certainly God's wrath over sin is no illusion; the law always condemns because it always encounters *homo peccator*. Yet only the gospel shows that the wrath of God's severity is in fact the wrath of his fatherly goodness; it alone shows that such wrath is his "strange work" standing in service of, and culminating in, that ineffable mercy which is his "proper work." [42] For Luther this unity of law and gospel is ultimately rooted in the unity of the being and work of God the Holy Spirit, who is himself the acting subject in the proclamation of law and gospel.—The God who judges through the word of condemnation is none other than the God who acquits through the word of promise. Even as God the Judge and Savior is one, so also his word is one, which is to say that *both* forms of the word, law and gospel, must be proclaimed and always *together*. Regin Prenter has aptly summed up Luther's consistent position on the requisite "togetherness" of law and gospel: "The spiritual use of the law does not in the strict sense belong to the realm of the law, but to the realm of the gospel. In the spiritual use of the law

[41] WA 39-I, 446, 22 ("Secunda disputatio contra Antinomos," 1538). Cf. 446, 1: "And so the law ought to be interpreted through the gospel and be led back through that which is impossible to its salutary use, namely, to Christ and to the gospel, which by its power makes a disciplinarian [*paedagogum*] out of a robber and takes hold of the person who was killed by the law and brings him back to Christ; for this is what the law cannot do."

[42] *Romans Lectures*, pp. 44-45. Cf. p. 42: "There is so much blindness in a sinner that he misuses what is given to him for his good, thus causing his own ruin. On the other hand, there is so much light in a righteous and religious man that he uses for his good what is given to him for ill. Hence, the godless man does not know that the goodness of God leads him to repentance, but the righteous man understands that the severity of God also works toward his salvation. For he breaks down and heals, 'he kills and makes alive.' "

the law is no longer an independent power but is subordinated to the gospel and placed at its disposal." [43]

Thus Ritschl rejected the law-gospel formula in opposition to nomistic piety, out of intended fidelity to the Lutheran "grace alone." But Luther himself insisted on the necessity of this formula *precisely in order to destroy nomistic piety once and for all*. The law must be preached for the sake of the gospel, in order to establish the latter as genuine "good news." When an individual hears the law proclaimed in its authentic form as *God's* just demand, as the total claim on the total person calling for perfect love toward God and the neighbor, then in his conscience he realizes the impossibility of ever standing before God on the basis of any presumed legal righteousness. For since it is a question of righteousness before God predicated on obedience to God's own commands, rather than one's vaunted righteousness before others predicated on conformity to one's own sense of rectitude, every notion of legal righteousness is a mockery of God. In itself, to be sure, God's law is truly good, holy, and just, but because it encounters and exposes *homo peccator* it always accuses, never justifies. The road to God along the way of nomistic piety is forever blocked by God's own law which renders every man a sinner without excuse. Precisely at this point—when every presumptuous claim to virtue or legal rectitude or even relative perfection has been abolished by the law itself—the absolute wonder of the gospel first comes to light: God confounds the wise by justifying the ungodly, doing so not only in spite of the law's just demands but in truth *contra legem*.

Had Ritschl fully perceived the meaning of the law-gospel distinction for Luther, he could scarcely have considered the believer's own sense

---

[43] Prenter, *Spiritus Creator*, p. 220. So also Althaus, *The Theology of Martin Luther*, p. 260: "Both belong together and both must be preserved in the church: anxiety and pain under the law, and comfort and joy under the gospel. These two together constitute true evangelical repentance. Evangelical repentance is thus worked by the law and gospel together. In this process the law precedes the gospel." If justice is to be done to Luther's position, it cannot be sufficiently stressed that the unity of law and gospel in effecting repentance is not to be understood merely as a theological construct, as a unity achieved by a theoretical adjustment or dialectical balance of conflicting forces, a unity seen from the vantage point of a third person or "spectator." Rather, it is ever a unity which is *experienced and confessed* by the believer in his *Anfechtung*, when the word of divine judgment strikes his conscience and empties him of all pretense to goodness, a "shaking of the foundations" which would surely end in utter despair were it not for the accompanying proclamation of divine pardon which liberates the conscience with the promise, "Son, be of good cheer, your sins are forgiven you." In sum, through the hearing of this twofold word, and amid the experience of "salutary despair" which attends such hearing, evangelical repentance is worked by the Spirit and the unity of law and gospel is "lived out."

of moral honor as a contributing factor in evangelical repentance. By recognizing Christ's life as the "model of what life should be," said Ritschl, we at the same time "do homage to our own ideal . . . from the standpoint of our own honor and dignity." [44] As Luther was at pains to show in his *Romans Lectures,* just such a standpoint still lay wholly within the bounds of egocentric and nomistic piety. It represented the self-satisfied outlook of the *homo religiosus,* who felt no qualms at juxtaposing his own moral dignity alongside the honor of Christ and his own sense of rectitude alongside the demands of God's law. Yet "in the Church," insisted Luther, "we must not merely see to it that our righteousness and wisdom, which are not worth anything, are neither upheld by our own sense of glory nor extolled by the good opinion of others, but rather, we must take pains that they are destroyed and plucked up from our own complacent inner feeling." [45] In short, if the law is not preached in all its severity then the gospel does not appear in all its splendor; if "everything that is in us" is not overthrown, then "everything that is outside us and in Christ" is not established for our salvation. "For even if by his native and spiritual gifts a man is wise, righteous, and good in the sight of men," concluded Luther, "he is not so regarded by God, especially if he considers himself as such. Therefore we must keep ourselves humble in all these respects, as if we were still bare, and look for the naked mercy of God that he may reckon us righteous and wise." [46]

I conclude, therefore, that Ritschl's dismissal of the law-gospel formula cannot be sustained, at least for the specific reasons he advanced. He wrongly attributed to the late Luther what belongs to the total Luther. He asserted discontinuity in Luther's theological development where there is massive evidence of continuity. He mistakenly assimilated Luther's position to that of Pietism (as he understood this latter phenomenon). Most significantly, perhaps, he simply failed to probe the subtleties of Luther's position.[47] Certainly the law-gospel distinction bears its own

---

[44] J. & R. III, 166-67.

[45] *Romans Lectures,* pp. 3-4.

[46] *Ibid.,* pp. 4-5. One might contend that Ritschl—by giving scope in the matter of repentance to the believer's own sense of moral honor and dignity—simply broke apart the sharp dualism of Luther's *coram Deo/coram hominibus* and *justitia aliena/justitia propria* distinctions. For Luther, owing to his uncompromising attack on religious eudaemonism, precisely this sense of worth as a "moral personality" must be broken down and stripped of its presumed value if the *sola gratia* and the *sola fides* are to emerge in their true radicality. On Luther's view, true repentance is not the result even in part of the religious man's *amor boni* but strictly of the Spirit-wrought *accusatio sui.*

[47] According to Ritschl, Luther and Melanchthon—by adopting the view that

complexities, ambiguities, and problems. Yet it runs like a guiding thread throughout Luther's total theology, and the Reformer never wavered in according it absolute centrality. Hence it is all the more remarkable that Ritschl should have dealt with this leitmotif in such a cursory and deprecatory fashion. One suspects—a point to which I shall return—that in this instance Ritschl the systematician prevailed over Ritschl the historian. For a variety of reasons he could make no room for the law-gospel formula in his own dogmatics; little wonder he found it such a rock of offense in his dear Luther.[48] Still, by assigning this formula to the "defective" Luther, he could conscientiously maintain his fidelity to the "genuine" Luther.

---

evangelical repentance is based on the twofold proclamation of law and gospel—in effect "abandoned the thought that the congregations before them were Christian, however incomplete might be their moral condition; and instead of this set out with the presupposition that they had to do with the 'common rude man,' who first of all needed to be converted to Christianity, and from whom the logically correct and alone effective view of the conditions of conversion had to be carefully withheld" (J. & R. I, 184). This blanket condemnation simply obscures the subtle and significant distinctions which the mature Luther made apropos the law's role in the Christian life. In the case of both the unbeliever and the believer (or the unregenerate and the regenerate man), the preached law attacks the conscience and always accuses of sin. But in the former case, where faith in Christ is absent, the law rules in the conscience and either induces abject despair or is "rationalized" by the "moral man" who uses this very law as an instrument of self-justification. When this same accusing law strikes the conscience of the Christian, however, faith opposes its Lord Christ, the victor over law, sin, and divine wrath, to these insistent threats of the law. Thus faith (namely, the *Christus victor* who is really present in and for faith) drives the accusing law out of the conscience, where it seeks to rule, into the "members," i.e., faith makes of the law a curb to the continuing "fleshly" impulses of the Christian. In the following graphic reply of the Christian to the accusing law, Luther illustrates this transfer of law from the believer's conscience to his recalcitrant flesh: "Law, what is it to me if you make me guilty and convict me of having committed many sins? In fact, I am still committing many sins every day. This does not affect me; I am deaf and do not hear you. Therefore you are telling your story to a deaf man, for I am deaf to you. But if you really want to argue with me about sins, then go over to my flesh and my limbs which are my servants. Teach them; discipline and crucify them. But do not trouble my conscience, which is lord and king; for I have nothing to do with you. For I am dead to you; I now live to Christ, where I am under another Law, namely, the Law of grace, which rules over sin and the Law" (LW 26, 158). For Luther, therefore, the preaching of the law is existentially conditioned according to what person it is confronting: one and the same law ultimately effects different responses in different persons according to their faith or unfaith. Accordingly, Ritschl must be faulted for neglecting Luther's manifest sensitivity to the distinction between the regenerate and the unregenerate conscience—a distinction which certainly militates against the notion that the preaching of the law necessarily entails the dislocation of the idea of the Church.

[48] See above, p. 34, n. 18, for a list of Ritschl's primary objections to the law-gospel formula.

‍₁ᵤ THE BASIC DEFECT OF RITSCHL'S
‍ LUTHER INTERPRETATION

In the previous chapter Ritschl's interpretation of the young Luther was closely examined and found seriously wanting at crucial points. A number of Luther's most characteristic themes, cardinal insights, and dominant concerns were obscured, minimized, or simply left out of account. In Ritschl's presentation one finds virtually no indication of Luther's so-called Copernican revolution in theology, whereby the drama of salvation was transferred from the stage of man's religious and moral endeavors to the forum of heaven and God's self-giving love.[1] Owing to his relentless, uncompromising assault on religious eudaemonism—an attack predicated on his understanding of God's righteousness and the attendant human predicament *coram Deo*—Luther engineered a dramatically new comprehension of the God-man relationship which was at once more radical and creative than Ritschl's interpretation allows.[2] Yet Ritschl was supremely confident that he had recovered Luther's practical theology in its original, pristine form. If this critique is accurate, such self-confidence must be deemed premature and ill-founded (although such a judgment, as will be shown in the concluding chapter, cannot be the final verdict). In spite of his impressive analytical and expository skills, Ritschl failed to lay hold of the authentic Luther.

This failure raises the larger question of historical explanation. Why in fact did Ritschl fail to comprehend Luther aright? Is it possible to

[1] See Philip Watson, *Let God Be God: An Interpretation of the Theology of Martin Luther* (Philadelphia, 1947), pp. 33-38.
[2] Cf. Luther's exposition of Psalm 51 (1532/1538) in LW 12, 311, where he specifies the subject matter of theology as *homo peccator* and *Deus justificans:* "The content of the psalm is the theological knowledge of man and also the theological knowledge of God. Let no one, therefore, ponder the Divine Majesty, what God has done and how mighty He is; or think of man as the master of his property, the way the lawyer does; or of his health, the way the physician does. But let him think of man as sinner. The proper subject of theology is man guilty of sin and condemned, and God the Justifier and Savior of man the sinner. . . . The issue here is the future and eternal life; the God who justifies, repairs and makes alive; and man, who fell from righteousness and life into sin and eternal death. Whoever follows this aim in reading the Holy Scriptures will read holy things fruitfully."

pinpoint a basic, underlying defect in his interpretation which might account for specific errors or flaws therein, as well as for a number of misdirected criticisms which he leveled against Luther the theologian? Or, to pose the same question in a different form, is there a controlling center in Luther's theology to which Ritschl did not accord sufficient attention, with the predictable result that his interpretive focus was necessarily off-center? I have already contended that Ritschl was insensitive to the rigorously theocentric grounding of Luther's thought. In this chapter I go on to maintain that Ritschl also failed to do justice to the kerygmatic character of Luther's theology.[3] This is not to suggest that Luther's theocentrism somehow stands in competition with, or is of less import than, his theology of the Word. The point is that Luther's theocentrism is most clearly expressed in his view that God exercises his sovereign lordship by speaking: God shows himself to be God precisely through his creating, judging, redeeming, and sanctifying Word. When, for example, Ritschl turned to Luther's *On Christian Liberty,* he did so primarily because he found there the classic expression of the Christian life ideal as religious dominion over the world. In that same treatise, however, as the following quotation bears out, Luther closely linked this motif of Christian kingship with its transcendent presupposition, the Word of God:

One thing, and only one thing, is necessary for Christian life, righteousness, and freedom. That one thing is the most holy Word of God, the gospel of Christ. . . . Let us then consider it certain and firmly established that the soul can do without anything except the Word of God and that where the Word of God is missing there is no help at all for the soul. If it has the Word of God it is rich and lacks nothing since it is the Word of life, truth, light, peace, righteousness, salvation, joy, liberty, wisdom, power, grace, glory, and of every incalculable blessing.[4]

[3] The reader should perhaps again be cautioned against drawing the unwarranted conclusion that Ritschl interpreted Luther in an anthropocentric fashion (or that Ritschl himself, in his systematic theology, took man to be the measure of things). Ritschl repeatedly emphasized that for Luther justification was a creative act of the divine will, specifically God's "synthetic" judgment (and, in like manner, Ritschl himself construed justification as God's free resolve to pardon the sinner apart from any "merit or worthiness" on the latter's part). Ritschl, however, did fail to grasp Luther's view of justification as God's continuous *creatio ex nihilo* through the Word of promise, to the end that the believer's faith or consciousness of forgiveness ever remains subject to this God who speaks, and so remains a gift and is never a permanent possession. It is my claim, then, that Ritschl's interpretation neglects to indicate the *specific way* in which Luther's teaching on justification is at once theocentric and kerygmatic (one might say, theocentric *because* kerygmatic).

[4] LW 31, 345.

It may readily be granted that Ritschl in part recovered and revitalized Luther's grand motif of Christian freedom. I have shown in Chapter I that Ritschl self-consciously attempted to give new currency to many of Luther's leading themes by taking them into his own systematic theology. At this point, however, one must pose the fundamental question: Did Ritschl satisfactorily comprehend the presupposition of these motifs, namely, the gospel of Christ, or *Christusverkündigung?* My answer is that he did not.

This latter assertion obviously requires closer scrutiny and supporting documentation. The aim in this chapter, therefore, will be twofold: (1) to elaborate what is meant by designating Luther a kerygmatic theologian and by asserting that the Word of God is the controlling center in his theology; and (2) to specify in what respects Ritschl manifests his reputed neglect of Luther's theology of the Word. I propose to carry out this twofold aim by closely examining the following central features of Ritschl's Luther interpretation: his focus on Luther's presumed recovery of medieval piety as the original dynamic of Church reform in the sixteenth century; his concentration on the experiential bearing of justification; and his assertion that Luther failed to frame a satisfactory teleological doctrine of justification. Within this framework I shall endeavor to show that Ritschl did not perceive to what extent the Reformation itself was an exegetical phenomenon, originating in Luther's creative encounter with Scripture. I have previously noted that Ritschl sharply repudiated the law-gospel formulation as an unwarranted holdover from Luther's monastic training, apparently without realizing that this distinction functioned as Luther's chief principle of scriptural interpretation and lay at the heart of his biblical theology. In like manner—one might truly say *because* of this repudiation—his treatment of the young Luther on justification obscured the role of the dynamic Word in God's handling of the sinner, for God crushes and heals specifically through his *verbum efficax.* Further, upon careful analysis, Ritschl's censure of Luther as a theologian will be seen to turn largely on his own failure to give due weight to Luther's cardinal motif of "Word and faith."

1. THE REFORMATION AS AN EXEGETICAL PHENOMENON

In October, 1512, acting in obedience to a directive from Staupitz, Martin Luther became a Doctor of Sacred Scripture. For the remaining years of his life he faithfully fulfilled the office of lecturer in Scripture at the recently founded (1502) Wittenberg University. The Lutheran Reformation was thus the work of a professor of biblical theology. Modern scholars from Holl onward have increasingly approached Luther as primarily a biblical theologian, whose theology was not only pregnant with scriptural allusions and patterns of thought but which actually purported to be nothing other than exegetical theology.[5] Before his adversaries Luther boasted, "I know and am assured, by the grace of God, that I am more learned in the Scripture than all the sophists and papists," while friend and foe alike acknowledged his amazing grasp of the biblical material.[6] During his self-imposed exile in the Koburg (April to October, 1530), he wrote on the wall the prophetic words of Psalm 118:17: "I shall not die but shall live, and shall recount the deeds of the Lord"—and for Luther declaring God's works meant proclaiming his promises attested in Scripture. In later Lutheranism the *sola scriptura* theme may have hardened into a formal principle; for Luther himself this motto connoted the living center of his thought. "My conscience," he testified at Worms, "is captive to the Word of God." [7]

In Luther's hands Scripture invariably sprang to life and even today his commentaries pulsate with contemporary relevance, as indeed one might expect from a theologian who was not only a professor but also a preacher and pastor (as well as a biblical translator, impassioned pamphleteer and polemicist, devotional writer, composer of hymns, counselor to magistrates, and not least a paterfamilias). In fact precisely his lifelong vocational commitment to both the lecture platform and the pulpit supplies a significant index to Luther's own understanding of his work and thought. At root his theology is kerygmatic through and through, a theology of and for proclamation, centered on God's creative and dynamic Word which ever goes forth to make all things new. Fidelity to

[5] See Karl Holl, "Luthers Bedeutung für den Fortschritt der Auslegungskunst," in *Gesammelte Aufsätze zur Kirchengeschichte*, I: *Luther* (7th ed., Tübingen, 1948), 544-82; Gerhard Ebeling, *Evangelische Evangelienauslegung: Eine Untersuchung zu Luthers Hermeneutik* (Munich, 1942); Heinrich Bornkamm, *Luther und das Alte Testament* (Tübingen, 1948); Walther von Loewenich, *Luther als Ausleger der Synoptiker* (Munich, 1954); H. Ostergaard-Nielsen, *Scriptura sacra et viva vox* (Munich, 1957); Jaroslav Pelikan, *Luther the Expositor* (St. Louis, 1959); and James S. Preus, *From Shadow to Promise: Old Testament Interpretation from Augustine to the Young Luther* (Cambridge, Mass., 1969).

[6] LW 40, 55 ("Letter to the Princes of Saxony Concerning the Rebellious Spirit," 1524). Mosellanus, who presided at the Leipzig Debate, recorded this impression of Luther: "Luther is extraordinarily learned. Above all, he possesses such an astonishing knowledge of the Bible that he knows almost all of it by heart." Heinrich Boehmer, *Martin Luther: Road to Reformation* (New York, 1957), p. 288.

[7] LW 32, 112 ("Luther at the Diet of Worms," 1521).

Luther's own self-understanding and historical achievements requires a critical sensitivity both to his status as a biblical theologian and to the actual shape of his theology as a witness to the Word.

Ritschl's basic failure as a Luther interpreter is evidenced, perhaps most dramatically, in his depreciation of the central role of scriptural interpretation in Luther's theological development as well as in the Reformation *Ansatz*. Contemporary Luther scholars may diverge sharply on the dating of Luther's so-called tower experience (and may even suggest that it was not a single isolated discovery at some specifiable moment); but they generally agree that it was an exegetical phenomenon, predicated on Luther's agonizing long-term struggle with basic biblical concepts, especially the idea of God's righteousness.[8] Luther himself related how, "meditating day and night" upon Rom. 1:17, he at last began to understand that God's righteousness is not that "formal or active righteousness . . . with which God is righteous [in himself] and punishes the unrighteous sinner," but rather that "passive righteousness with which merciful God justifies us by faith." [9] It was Luther's existential grappling with Scripture which supplied his major theological categories; prompted his radical attack, in the name of the gospel, on scholastic theology, the papacy, monasticism, and the sacramental system; led to the transformation of the academic curriculum; and brought about the revitalization of Christian teaching and preaching. Luther clearly sounded the dominant note of his reformation activity when he wrote to Pope Leo X in 1520: "I have no quarrel with any man concerning his morals but only concerning the word of truth. In all other matters I will yield to any man whatsoever; but I have neither the power nor the will to deny the Word of God." [10] When in later years he reflected upon the remarkable course of the Reformation, Luther repeatedly ascribed its success to the agency of the Word alone.[11]

---

[8] See the collection of articles in Bernhard Lohse, ed., *Der Durchbruch der reformatorischen Erkenntnis bei Luther* (Darmstadt, 1968).

[9] LW 34, 337 ("Preface to the Complete Edition of Luther's Latin Writings," 1545). Cf. LW 54, 195-96 ("Table Talk").

[10] LW 31, 335 ("An Open Letter to Pope Leo X," 1520).

[11] In 1522 Luther asserted: "I simply taught, preached, wrote God's Word: otherwise I did nothing. And then, while I slept, or drank Wittenberg beer with my Philip and my Amsdorf, the Word so greatly weakened the Papacy that never a Prince or Emperor inflicted such damage upon it. I did nothing. The Word did it all. Had I desired to foment trouble, I could have brought great bloodshed upon Germany. Yea, I could have started such a little game at Worms, that the Emperor would not have been safe. But what would it have been? A mug's game. I left it to the Word." Cited in Gordon Rupp, *Luther's Progress to the Diet of Worms* (New York, 1964), p. 99. Cf. LW 51, 77-78 ("Eight Sermons at Wittenberg," 1522).

One can readily understand, then, why Luther wished to be remembered only as a faithful servant of the Word.

Ritschl, however, located the immediate source of Luther's Reformation consciousness, and of his practical fundamental principle of justification, in Luther's personal appropriation of a venerable ecclesiastical tradition, not in his personal encounter with Scripture. "I think I may venture to affirm," he wrote, "that neither Zwingli nor Luther either discovered the thought which was the leading one with them as Reformers, or rediscovered it merely by study of the Bible, but that they imbibed it from a tradition current within the Church." [12] Ritschl viewed Luther's central concept of justification by faith—that the believer regulates his religious self-estimate solely in the light of grace alone—as standing in an indisputable continuity with the highest piety of the Western Church, from St. Augustine through St. Bernard down to Johann Wessel and Johann von Staupitz. He vigorously polemicized against those "blind partisans of Luther" who out of myopic respect for Luther considered it "necessary to assume that in the thought of justification through Christ by faith he propounded something that up to his time had been utterly unheard of," and who further asserted that Zwingli was but a superficial borrower of Luther's new insights.[13] In response Ritschl contended that both Reformers independently appropriated a common medieval tradition of *sola gratia* piety:

> They actually established, as the practical standard in accordance with which the religious life of the Church should be constantly renewed, simply that thought in accordance with which the self-estimate of the most conspicuous characters of the middle ages was formed, and in which, as a whole, the loftiest and purest piety of the medieval church finds expression—the thought, namely, that with the Christian, whether he be conscious of relative perfection or relative imperfection, grace alone, and not merit, is the ground of his acceptance with God. [14]

Certainly Ritschl was fully justified in rejecting the thesis of absolute discontinuity between Luther's theology of grace and his medieval antecedents. Luther's precise relation to such medieval phenomena as the *via antiqua* and *via moderna*, the *devotio moderna*, speculative and practical mysticism, etc., has been the object of extensive research since Ritschl's

[12] J. & R. I, 166.
[13] *Ibid.*, pp. 163-64.
[14] *Ibid.*, p. 133.

day, and the accumulated evidence supports Ritchl's insistence that Luther was a genuinely catholic theologian who gratefully acknowledged his indebtedness to a cloud of witnesses in the Latin Church. Ritschl's remarks also provide a salutary reminder that the Reformation principle of *sola scriptura* did not exclude a positive adhesion to the theological tradition.[15] At the same time Ritschl greatly oversimplified an exceedingly complex problem with his own thesis of an unbroken continuity in piety (if not in doctrine and *Weltanschauung*). He failed to discern that Luther's biblical theology involved far more than an insistence on the priority of grace or even the exclusive value of grace for the troubled conscience, but had to do with the very meaning of grace and all its concomitants. The Reformation brought about and gave expression to a far-reaching transvaluation of values. Luther's exegetical labors led him to distinctly new positions on such questions as: How is grace *bestowed?* On *whom* (what manner of person) is it bestowed? How is it personally *appropriated?* Yet Ritschl so narrowly concentrated on the subjective value of the very thought of grace for the believer, as the answer to his inchoate righteousness, that he missed the truly revolutionary features of Luther's attack on the medieval tradition and failed to probe the depths of Luther's teaching.[16]

Surely Ritschl was also correct in asserting that it was not simply a *doctrine* of justification by faith which was "the lever of the Reformation." [17] For, as he rightly maintained, what came to expression in the clash over theological formulas was a new *consciousness* of the Christian's relationship to God, the Church, and the world.—But the "motive power that produced the Reformation" cannot be directly equated with that particular "attitude of the religious subjective consciousness" which Ritschl himself specified, namely, the awareness of "God's grace as the counterpoise of imperfect works"—an awareness which was simply a derivative and continuation of the loftiest Catholic piety of the Middle Ages.[18] Luther's religious consciousness, while inevitably shaped by ecclesiastical tradition and especially by his setting in late medieval theology and piety, was decisively informed by his personal encounter with Scrip-

---

[15] See Gerhard Ebeling, " 'Sola Scriptura' and Tradition," in *The Word of God and Tradition* (Philadelphia, 1968), pp. 102-47; and Peter Fraenkel, *Testimonia Patrum: The Function of the Patristic Argument in the Theology of Philip Melanchthon* (Geneva, 1961).

[16] Cf. above, p. 99, n. 19; and p. 101, n. 25.

[17] J. & R. I, 167.

[18] *Ibid.*, pp. 171, 138, 133.

ture, a profound dialogue between interpreter and text which literally shook the foundations on which the Church had rested for centuries.[19] Whether or not Luther could have found his radical theology of sin and grace in the tradition is not at issue. The point is that he in fact forged it for himself out of Scripture on the basis of continual *oratio, meditatio,* and *tentatio.* And what he discovered in the process was revolutionary enough to bring about the dividing of Christendom.

2. JUSTIFICATION AND PROCLAMATION

Earlier Ritschl's interpretation of the young Luther's idea of justification was questioned chiefly on the grounds that he did not accord sufficient weight to the theocentric context of Luther's teaching. This criticism may now be amplified and further substantiated by pointing out his neglect of the kerygmatic context of Luther's position. According to Ritschl, what Luther meant by justification through faith in Christ was "a subjective religious experience of the believer within the Church, and not an objective theological *dictum* in the Church's system of doctrinal beliefs." [20] In effect Ritschl poses two options: either justification is a personal religious experience of the believer, complete in itself and continuous; or it denotes a doctrinal proposition which must be believed on scriptural and ecclesiastical authority, without regard to any subjective determinants. I have previously observed that in other instances Ritschl's particular *Fragestellung* was largely informed by polemical rather than purely expository interests. It is obvious that by stating the issue of justification in this precise form he was explicitly striking out against the objectivizing and legalizing tendencies of neo-scholastic Orthodoxy. In this instance Ritschl believed he could demonstrate on historical grounds that Lutheran Orthodoxy stood judged and condemned by Luther himself (at least by the real Luther of the Reformation's early years). In view of Orthodoxy's crystallization of justification into the so-called material principle of Scripture, one may readily grant the weight of Ritschl's underlying polemic and recall its significance for the theological *status controversiae* of his own day. The question remains, of course, whether Ritschl correctly expounded the authentic Luther. Perhaps Orthodoxy and Ritschl *both* went wide of the mark in asserting their respective claims to represent true Lutheranism.

[19] See Gerhard Ebeling, "The New Hermeneutics and the Early Luther," *Theology Today* 26 (1964): 34-46.
[20] J. & R. I, 121.

Certainly Ritschl cannot be faulted for his emphasis on the experiential dimension of Luther's teaching. The repristinating Lutheran Orthodoxy of Ritschl's day fought with blunted instruments when it repudiated Schleiermacher's "ego-piety" in the name of Luther's supposed objectivism.[21] The late Paul Althaus of Erlangen, a dean of modern Luther research, justly asserted: "There can be no doubt that experience is one of the principles of [Luther's] theology. It is, of course, not a source of knowledge in and by itself, but it definitely is a medium through which knowledge is received." [22] Nor can there be any doubt that Ritschl rightly underscored Luther's intense concern with the *pro me* character of God's justifying activity. The Luther renaissance of the twentieth century has in no little measure been a recovery of the existential Luther, and Ritschl himself helped direct the course of scholarship into this fruitful channel. As is already evident from the previous discussion, however, Ritschl must be faulted for obscuring Luther's fundamental view of justification as a kerygmatic phenomenon, namely, God's redemptive work of pardoning and purging the sinner through the agency of his Spirit who is himself the acting subject in the proclamation of law and gospel. What follows is an attempt to draw together several of Luther's leading themes which have already been adumbrated in order to bring them to focus on the kerygmatic context of his teaching.

Luther's theology is completely theocentric, and that not only because God's righteousness provides the standard for appraising the human situation, but no less because justification is from start to finish God's own work: "The movement of justification is the work of God in us." [23] What must be stressed at this point is, first, that the specific form which this divine operation takes is that of the preached Word (*verbum vocale*) as law and gospel. "God has arranged to heal [men] through his speaking," wrote Luther in his *Romans Lectures*, and this healing Word which God speaks is at once judgment and mercy.[24] For Luther, therefore, God is always most properly thought of as the God who speaks, who clothes himself in words. Furthermore, God *acts* by his speaking, for "when God speaks a word, the thing expressed by the word immediately

---

[21] The Lutheran theology of the so-called Erlangen School implicitly sided with the main currents of nineteenth-century religious thought, and so with Ritschl no less than with Schleiermacher, when it attempted to articulate an *Erfahrungstheologie* grounded on a biblical and Reformation base.

[22] Althaus, *The Theology of Martin Luther*, p. 8.

[23] LW 34, 177 ("The Disputation Concerning Justification," 1536).

[24] *Romans Lectures*, p. 69.

leaps into existence." [25] The reason God's Word effects what it declares is that it is the instrument of his Spirit, and so is necessarily a living, dynamic, creative Word. Finally, the actual mode of God's working through his Word is always *sub contrariis,* under the form of opposites: he afflicts in order to heal; he kills in order to make alive; he humbles the proud so that he may exalt the humbled. "Because *we* live in a lie," states Prenter, summarizing Luther's position on the hiddenness of God's acting, "the truth, when it shall come to us, must appear *adversaria specie.* Therefore, if we want to hear, we must permit our own thoughts to be corrected by the Word, which comes to us as a message from the outside." [26]

God's salvatory working is thus encompassed in his Word and effected through his Spirit under the form of contraries. Accordingly, when viewed in this context, what justification entails is taking God at his Word, acknowledging as true what God declares one to be, namely, a sinner in thought, word, and deed—in direct opposition to one's own senses and reason and in spite of the "foolishness" of this Word which points to weakness, suffering, and the cross.[27] In the *Romans Lectures* Luther can assert that precisely this passive justification of God—letting God be God and one's self a liar—is in fact the active justification by God:

> By this "justification of God" we are justified. And this passive justification of God by which he is declared righteous by us is our active justification by God. For he reputes the faith as righteous that regards his words as righteous. . . . For he justifies (and triumphs) in his word when he makes us such as his word is, namely, righteous, true, wise, etc. And thus he changes us into his word, but not his word into us. And he makes us such as we believe his word to be, namely, righteous and true. For then certainly there is conformity between the word and the believer, i.e., in truth and righteousness. Therefore, when he is declared righteous, he makes righteous, and when he makes righteous, he is declared righteous.[28]

[25] LW 13, 99 ("Commentary on Psalm 90," 1534-35).

[26] Prenter, *Spiritus Creator,* pp. 118-19. Cf. *Romans Lectures,* p. 298: "But, in reality, the word of God comes, when it comes, in opposition to our thinking and wishing. It does not let our thinking prevail, even in what is most sacred to us, but it destroys and uproots and scatters everything. As we read in Jer. 1.10 and 23.29: 'Are not my words as fire and as a hammer that breaks the rock in pieces?' "

[27] Cf. *Romans Lectures,* pp. 69-70: "For the words which God lets go forth to men are regarded [by the godless and the proud] as foolish, mendacious, and meaningless, as if they were not God's. . . . Whoever, therefore, is satiated with his own truth and wisdom is incapable of comprehending the truth and wisdom of God, for they can be received only in emptiness and a vacuum."

[28] *Ibid.,* p. 77. See LW 26, 227 for a related emphasis in the mature Luther.

In this last passage Luther's train of thought is somewhat elliptical since he apparently neglects the christocentric ground of justification, i.e., the "for Christ's sake." Upon further consideration, however, this ambiguity is clarified and resolved. In the first place, the movement away from one's self, away from one's own domestic righteousness—which is the meaning of regarding God's words as just and true—is really the movement of faith to the alien righteousness of Christ and involves the actual bestowal of the latter as a gift. Luther explains his position as follows:

The passive and active justification of God and faith or trust in him are one and the same. For when we acknowledge his words as righteous, *he gives himself to us,* and *because of this gift* he recognizes us as righteous, i.e., he justifies us.[29]

The self-accusation wrought by the Spirit is at the same time the sinner's groaning for Christ and his righteousness, wherein alone he can stand before God; and to the broken and contrite spirit God gives himself in Christ. Secondly, it must be remembered that for Luther the Word to which God conforms us through his Spirit, when "he makes us such as his word is," is in the truest sense God's own "substantial" Word: the incarnate, crucified, and risen Christ. The supreme paradigm or Exemplar of God's mode of working under contraries is Christ himself, who was "first humbled and then glorified through the Holy Spirit." [30] Hence the believer must recognize that God now deals with him as he dealt with his Lord, "for all that comes from God must be crucified in this world (and so long as it is not led to the cross, i.e., the readiness to endure shame, it cannot be recognized as coming from God)." [31] Properly speaking, therefore, to be conformed to God's true and righteous Word—becoming "inwardly nothing, emptied of everything, and completely rid of ourselves" in order to be filled with the righteousness of God—is to be conformed to Christ.[32]

The believer's role throughout this divine operation is simply that of a *passio* under God's effective Word of judgment and pardon. Faith is itself Spirit-worked and is truly a *fides passiva* which suffers God's humbling action and receives his gift of Christ's alien righteousness. Thus the believer's sole work is one of hearing, for his faith is always a *fides ex auditu:*

[29] *Romans Lectures*, p. 78 (italics added).
[30] *Ibid.*, p. 14.
[31] *Ibid.*, p. 43.
[32] *Ibid.*, p. 70.

For if you ask a Christian what is the work with which he is made worthy the name of Christian, he can give no other answer than that hearing of the Word of God which is faith. Thus the ears alone are the organs of a Christian man because not by the works of any other members, but by faith he is justified and judged as a Christian.[33]

Luther repeatedly speaks of this faith which comes by hearing as a "hidden understanding," since the Christian lives not by his eyes (*sensus et ratio*) but solely through heartfelt trust in the hidden God who works under contraries, who in his revelation in Jesus Christ veiled himself in weakness, suffering, and an ignominious death, and who even now makes himself present redemptively through the humble and humbling Word of the cross.

One searches Ritschl's Luther interpretation in vain for a sustained exposition of the sequence of thoughts delineated in the preceding paragraphs. Yet in this thought complex lies the center of gravity of Luther's theology. Time and again Ritschl interprets justification in Luther to mean a "subjective experience of the believer within the Church," but he consistently fails to locate this experience within the overarching context designated by Luther himself: the framework of Word and faith. Lest this criticism be misconstrued, it should be added at once that Ritschl is not being accused of an un-Lutheran psychologism or subjectivism. As noted previously in Chapter III, it is a false antithesis to oppose Luther as an objectivist to Ritschl as a subjectivist. Ritschl is generally to be criticized less for what he asserts than for what he overlooks or fails to underscore. In this instance he must be faulted not for the emphasis on subjective experience, but for *neglecting to ascertain the precise manner in which Luther comprehends this experience from the perspective of his theology of the cross*, in the light of the Word of the cross. In brief, viewed from Luther's perspective, the believer's consciousness of justification cannot rightly be spoken of *apart from specifying the way this consciousness is continually regulated by the word of preaching*.

Luther repeatedly maintained that God's free pardon of the sinner—understood as both the divine act itself and the resultant personal awareness that God is gracious in spite of one's root sinfulness—does not take the form of insight or enlightenment or memory or even historical perception, which, once attained, continues in effect without interruption. Rather it is an event which ever again *occurs* through the faith which

[33] WA 57, 222, 5 ("Lectures on Hebrews," 1517-18), as translated by Gordon Rupp, *The Righteousness of God*, p. 211. Cf. LW 29, 224.

comes by hearing, in the course of the ongoing proclamation of the Word. Luther can speak of this Word event as follows:

So you see that the gospel is really not a book of laws and commandments which requires deeds of us, but a book of divine promises in which God promises, offers, and gives us all his possessions and benefits in Christ. . . . When you open the book containing the gospels and read or hear how Christ comes here or there, or how someone is brought to him, you should therein perceive the sermon or the gospel through which he is coming to you, or you are being brought to him. *For the preaching of the gospel is nothing else than Christ coming to us, or we being brought to him.* When you see how he works, however, and how he helps everyone to whom he comes or who is brought to him, then rest assured that faith is accomplishing this in you and that he is offering your soul exactly the same sort of help and favor through the gospel. If you pause here and let him do you good, that is, if you believe that he benefits and helps you, then you really have it. Then Christ is yours, presented to you as a gift.[34]

The Christ who once came to sinners on the plane of history still comes today in the Word of promise, and, when that gracious coming is personally received in faith, all the possessions and benefits of Christ accrue to the believer.

In such a context one cannot properly speak of the promise without faith, or of faith apart from the promise. Both must be held together in their tensive unity: *fides et promissio sunt correlativa.* Hence to concentrate primarily on the experiential dimension of justification, as Ritschl was wont to do, is, from Luther's perspective, to run the risk of separating the gift from the Giver. It is to suggest that the religious self-understanding (or faith) finds in itself its own *raison d'être*, or has a kind of self-contained validity. For Luther, furthermore, the experience of faith has a distinctly unique character since it is precisely faith in the Word of the cross, heartfelt trust in a divine goodness which expresses itself in judgment and which hides itself under its opposite. Thus faith is ever subject

---

[34] LW 35, 120-21 ("A Brief Instruction on What to Look for and Expect in the Gospels," 1521; italics added). In "Christus und die Heilige Schrift," *Lutherforschung heute,* ed. Vilmos Vajta (Berlin, 1958), Ruben Josefson appropriately remarks: "Along with the Word the subject itself is given: together with the message of the words and works of Jesus Christ, he himself is given as the Present One. According to Luther, his presence is always a presence in the Word and through the Word" (p. 58). Likewise Walther von Loewenich, *Luther als Ausleger der Synoptiker* (Munich, 1954), p. 107, summarizes Luther's train of thought as follows: "In the Word Christ is present (WA 27, 438, 6); it is the spiritual advent of Christ (45, 424, 37; 425, 8; 426, 1, 7). The reign of this King 'is bound up in the Word' and we are to bind this Word in our hearts; indeed every action of Christ is comprehended in the Word, for both in and through the Word he desires to give us everything, and vice versa (36, 46, 5)."

to repeated conflict with itself—when God is felt to be absent and doubt about his mercy grips the conscience—a profound inner conflict which, paradoxically, can be overcome in no other way than by hearing anew the Word of the cross. For in such hearing anew, faith acknowledges that it is truly a *gift* of God, not a permanent human possibility but an always new creation of Word and Spirit. The certainty of forgiveness, therefore, must always be won anew in the midst of *Anfechtung*, through that venturesome trust and combative faith whereby one suffers himself to be humbled under God's judgment, in confidence that he who creates out of nothing through his Word alone, and who has forever pledged himself to sinners in his Word made flesh, will exalt the humbled and raise up the dead even as he raised Christ from the dead and exalted him to the right hand of his majesty.[35]

In summary, according to Luther, faith—or the personal experience of justification—must not be abstracted from the Word. Faith has no independent status; it is the creation of the Word and must ever be controlled by the Word. To be sure, Ritschl asserts that faith is regulated by the community's religious consciousness, by the cultic sharing of its common memory of God's historic redemptive acts. One cannot claim that Ritschl, any more than Luther, turned the believer's religious self-understanding into some purely autonomous phenomenon. Yet Ritschl was not sufficiently attuned to Luther's insistence that the believing com-

---

[35] Because faith has to do with a concealed reality—the God who hides himself even in his revelation, whose grace is hidden under his wrath and whose saving power appears in the form of helplessness and weakness—it "must believe against reason, against its own feeling and intuition, and against its understanding which grasps and admits the validity only of that which is empirical" (Althaus, *The Theology of Martin Luther*, p. 57, n. 42). Thus there is no unambiguous experience of faith which is not shadowed by doubt and temptation, although Luther also acknowledges a positive experience arising from faith, e.g., the awareness of the renewing power of grace as displayed in good works. But *because there is no simple, unequivocal, transparent relation between faith and experience, or between faith and empirical righteousness, the believer must cling to the promise alone.* Althaus writes: "To believe means to live in constant contradiction of empirical reality and to trust one's self to that which is hidden. Faith must endure being contradicted by reason and experience; and it must break through the reality of this world by fixing its sights on the word of promise. This presupposes that faith is not a position on which one takes a stand but a constantly new movement. The empirical reality of human existence and of the world, the experience of trouble, of wrath, and of death, does not cease and cannot be avoided. The Christian can only overcome it constantly by holding fast to the word in faith" (p. 33). Ritschl certainly appropriated Luther's emphasis on the positive relation between faith and experience, as shown, for example, in the "practical" realization of spiritual lordship over the world through trust in God; yet he failed to apprehend that theology of *Anfechtung* which entirely permeates and shapes Luther's understanding of faith and experience.

munity, no less than the individual believer, must live continuously under and out of its daily encounter with the Word. Certainly the Church, as Ritschl rightly maintained, is the mother which gives birth to and nourishes every Christian, and so is prior to the individual; but at the same time the Church is also the creation of the gospel. Luther forcefully expressed the Church's total dependence on the Word when he advanced the following ecclesiological axiom: *"Tota vita et substantia Ecclesiae est in verbo Dei."* [36] As Philip Watson has stated: "It is the preaching about Christ, the proclamation of the Word, that is constitutive of the Church; for if the Church is the mother of Christians it is not the mother, but the daughter of the Word." [37] The Word as law and gospel must continuously be preached in the Church in order to uncover the depths of sin even among the religious, to reveal and root out human egocentricity masking itself as piety; and simultaneously to disclose anew the depths of divine mercy in Christ, to attest God's ongoing fidelity to his promises as the one sure ground of religious certainty, and to bestow the Creator Spirit as God's own answer to the Christian's daily battle with the flesh. I conclude, therefore, that while Ritschl justly repudiated Orthodoxy's distortion of justification into a doctrinal proposition, he himself, no less than Orthodoxy, obfuscated Luther's seminal insights into the *viva vox Dei* as the regulative principle of justification by faith. [38]

3. THE *FIDES CHRISTI* AND THE RELATION OF FAITH TO ETHICS

Ritschl held that already prior to 1517 Luther had arrived at his "practical consciousness of justification through Christ as the basis of

[36] WA 7, 721, 9 ("Ad librum Catharini responsio," 1521): "For the gospel— even more than the bread and baptism—is the unique, most certain and noblest sign of the Church, since it is through the gospel alone that the Church is conceived, formed, nourished, born, trained, fed, clothed, adorned, strengthened, armed and preserved. In short: the entire life and substance of the Church is in the Word of God. . . ."

[37] Watson, *Let God Be God*, p. 169.

[38] Ritschl, to be sure, observed that Word, faith, and community were reciprocally related concepts in Luther's theology. He correctly noted that, according to Luther, "no one attains unto faith unless as having a standing in the Church by means of the Word of God, and that God has given this key of the kingdom of heaven to the community of believers" (J. & R. I, 158). But Ritschl did not accord sufficient weight to this observation, nor did he "unpack" the full significance of Luther's correlation between Word and faith for life in the community. It is difficult to escape the conclusion that, on Ritschl's interpretation, the Church *has* the Word as its own instrumentality, rather than being constantly dependent on that Word for its ongoing existence.

Christian life in the Church." [39] In the course of the controversy over indulgences and penance, Luther defended this fundamental principle, exhorting the distressed penitent to look away from his works to the merit of Christ alone, it being assumed that he would continue performing good works. Subsequently, however, the controversy extended to the idea of justification per se, and now the specific question arose: How, on Luther's view, are good works possible at all, indeed, why are they even necessary, if everything depends on grace and faith alone? Does justification work any actual change in the believer himself? According to Ritschl, Luther accommodated himself to this line of questioning and undertook to explain, within the framework of the law-gospel distinction, the manner in which the sinner is made righteous. The result of this endeavor was that the Reformation doctrine of justification, "in form and tendency" at least, approximated to the similarly named but "really so different" Roman doctrine. [40]

While Luther consistently maintained that justification is strictly an *actus forensis* or sentence of divine acquittal, he also asserted that "through the gospel not only is forgiveness of sins bestowed, but also the Holy Ghost unto newness of life; or, in other words, that in the faith which appropriates justification is contained also the ability and inclination to well-doing." [41] Ritschl could scarcely approve this position because it seemed to express merely an "external connection" between justification and regeneration, it being "merely asserted and proved by Bible-texts that the two results always go together." [42] What particularly disturbed Ritschl was the resultant hiatus between justification and regeneration "in respect of the purposes which they serve": justification (or the sentence of acquittal) transpires to the end of pacifying the anxious conscience; regeneration (or the gift of the Spirit as the power to produce good works) takes place so that God might be "well pleased, or that his eternal law may be kept." What was really required, continued Ritschl, was a homogeneous, internally self-consistent, "teleological" doctrine of justification:

The statement of the doctrine by Luther and Melanchthon never enters on the consideration that even in justification as such there must be traced a telic reference to regeneration and the fulfilling of the law by faith, in order to secure a strict sequence of ideas in the doctrine. . . . As long as these two elements are not united in one thought, the doctrine of Luther and Melanchthon

[39] J. & R. I, 169.
[40] *Ibid.*, p. 171.
[41] *Ibid.*, p. 172.
[42] *Ibid.*, pp. 172-73.

is incomplete, and fails fully to commend itself to men's convictions as against the Romish doctrine, in which the course of *justificatio* is directly framed in such a way as to satisfy at once man's need, as also the demand of God's law, by laying the foundation for the ability to produce meritorious works.[43]

In sum, the Reformers never framed an adequate doctrine in which justification and sanctification, or faith and ethics, could be "united in one thought." They simply allowed their original religious consciousness to work on independently of their scientific labors and remained content to assert that faith possesses its own inner impulse to good works. Yet Luther sensed the inadequacies of his position and sought to unite more closely the two thoughts of justification and renewal. He did so by reverting to an earlier mode of speaking found occasionally in his writings prior to 1517 but especially in those of the years 1519-1522. This position was one which was basically identical with that later articulated by Andreas Osiander, according to which justification involves not only the imputation of righteousness but "a real infusion of righteousness." [44] In effect Luther brought together justification through Christ and the gift of the Spirit "in such a way as to make justification or forgiveness of sins dependent upon the Spirit of God, which is in believers the efficient cause of actual goodness." [45] In the famous correspondence between Melanchthon and Johannes Brenz in May, 1531, in which Luther himself participated by way of a postscript to Melanchthon's letter, Luther separated himself from Melanchthon's correct view that justification depends on faith alone, which lays hold of Christ's imputed righteousness, and not on any newness or quality of love in the believer. Luther went on to postulate an actual immanence of Christ in the believer, and while he later ceased "to maintain the error of making the forgiveness of sins dependent on that [immanence]," he committed the far graver error of passing over the relation of the believer to the Jesus of history by becoming entangled in a form of Christ mysticism.[46] At this point Ritschl invoked against Luther a dictum used in the Middle Ages anent certain propositions of Peter Lombard: *in hoc magister non tenetur!*

[43] *Ibid.*, p. 172.
[44] *Ibid.*, p. 174. Ritschl argues: "By Luther's sense of the disparity of his doctrine and of the need for bringing into closer connection the two thoughts of justification and of renewal by the Holy Ghost, I think it is possible to explain the fact that in certain of his expressions Luther defined the idea of justification in a way identical with that which was subsequently elevated to the rank of a principle by Andreas Osiander."
[45] *Ibid.*, p. 175.
[46] *Ibid.*, p. 176.

In substance I have already indicated the untenability of Ritschl's critique. Luther understood justification as a making righteous, and employed the law-gospel distinction, from the time of his earliest lectures, doing so apart from any purely apologetic or polemical considerations. The idea of renewal by the gift of the Spirit was not a later addition to the fundamental thought of forensic justification, introduced only to answer the question of how good works can be produced within the context of the *sola fides*. At no time in his career did Luther explain justification in purely forensic terms; he always conjoined the thought of man's actually becoming righteous through God's total act of justifying the sinner. The key to Luther's position, as has been shown, is that from beginning to end justification is God's work, and when God declares the sinner righteous for Christ's sake through faith he makes him righteous through his Creator Spirit. Hence justification and regeneration cannot be separated in practice, although they may (and, says Luther, must) be distinguished in theory. "Indeed, they might well be said to be simply different aspects of the same thing." [47] Their unity is grounded in the unity of the divine operation, for God's dynamic Word effects what it proclaims. God speaks and it is done. His Word does not return empty but accomplishes its salvatory purpose: the real justification of the ungodly. The "telic reference" of justification to sanctification, therefore, resides for Luther in the inherent purposefulness of the total *operatio Dei*. God purports to make us "like he is," an intention that is already being realized in the Church, where God continually creates saints through his Word and Spirit, but whose consummation is yet to come in the eschatological Kingdom. In his critique Ritschl once again missed the significance of Luther's cardinal motif of the creative Word, in which the original biblical (and especially Hebraic) understanding of this concept came powerfully to the fore and achieved new currency.

Ritschl of course approached Luther's delineation of the relation of justification to sanctification primarily from the viewpoint of faith as a subjective principle, rather than from the objective perspective of the divine operation. It is when the problem is thus posed from below, so to speak, that the tensions and hiatus in Luther's position presumably come to light. Luther (as well as Melanchthon and Zwingli) defined faith chiefly as *fiducia cordis,* or heartfelt trust in God's unmerited forgiveness, to the end that the distressed conscience is consoled. Hence, says Ritschl, the idea that faith contains its own spontaneous impulse to good works, and

[47] Watson, *Let God Be God*, p. 171.

leads to the fulfilling of the divine law, must necessarily appear as an appendix to this primary definition. But how can justifying faith be regarded as simultaneously passive and active without falling into logical contradiction or threatening the principle of grace alone? Certainly the Reformers always insisted that faith is both the "receptive organ for the appropriation of justification" and the "active instrument of all Christian life and action"; but they never moved beyond the level of assertion to that of demonstration.[48] Thus they failed to secure their position against serious misunderstanding as well as the charge of incoherence.

Turning to Luther himself, however, one sees that the relation of justification to sanctification, even from the perspective of faith, does not really pose such an antinomy between the passivity and activity of the believer. True, if faith were in fact the believer's own *work*, then any reference beyond faith's pure passivity to its reputed activity would seem to mark a reversion to the Roman concept of faith formed by love and so to the language of merit. Luther obviously foresaw the possibility that Evangelicals might come to understand faith in such wise, and so he never ceased pointing out that faith itself is God's own creation and gift. Through his Word and Spirit, God not only makes Christ present for faith but actually justifies a person by giving him faith. The Word which brings Christ also creates the receptivity to Christ and makes Christ and faith one indivisible reality. Hence on occasion Luther could say that justification transpires not only through faith (*per fidem*) but on account of faith (*propter fidem*), since faith is nothing other than Christ living and acting in the believer.[49] For Luther, therefore, faith is best comprehended as the *fides Christi*: Christ's real presence in and for faith, and faith's tenacious grasp on Christ, "as a ring holds a gem" (*fides apprehensiva*). The essence of

[48] J. & R. I, 138. Rather than speaking of faith as both receptive and active, Ritschl can also say, following Luther's specific usage, that "faith is the earnest of 'Christ in us,' as well as of 'Christ for us.'" In explanation, Ritschl adds: "This view is not insisted on merely for the purpose of guarding against the mistaken inference that the inclination to continuance in sin might possibly be conjoined with faith in Christ's merit. Luther needed this twofold view of faith also in order to secure for the moral works of the regenerate that unconstrainedness, the absence of which betokens effort after work-righteousness." From these explanatory remarks it is evident that Ritschl correctly noted the presence, but failed to grasp the paramount importance, of the *fides Christi* motif in Luther's concept of justification through faith. While the notion of Christ's real presence in faith certainly militates against false antinomian inferences and also serves to explain the spontaneity of the believer's good works, this motif—as I shall show in the following pages—is nothing less than the *sine qua non* of Luther's total doctrine of justification.

[49] Hence Luther can also maintain that "faith is my righteousness" as well as "Christ is my righteousness," since in both cases he is making the *same* claim.

faith is not that the believer assents to a particular teaching about Christ's person and work (as Ritschl so justly maintained against Orthodoxy); not even that the believer personally applies to himself the community's assurance of divine forgiveness as the covering for his own imperfection and as the antidote to self-righteousness (which was Ritschl's own leading thought); but that faith "unites the soul with Christ as a bride is united with her bridegroom." [50] Precisely in the treatise *On Christian Liberty*, Ritschl's favorite writing, Luther set forth with clarity and power his view of justification and sanctification as based on this union, this *incorporatio Christi*, effected by the Word. In faith there takes place a "joyful exchange" between Christ and the believer, "for if Christ is a bridegroom, he must take upon himself the things which are his bride's and bestow upon her the things that are his." [51] Luther depicted this "royal marriage" as follows:

Christ is full of grace, life, and salvation. The soul is full of sins, death, and damnation. Now let faith come between them and sins, death, and damnation will be Christ's, while grace, life, and salvation will be the soul's. . . . Who can understand the riches of the glory of this grace? Here this rich and divine bridegroom Christ marries this poor wicked harlot, redeems her from all evil, and adorns her with all his goodness. Her sins cannot now destroy her, since they are laid upon Christ and swallowed up by him. And she has that righteousness in Christ, her husband, of which she may boast as of her own and which she can confidently display alongside her sins in the face of death and hell. . . . [52]

Because Christ is present in and for faith with his righteousness, there is no more law, sin, condemnation, death, hell, i.e., justification has occurred and God has passed his sentence of acquittal:

Living in me as He does, Christ abolishes the Law, damns sin, and kills death; for at His presence all these cannot help disappearing. Christ is eternal

[50] LW 31, 351 ("The Freedom of a Christian," 1520). Cf. LW 26, 168-69 ("Lectures on Galatians," 1535): "But faith must be taught correctly, namely, that by it you are so cemented to Christ that He and you are as one person, which cannot be separated but remains attached to Him forever and declares: 'I am as Christ.' And Christ, in turn, says: 'I am as that sinner who is attached to Me, and I to him. For by faith we are joined together in one flesh and one bone.' Thus Eph. 5.30 says: 'We are members of the body of Christ, of His flesh and of His bones,' in such a way that this faith couples Christ and me more intimately than a husband is coupled to his wife. Therefore this faith is no idle quality; but it is a thing of such magnitude that it obscures and completely removes those foolish dreams of the sophists' doctrine—the fiction of a ' formed faith ' and of love, of merits, our worthiness, our quality, etc."

[51] LW 31, 351. The phrase "joyous exchange" ("*fröhlicher Wechsel*") is found in the German text of this treatise (the Latin text being the basis of the translation in LW 31). Cf. WA 7, 25, 28.

[52] LW 31, 351-52.

Peace, Comfort, Righteousness, and Life, to which the terror of the Law, sadness of mind, sin, hell, and death have to yield. Abiding and living in me, Christ removes and absorbs all the evils that torment and afflict me. This attachment to Him causes me to be liberated out of my own skin, and transferred into Christ and into His kingdom, which is a kingdom of grace, righteousness, peace, joy, life, salvation, and eternal glory. Since I am in Him, no evil can harm me.[53]

Because Christ is present in and for faith with his life and power, the dominion of sin has been broken and good works spontaneously well forth and abound, i.e., sanctification has occurred and God is beginning his work of healing:

Therefore we conclude with Paul that we are justified solely by faith in Christ, without the Law and works. But after a man is justified by faith, now possesses Christ by faith, and knows that He is his righteousness and life, he will certainly not be idle but, like a sound tree, will bear good fruit (Matt. 7:17). For the believer has the Holy Spirit; and where He is, He does not permit a man to be idle but drives him to all the exercises of devotion, to the love of God, to patience in affliction, to prayer, to thanksgiving, and to the practice of love toward all men. Therefore we, too, say that faith without works is worthless and useless.[54]

Thus Christ is not only the object of faith but also its acting subject: *in ipsa fide Christus adest*.[55] It is Christ himself who through his Spirit progressively conforms the believer to his death and resurrection, which is to say that the believer daily dies to sin and rises to new life; or that justification and sanctification constitute one unified event under the joint working of Word, Spirit, and indwelling Christ; or that the believer is at once passive and active, according to whether the accent falls on the Spirit's creation of faith or the activity of Christ in faith. In any event, faith is no mere historical faith oriented to the distant past, but nothing else than faith formed by Christ (*fides Christo formata*) wherein the living Christ exercises present lordship over the total life of the disciple.[56]

---

[53] LW 26, 167.

[54] *Ibid.*, pp. 154-55.

[55] WA 40-I, 228, 33. Cf. LW 26, 129: "But if it is true faith, it is a sure trust and firm acceptance in the heart. It takes hold of Christ in such a way that Christ is the object of faith, or rather not the object but, so to speak, the One who is present in the faith itself."

[56] WA 39-I, 204, 12 ("Die Promotionsdisputation von Palladius and Tilemann," 1537): "Christ is truly formed in us continually—and we are conformed to his image —as long as we live." Cf. LW 26, 129: "Such are the dreams of the scholastics. But where they speak of love, we speak of faith. And while they say that faith is the mere

Luther's profound concept of the *fides Christi* can be traced throughout his career and forms the basic presupposition of his teaching on the unity of justification and renewal. And specifically at this point Luther's deepest difference from Melanchthon comes to light. Contrary to Ritschl's assertion, Luther's contribution to the aforementioned Brenz-Melanchthon correspondence did not mark a random aberration from his own predominant outlook, which Melanchthon continued to affirm in spite of Luther's defection.[57] Here Luther in fact displayed a fundamental insight which he struggled to express with ever more precision and forcefulness: Christ must never be comprehended as relating himself to the believer only from without; rather he must be understood as actualizing and incarnating himself whenever the Word is received with joy and trust.[58] Melanchthon

---

outline but love is its living colors and completion, we say in opposition that faith takes hold of Christ and that he is the form that adorns and informs faith as color does the wall." Also LW 26, 167: "This is why [Paul in Gal. 2:20] says: 'Not I, but Christ lives in me.' Christ is my ' form,' which adorns my faith as color or light adorns a wall. (This fact has to be expounded in this crude way, for there is no spiritual way for us to grasp the idea that Christ clings and dwells in us as closely and intimately as light or whiteness clings to a wall.) 'Christ,' he says, 'is fixed and cemented to me and abides in me. The life that I now live, He lives in me. Indeed, Christ Himself is the life that I now live. In this way, therefore, Christ and I are one.'"

[57] On the Brenz-Melanchthon correspondence, see Wilhelm Pauck, "Luther and Melanchthon," pp. 21-22, and Robert Stupperich, "Die Rechtfertigungslehre bei Luther und Melanchthon, 1530-1536," pp. 81-82, in *Luther and Melanchthon*, ed. Vilmos Vajta (Philadelphia, 1961). Pauck translates Melanchthon's reply to Brenz as follows: "You are still confined to Augustine's way of thinking . . . for he thinks that we are regarded as righteous because of the fulfillment of the law which the Holy Spirit accomplishes in us. And you too think that the doctrine that we are justified by faith means that by receiving in faith the Holy Spirit we can be righteous through the fulfillment of the law which the Holy Spirit accomplishes. This idea identifies righteousness with our fulfillment of the law, with our purity and perfection, but properly speaking, this renewal must be understood as a result of faith. Now you must dismiss from your mind this idea of renewal and the law, instead, you must direct your attention to Christ's promise in order that you may see that it is for Christ's sake and not because of this renewal that we are righteous, i.e., acceptable in God's sight and capable of being consoled in our conscience. For the fact of our having become new is not sufficient for this. We are therefore righteous by faith alone, not because, as you express yourself, it is the root of renewal, but because it is directed to Christ. It is because of him that we are acceptable to God, regardless of our renewal, whatever that may be. This renewal is the necessary consequence of faith, to be sure, but it cannot give consolation to our consciences. . . . Faith therefore justifies us not because it is the work of the Holy Spirit in us but because it apprehends Christ. It is for his sake and not because of the gifts of the Holy Spirit which may be ours that we are acceptable in God's sight."

[58] In Pauck's translation, Luther's postscript reads: "Let me add to this on my part, dear Brenz, that in order to understand this matter properly, I make it a rule to remind myself that there is in my heart no quality of any kind that could be called faith or love. But I put in their stead Jesus Christ and say: There is my righteousness!

certainly understood Luther's authentic theological intentions, and Luther even pronounced his *Loci communes* of 1521 worthy of canonical status. Yet it remains true that Melanchthon's "manner of theologizing did not mirror that immediate, dynamic actuality of the gospel of Christ which Luther was able to express so directly and forcefully." [59] Melanchthon sought to capture and define through doctrinal formulas what for Luther was an ongoing contemporaneous event, the justification of sinners, which takes place, as God wills, whenever Word and faith meet. For Luther the teaching about justification must never obscure the latter's event-like nature, since justification has to do with what God is now doing, not merely with what he once has done.

It will readily be seen that Luther's characteristic mode of speaking actually lay much closer to Ritschl's own deepest theological concerns than did Melanchthon's outlook. For Ritschl wished to overcome the theological formalism, doctrinalism, and externalism of Melanchthonian Ortho-

---

He is in fact what this quality and this so-called formal righteousness in me are supposed to be. Hence I no longer need to concentrate my attention upon the law and good works nor upon a Christ who confronts me from without and whom I must take to be a teacher or a donor of something. Instead I understand him to be the one who is in and by himself what he teaches me and gives me as his gift. I therefore have everything. Remember that he himself says: 'I am the way, the truth, and the life.' He does not say: I give to you the way and the truth and the life, as if he effected all this in me from without. It is within me that he must be, stay, live, speak . . . so that we are righteous in God's sight in him and not in love and in the gifts that flow from faith." Cf. LW 26, 167: "But so far as justification is concerned, Christ and I must be so closely attached that He lives in me and I in Him."

[59] Wilhelm Pauck, "Luther and Melanchthon," p. 21. Lauri Haikola, "Melanchthons und Luthers Lehre von der Rechtfertigung: Ein Vergleich," in Vajta, *Luther and Melanchthon*, p. 103, attributes Melanchthon's inability to hold together the forensic and effective dimensions of justification to his defective understanding of Christ's real presence in Word and faith. According to Luther, "God's wrath and the law continue to be living realities [even after the historical reconciliation through Christ] which tyrannize the sinner and hinder him from faith. These tyrants must be overcome in a man's personal life. The appropriation of Christ's work, therefore, not only involves the transfer of Christ's merit from the historical past into the present, but also means that the living Christ is now present in his divine and human nature for the purpose of conquering the enemies of man. Christ in all his invincible righteousness is present in the Word. Given these presuppositions one can readily understand why for Luther the preaching of the Word must have an altogether different and more dynamic character than for Melanchthon. The Word awakens faith in man and gives him Christ with all his righteousness. Christ lives in faith. His merit, which is imputed to the sinner, bestows the forgiveness of sins; his divinity brings about renewal in the faith. Word and sacrament represent the humanity of Christ. Thus forgiveness of sins and renewal —the forensic and the effective dimensions of justification—cannot be separated from each other any more than Christ's person can be separated from his work. It is here, finally, that one must seek the explanation for the fact that Luther does not know the basic difficulty of the Melanchthonian theology: the problem of holding together the forensic and the effective sides of justification."

doxy by recovering the experiential and existential ("practical") theology of the young Luther. It is all the more remarkable, therefore, that he should have dismissed Luther's concept of communion with Christ, predicated on the Church's preaching of Christ, as an aberration which Melanchthon was unable to correct. Indeed on this crucial point Ritschl preferred Melanchthon to Luther and so in effect preferred Orthodoxy to Luther, merely assimilating Luther's position to Osiander's through a hasty and unwarranted generalization. In fact Ritschl's conclusions on this topic have stimulated the pursuit of what Regin Prenter has rightly called an unfruitful question: whether Luther's views on justification tended to be more Melanchthonian or more Osiandrian.[60] Thus Ritschl also posed those sterile choices which ever since have led to repeated controversies and a polarization of viewpoints in Luther research: in the matter of justification one must supposedly opt for either imputed righteousness or infused righteousness; either God's forensic sentence outside us (*extra nos*) or his sanative process within us (*in nobis*); either the "for Christ's sake" or the "in view of the new obedience." Luther himself would not have recognized these options as mutually exclusive. His theology of the real presence of Christ, effected in the believer by the Spirit through faith in the living Word, held together what his interpreters have not infrequently put asunder.

In fairness to Ritschl, however, one must give heed to the explicit rationale underlying his rejection of Luther's "error." On his view Luther's postulate of Christ's immanence in the believer "would fain pass over the intuition of the Christ of history, and thus treat as merely an initial stage of the believer's consciousness that has soon to be got over, that relationship between the believer and the historical appearance of Christ which is justly described to be the abiding ground of the subjective consciousness of salvation." [61] If Christianity is truly a historical religion, then its unique ties to its Founder must not be threatened with dissolution through an ahistorical Christ mysticism. Luther, of course, never intended any such

---

[60] Prenter, *Spiritus Creator*, p. 63. Prenter also enters an appropriate caveat against equating Luther's *fides Christi* theme with a "Christ mysticism": "The many-sided and too much emphasized phrase 'Christ mysticism' should in any case be kept as far away as possible from Luther's presentation of the real presence of Christ. Luther does not know of any other reality of Christ than that of faith. And faith is a strenuous affair, *argumentum non apparentium*. But—and this must never be forgotten—faith, as *argumentum non apparentium*, is in contact with God and with Christ as a present reality, not just as a mere idea. The *res non apparentes* of faith is simultaneously the *res valde praesentes* of faith" (p. 45).

[61] J. & R. I, 176.

thing. His teaching on the *fides Christi* was in fact his solution to the so-called hermeneutical problem, the problem of the contemporary actualization or re-presentation of a past event. Luther stated his case very plainly in the *Large Catechism* during the course of his explanation to the Third Article of the Apostles' Creed:

> Neither you nor I could ever know anything of Christ, or believe in him and take him as our Lord, unless these were first offered to us and bestowed on our hearts through the preaching of the gospel by the Holy Spirit. The work is finished and completed, Christ has acquired and won the treasure for us by his sufferings, death, and resurrection, etc. But if the work remained hidden and no one knew of it, it would have been all in vain, all lost. In order that this treasure might not be buried but put to use and enjoyed, God has caused the Word to be published and proclaimed, in which he has given the Holy Spirit to offer and apply to us this treasure of salvation. Therefore to sanctify is nothing else than to bring us to the Lord Christ to receive this blessing, which we could not obtain by ourselves.[62]

According to Luther, therefore, the redemptive activity of the Incarnate Word realizes itself again in the present through the preached (and the sacramental or "signed") Word, whereby the exalted Lord through his Spirit continues to redeem and sanctify those who hear in faith. Ritschl himself appeared to solve the hermeneutical problem by an appeal to exact memory and to the concrete historic reality of the religious community in its exercise of worship (the "Church" properly speaking) and in its extension as the moral society of nations (the kingdom of God).[63] Regardless of the validity of the one position or the other, Ritschl qua historian must be faulted for not uncovering the full dynamics of Luther's viewpoint, owing to a superficial analysis and predilection for sweeping judgments.

[62] BC, pp. 415-16.

[63] In Ritschl's theology the religious community is always superordinate to the individual believer. From the time of Jesus' calling of the disciples, the Church has existed as the new covenant community; thus it is the Church itself, in its continuing existence on the plane of history, which bridges the gap between past and present. It must also be remembered that, according to Ritschl, God's sentence of justification does not pertain directly to individuals but to the original community which Jesus founded. Hence the believer's present experience of forgiveness derives from his personal appropriation of the community's consciousness of reconciliation with God. Luther's emphasis on the immediate personal encounter between Word and faith is ultimately rejected by Ritschl as an instance of pietistic "individualism." Cf. J. & R. III, 591.

4. CONCLUSIONS

"One thing, and only one thing, is necessary for Christian life, righteousness, and freedom. That one thing is the most holy Word of God, the gospel of Christ." In the course of this chapter I have sought to elucidate the meaning of this claim for Luther by showing how he organized his theology, as well as his Reformation activity, around this one thing needful. In view of Luther's explicit precept and demonstrable practice, I have contended that Ritschl is to be criticized primarily for his failure to accord pride of place to, and unfold the content of, Luther's distinctive teaching on God's creative Word. Certainly one cannot deny that Ritschl properly emphasized the centrality of grace and faith in Luther's teaching on justification, as opposed to the Roman teaching on grace and merit. But in this connection Ritschl did not satisfactorily bring into prominence the centrality of the *Christusverkündigung*, for grace is always bestowed by the Word of promise. Grace, concretely speaking, is nothing other than Christ's real presence for faith in the Word; and faith, which unites the believer with his Lord, is created, sustained, and regulated by this Word. The entire life of the Christian, therefore, is *wortförmig.* Such conformity to the Word, however, is specifically conformity to Christ. It is participation in his righteousness (forgiveness) and his power (renewal). Where Christ is present with his Spirit, there the *telos* of God's justifying activity has been realized, i.e., the new creation has dawned and the kingdom of God has come among men.[64] But this end can never be abstracted from its source in the *viva vox Dei.* In Luther's Reformation, therefore, the pious praxis of faith, on which Ritschl riveted his attention, was of far less moment than the right comprehension of the Word. For without the latter the former might well be a praxis of the noblest piety of the human spirit, and yet not truly be a new life under the leading of the Holy Spirit, a life with Christ comprehended in the Word of the cross.

Such considerations, coupled with the findings in Chapter III, warrant the conclusion that Ritschl did not achieve that definitive *Lutherbild* to which he both aspired and laid claim. This is not to say that he was preoccupied with merely peripheral matters in Luther's thought. Ritschl was a discerning scholar and, as was shown in detail in Chapters I and II, he successfully recovered some of Luther's most significant principles and

[64] See T. F. Torrance, "The Eschatology of Faith: Martin Luther," Chapter II in *Kingdom and Church: A Study in the Theology of the Reformation* (Fair Lawn, N. J., 1956), pp. 7-72.

worked them into his doctrinal system. Yet, on even the most sympathetic reading, his Luther interpretation falls short on many counts. His rigid distinction between the original and the deformed Luther had a deleterious effect since it blinded him to the pervasive continuity between Luther's early and later theology and, more importantly, served to preclude a depth confrontation with the full range of Luther's thought. Furthermore, Ritschl's insensitivity to the subtleties and complexities of Luther's thought points to a characteristic weakness in his historical method, or, more accurately, in the execution of that method. Otto Ritschl tells us that his father's methodology was grounded on the axiom, *qui bene distinguit et bene comprehendit, bene docet*, and certainly one cannot fail to be impressed by Ritschl's analytic and synthetic powers.[65] He particularly prided himself on his acknowledged talent for construction; indeed he took the *bene comprehendere* to be the mark of the genuine theologian. One must also remember that Ritschl pursued his Luther scholarship with a view to serving his dominant systematic interests. In fact this constructive impulse underlay all his historical labors. But the lasting impression conveyed by his Luther interpretation is that the *bene distinguere* was ultimately subordinated to the overriding systematic concern, rather than being accorded equal weight and moment. In brief, Ritschl was finally more intent on "placing" Luther in his doctrinal system than on "hearing" Luther on Luther's own terms.

Surely it is incontestable that essential features of Luther's theology, especially certain all-important facets of his teaching on justification, found little or no echo in Ritschl's presentation. In his delineation of the Reformation principle Ritschl maintained that Luther, in opposition to Rome's legalistic penitential praxis and its distorted ecclesiology, had successfully reinstated the traditional Augustinian theme of grace alone and had simultaneously reappropriated and revalidated the classical concept of the Church as the fellowship of believers. While there is much to recommend such a perspective—particularly its anchorage of Luther's teaching on justification within the context of the penitential system—it remains vulnerable to criticism because of what it glosses over or neglects to say. Ritschl's Reformation principle has a decidedly prosaic ring to it when compared with Luther's own Reformation consciousness as evidenced in his vocational *tentatio*. Luther believed that he was breaking decisively with the prevailing doctrinal tradition of the whole of medieval Scholasticism, not simply with the more overt Pelagian tendencies of

[65] *Leben*, II, 167-68.

such nominalist theologians as Occam, d'Ailly, and Biel.[66] Nor did Luther exempt Augustine himself from incisive criticism.[67] Hence he could not suppress such disquieting questions as: "Do you suppose that all previous teachers were ignorant? Are our forefathers all fools in your eyes? Are you the one latter-day nest egg of the Holy Spirit? Would God have permitted his people to wander in error for years?"[68] At such times Luther consoled himself with the thought that his "new doctrine" had but one fundamental intent: to let God be God, to give God alone the glory.[69] It is precisely Luther's absolute commitment to this *soli Deo gloria* theme—as attested in his doxological confession of God's "Godness," his overwhelming sense of the Holy, his profound awe and gratitude that the Righteous One freely pardons the unrighteous—which one misses in both Ritschl's interpretation of the young Luther and his exposition of the Reformation's leading theme.

It is no less regrettable that Ritschl proved unable to penetrate the vital center of Luther's thought, his theology of the Word of the cross (*theologia crucis*), and thus did not enter into a genuine, sustained dialogue with Luther's guiding theme. Had he done so he would undoubtedly have been compelled to renounce his overly facile depreciation of Luther

---

[66] See Heiko A. Oberman, "'Iustitia Christi' and 'Iustitia Dei': Luther and the Scholastic Doctrines of Justification," *Harvard Theological Review* 59 (1966): 1-26. Cf. p. 19: Luther "attacked the whole medieval tradition as it was later confirmed at the Council of Trent."

[67] Luther especially rejected the Augustinian notion of a *caritas ordinata* in which self-love was accorded a legitimate place, since for Luther *amor sui* is the very root of all sin and the source of religious eudaemonism. Luther, however, apparently did not perceive to what extent scholastic theology could rightfully invoke Augustine's authority in support of some of its basic tenets. See Wilhelm Pauck's "General Introduction" to his translation of the *Romans Lectures*, pp. xlii-1.

[68] LW 43, 160 ("A Letter of Consolation to the Christians at Halle," 1527).

[69] Cf. LW 26, 66: "I recall that when my movement first began, Dr. Staupitz, a very worthy man and the vicar of the Augustinian Order, said to me: 'It pleases me very much that this doctrine of ours gives glory and everything else solely to God and nothing at all to men; for it is as clear as day that it is impossible to ascribe too much glory, goodness, etc., to God.' So it was that he consoled me. And it is true that the doctrine of the gospel takes away all glory, wisdom, righteousness, etc., from men and gives it solely to the Creator, who makes all things out of nothing. . . . My doctrine is one that preaches and worships God alone, and it condemns the righteousness and the wisdom of all men. Here I cannot go wrong, for both to God and to man I ascribe what properly and truly belongs to each." Cf. also LW 12, 187 ("Commentary on Psalm 26," 1525): "Concerning our life we dare not boast. Concerning our speech we should boast before God and men of our certainty that our teaching is correct. I can say, 'Thus my teaching stands, and so it is correct.' It is a good teaching. This is evident from the fact that it builds upon the Lord Christ, it lets God be our Lord God, and it gives God the glory. This teaching is correct, and it cannot go wrong; nor will anyone improve on it."

as theologian. It is a commonplace that Luther was not a systematic theologian in the mold of Melanchthon or Calvin, but he was a far more astute thinker and careful workman than Ritschl perceived.[70] By stereotyping Luther as an undisciplined religious genius, as well as by holding steadfastly to his discontinuity hypothesis, Ritschl virtually eliminated the very possibility of uncovering Luther's theological rigor and consistency. The result was that Luther's profound and amazingly fertile theology of Word and faith was literally "overcome" before it could stand forth in its own integrity and could at least pose a persistent challenge to Ritschl the reformer of church doctrine and life. The significance of Ritschl's Luther interpretation, therefore, cannot be located in any presumed recovery of the "integral Luther," albeit Ritschl himself believed that to be the case. What, then, is its significance? To this question I now address myself in conclusion.

---

[70] One thinks, for example, of Luther's masterful treatise *Against Latomus* (1521), with its compact formulations and closely reasoned argumentation.

12 THE SIGNIFICANCE OF RITSCHL'S LUTHER INTERPRETATION

As Ritschl was bringing to a close the first major subdivision of Volume Three of *Justification and Reconciliation,* he traced out for his readers the distinguished lineage or pedigree of his doctrinal formulations:

In defining justification or reconciliation, and in fixing their relations, I have made use of materials drawn partly from the dogmatic theologians of the classical age, partly from the Reformers and the Lutheran symbols. It has been impossible to combine and arrange these materials without modifying particular aspects to which importance has always been attached from the very outset. Conceptions, which we find alongside of each other in the pages of the theologians without correlation, have at the same time either been reduced one to the other or sifted out altogether. *But on the whole the doctrine of justification set forth . . . stands in the line of direct continuity with the intention of the Reformers and the standards of the Lutheran Church.* Especially is this the case as regards the practical aspect of justification, its significance as explaining the peculiar character of that view of the world and of life which we owe to the Reformation. On this point we get no help from the theology which is haunted by the prejudice that it must follow the symbolical books at every step. And yet it has shown itself, and that not merely in the present case, very indifferent to the standards of the Reformation.[1]

This claim—typically Ritschlian in its sweep, self-assuredness and polemical bent—has in effect served as the starting point and focus of the present investigation. The casual or hypercritical reader might well dismiss these remarks as gratuitous and self-serving, or at least highly questionable, given Ritschl's widespread reputation as the leading representative of a long discredited Culture Protestantism. I have proceeded on the assumption, however, that this assertion was no idle boast; on the contrary I have welcomed it as a valuable and revealing clue to Ritschl's self-understanding as an Evangelical churchman and theologian. In view of the findings detailed in the preceding chapters, one can justly maintain that here Ritschl was simply making explicit what was in fact implicit throughout his mature work: an intended fidelity to, and deep-seated sense of responsi-

[1] J. & R. III, 191 (italics added).

bility for, the heritage of the Reformation. These latter motives prompted Ritschl to undertake his critical reappropriation of the Reformers' central teaching on justification, particularly in its original practical form expounded by the young Luther.

Certainly the sincerity and pervasive significance of Ritschl's *intentions* are beyond doubt. Chapters I and II have shown at some length that Ritschl attempted to organize his systematic theology around Luther's major motifs and likewise elevated the Reformation principle to the rank of a dominant historico-axiological category. I have amply demonstrated, I believe, that Ritschl's comprehensive theological program cannot be properly surveyed or fairly evaluated without due consideration for the multifaceted relationship which it sustains to Luther's theology. I also believe that in pursuing the details of this relationship I have presented a fresh perspective on Ritschl's theology.

To be sure, Chapters III and IV also contain a sharply critical judgment on the ultimate adequacy of Ritschl's Luther interpretation. However sincere his intentions and confident his claims, Ritschl did not recover the authentic Luther because, as I have shown, he did not apprehend the integral Luther. He did not see Luther steady, nor did he see him whole. Perhaps my rigorous critique may have the unintended, but nonetheless real, effect of seeming to take away with the left hand what I have given with the right. One might forthwith conclude that Ritschl's simultaneous use and abuse of Luther simply cancel each other out, so that we must necessarily arrive at the unsatisfying yet inescapable verdict that we are here treating a classic instance of the failure of good intentions. From this vantage point the general significance of Ritschl's Luther interpretation would reside primarily in its negative value as a stern warning against the all too human tendency to advance lofty claims before making certain of actual achievements. If this were the case, all that would remain to be done is to ruminate on the folly and futility of grandiose designs, or to lament the characteristic foibles of scholars and their seemingly inexhaustible capacity for self-deception.

Such a dismal conclusion, however, is wholly unwarranted. Surely the serious defects of Ritschl's Luther interpretation can neither discredit nor discount the honored place and normative role which Ritschl in fact accorded both Luther and the Reformation principle. Hence there can be no question of simply balancing the one factor against the other. The final validity of Ritschl's Luther interpretation is not a test of its applicability within Ritschl's own system. The very fact of Ritschl's depth relationship to Luther and the Reformation—an involvement which serves to open up and illumine the whole of Ritschl's theology—must be granted its full weight *before* any evaluation of that relationship is allowed to enter the picture. Premature judgments would obscure the remarkable scope and intensity of the relationship and so lead to a fundamental distortion of perspective. For this reason I prescinded from critical remarks in Chapters I and II. The primary significance of Ritschl's Luther interpretation, therefore, resides in its manifest *hermeneutical value* vis-à-vis Ritschl's own theology: its capacity to shed light on what heretofore may have been obscure and to bring order out of an otherwise confusing welter of data. Of course the reader must decide for himself whether, and to what extent, my approach to Ritschl has displayed such an illuminating and ordering capacity. In effect, then, I have *already* underscored the paramount importance of Ritschl's Luther study by using this investigation as an interpretive device for uncovering the major structural components and underlying tenor of Ritschl's systematic and historical theology.

In addition to its hermeneutical value, however, Ritschl's Luther interpretation also possesses a definite *contextual* significance which first comes to light when this interpretation is studied in its own historical setting. In this closing chapter, therefore, I shall examine Ritschl's Luther study within its particular ecclesiastical and cultural context. Through such a procedure it should become clear that Ritschl's *Lutherdeutung* involves far more than a failure of good intentions, since it has its undeniable successes and attainments when once we see more clearly what Ritschl was striving to accomplish through it in his own time and place. Before turning to this contextual inquiry, however, I first intend to clarify and further substantiate the claim to be presenting a fresh perspective on Ritschl's theology. I shall do so by contrasting my approach to Ritschl with that viewpoint which is met with most frequently in the secondary literature, especially since the advent of neo-Orthodoxy. I shall also consider the noteworthy connection between Ritschl's Luther study and the epoch-making researches of Karl Holl, in order to stress the lasting indebtedness of twentieth-century Luther research to Ritschl the Luther scholar. In this way I propose to unfold what might be called the *corrective* significance of Ritschl's Luther interpretation.

1. THE CORRECTIVE SIGNIFICANCE OF RITSCHL'S LUTHER INTERPRETATION

To speak of a fresh perspective on Ritschl's theology implies that there is an alternative viewpoint which in the course of time has entered into general use, but whose broad acceptance is no guarantee of its final adequacy. Such in fact is the case. What can properly be called the standard perspective on Ritschl is at the same time palpably one-sided and biased and simply fails to do justice to Ritschl's total theological significance. This perspective is the familiar one which glosses over both Ritschl's depth involvement with classical Protestantism and the important role which he has played in the modern Luther renaissance. In this section I shall indicate the importance of Ritschl's Luther interpretation as a corrective to this recurrent viewpoint, and thereby further spell out the meaning of a fresh perspective on Ritschl's theology.

Ritschl and His Contemporary Critics

"Nobody either before or since Ritschl," wrote Karl Barth, "has expressed the view as clearly as he, that modern man wishes above all to live in the best sense according to reason, and that the significance of Christianity for him can only be a great confirmation and strengthening of this very endeavor." [2] Far from overcoming the Enlightenment, Ritschl "energetically seized upon the theoretical and practical philosophy of the Enlightenment in its perfected form. That is, he went back to Kant, but Kant quite definitely interpreted as an antimetaphysical moralist, by means of whom he thought he could understand Christianity as that which grandly and inevitably made possible, or realized, a practical ideal of life." [3] According to Barth, then, Ritschl's theology marked the ultimate triumph of a chastened Enlightenment rationalism and Kantian moralism within modern Protestantism. Indeed the "rounded, transparent and compact quality" of Ritschl's thought simply expressed in a sober and honest fashion what was in truth the secret intention of nineteenth-century theology as a whole: the steadfast resolve to place man in the center of things and to invoke God's providential care in order to secure for modern man his precarious self-assurance. [4]

As it stands in this unqualified form, Barth's judgment cannot be sustained. Barth, it has been aptly remarked, treats Ritschl somewhat as Ritschl treated Pietism! His intensely critical, unsympathetic stance is paradigmatic of a recurrent approach to Ritschl: the thoroughly one-sided attempt to interpret Ritschl's theology strictly as a development out of its eighteenth- and nineteenth-century antecedents. On this view the contribu-

---

[2] Barth, *Protestant Thought: From Rousseau to Ritschl*, p. 391.
[3] *Ibid.*
[4] *Ibid.*, pp. 391-92, 397.

tions of German idealism are dominant and all-determining. Ritschl's relationship to Reformation theology, if noted at all (Barth virtually overlooks it), is considered but a transient moment in this development, a mere appendix to an understanding of the Christian religion derived from modern sources. Kant and Schleiermacher, along with Baur, Rothe, and Lotze, but emphatically *not* Luther and Calvin, are the spiritual fathers of the Ritschlian system. The Reformation component is incidental to the idealistic element and has no self-contained significance.[5]

If nothing else, the present study has shown such a portrait to be a caricature. Not only does it precipitately dismiss Ritschl's avowed intentions and explicit claims, as well as discounting the weighty evidence supporting his pronouncements, it also leaves out of account Ritschl's express critique of the Enlightenment and especially his strictures on Kant's philosophy of religion and Schleiermacher's theology. In his *Festrede*, for example, Ritschl vehemently attacked the widely held assumption of the Illuminati that Luther had brought into being a purely individualistic concept of religious and spiritual freedom, or a simple message of release from all authority. In proclaiming Christian liberty Luther did not advocate complete religious freedom from common norms and viewpoints, so that presumably each person could establish his own religion for him-

---

[5] After my basic research and the greater part of my writing had been completed, there appeared Rolf Schäfer's valuable study of Ritschl's theological system, *Ritschl: Grundlinien eines fast verschollenen dogmatischen Systems* (Tübingen, 1968; Vol. 41 in *Beiträge zur historischen Theologie*, ed. Gerhard Ebeling). At a number of points Schäfer touches on the specific subject matter of this essay, and I am especially pleased to note his strong protest against those traditional interpretations of Ritschl which minimize Ritschl's indebtedness to the Reformation. For example, Schäfer takes issue with Gösta Hök's estimable book, *Die elliptische Theologie Albrecht Ritschls nach Ursprung und innerem Zusammenhang* (Uppsala, 1942), for neglecting to consider the impact of Reformation theology on the formulation of the famous Ritschlian "ellipse" (the relation of religion and morality). Schäfer's remarks are worth quoting in full: "To a much greater extent than Hök allows—inasmuch as he restricted the scope of his research to the 18th and 19th centuries—Ritschl was dependent on the Reformation theology and its attendant systematic problems. This becomes especially clear precisely in the relationship which he posits between religion and morality, since there . . . the old doctrine of faith and works, justification and sanctification, again makes its appearance almost point for point. There also lies the root for what Ritschl wanted to convey through the image of the ellipse. *Hence one will hit upon the center of Ritschl's theology in a much more reliable way if he rates the influence of the Reformation higher than that of idealism* (in addition to the influence of the Bible, which Hök also leaves aside). For Ritschl himself may not have been so far wrong in his self-estimate when he adjudged himself indebted in the first instance to the Bible and the Evangelical tradition. Once this has been clearly established, then one can proceed to take up at a second stage those questions which Hök is concerned to answer" (pp. 10-11; italics added).

self (as the young Goethe held, following Gottfried Arnold's *Unpartei-ische Kirchen- und Ketzer-Historie*). The truth, rather, is that

Luther intended Christian freedom—which he derived from that teaching for which he ever battled, namely, the doctrine of justification by faith—to be the content of a communal, churchly Christianity, which he intended to win back from the system prevailing up to that time. Nor did this teaching at all signify that a man could meet with approval before God through the inde- pendent resolve of his belief and disposition, which takes precedence over the multitude of prescribed deeds and accomplishments. Such an evaluation of the spontaneous religious and moral resolution would be nothing new or origi- nal. For even in the Catholic system this Christian attitude holds good as the basis on which all moral and ceremonial works are regarded as merits, which God will reward by granting salvation. But the freedom which Luther derived from the justification or reconciliation of the sinner with God through Christ attains a far higher plane.[6]

For Ritschl, therefore, following Luther, Christian freedom is the gift of a gracious God to the religious community of which Christ is Lord. It is a purely spiritual freedom over the world realized in faith alone, and predicated on Christ's own unwavering faithfulness to the will of the Fa- ther, to the end that Christ's standing in the love of the Father is imputed to the total community of which Christ is Founder and Head. Hence it is the freedom of Christians to claim with the apostle Paul: "We are more than conquerors through him who loved us" (Rom. 8:37). As such it is not to be compared with the autonomous moral disposition of the well- intentioned "reasonable" man, i.e., it is not a life simply lived in accord with a Kantian practical reason or with a Goethean *Humanitätsideal*.

Certainly one must not minimize Ritschl's self-acknowledged indebted- ness to Kant, Schleiermacher, and their successors. In the interest of estab- lishing Ritschl's relationship to the Reformation it is not necessary, and would be a falsification of the evidence, to deny his relationship to German idealism. One extreme interpretation would then be replaced by another no less extreme. But neither should one overlook nor make light of the specific rationale employed by Ritschl in his generally positive eval- uation of Kant and Schleiermacher. *Ritschl's primary criterion for assessing their significance is their fidelity to the Reformation.* Their greatness, he contended, lay in their epoch-making recovery of long neglected facets of Reformation theology. In various ways and to varying degrees they had appropriated the legacy of the Reformers. Kant, for example, through his

[6] *Festrede*, pp. 9-10.

uncompromising insistence on the absolutely binding character of the moral law, had provided Evangelical theology "with the means of establishing, on a surer basis than was afforded by the old Protestant doctrine of original sin, the corresponding subjective consciousness that we are in effect guilty in the eye of the law." [7] This guilt, furthermore, is of a radical nature, evidenced in willful selfishness countermanding the universal demands of the categorical imperative. For Ritschl, then, Kant's system of ethics "has this importance, that it secures that a man shall pass upon himself the very same moral judgment as is presupposed as the normal estimate of self by Christianity in its Protestant form." [8] In brief, Kant's ethical viewpoint "has at the same time the significance of a practical restoration of Protestantism," for he renewed "the *moral* view of the universe due to the Reformation." [9]

From the standpoint of the Reformation, however, Ritschl also adjudged Kant's position *religiously* defective. Kant had asserted man's moral autonomy to the neglect of his religious dependence, since for Kant the moral law is binding apart from any "supernatural sanction" and God is in effect postulated as an addendum to moral man's noumenal freedom. Thus Kant deduced religion from ethics contrary to the Reformers' grounding of ethics on the sinner's new "graced" relationship to God. Kant also attributed the conversion of the empirically evil man to that man's own unconditional power of self-legislating freedom, in open contradiction to his premise that the actual capacity for such conversion does not necessarily follow from man's autonomy, from his status as noumenon. Thus, concluded Ritschl, in spite of his insight into radical evil Kant

---

[7] J. & R. I, 388.

[8] *Ibid.*, p. 389.

[9] *Ibid.*, pp. 389-90. Cf. Karl Holl's similar judgment in *The Cultural Significance of the Reformation* (Eng. trans., New York, 1959), p. 127: Kant's "conception of human dignity as resting on submission to an unconditional law leads in its rigor even more definitely back to Luther [than does Kant's concept of the Kingdom of God]. It signifies for the conception of history the rejection of the concepts of happiness and welfare, which the Enlightenment treated as the highest measures of value. . . ." Likewise Otto Wolff, in *Die Haupttypen der neueren Lutherdeutung*, p. 129, asserted: "Luther's breakthrough of the scholastic relativizing of morality repeated itself here [in Kant's assault on eudaemonism] in a secularized, philosophical form." Wolff goes on to note that Ritschl's "theology grew out of the experience of the absolute 'ought' [*Soll*] which he, by way of Lotze's mediation, attached to Kant, and through which he felt himself led directly back to Luther" (*ibid.*). Those critics who speak almost exclusively of Ritschl's "Kantianism" generally neglect to consider Kant's "Lutheranism," and thus also fail to consider that "back to Kant" could also mean "back to Luther" for Ritschl.

ultimately regressed to a shallow *Aufklärung* optimism concerning man's presumed powers for self-justification.[10]

Ritschl's appraisal of Schleiermacher on the basis of the Reformation principle has already been discussed in Chapter II. Here it may again be noted that Schleiermacher's signal achievement was to unite the central Christian teaching on redemption with the thought of the religious and moral fellowship of believers. The Founder of the Christian religion was not a lawgiver or teacher of doctrines to a group of disciples (as were, respectively, Moses and Mohammed), but the Redeemer of the community to which he ever imparts his own perfect God-consciousness. "For the first time," asserted Ritschl, "there is taken up into theology, as a principle, that thought which, as a practical motive, dominates the Reformation and genuine Protestantism."[11] In other words, Schleiermacher recovered the Reformers' emphasis on the mutual reciprocity between the religious self-understanding and the religious Church understanding. The experience of reconciliation with God presupposes personal participation in the community of believers under the lordship of Christ. Religion is necessarily social in nature; true piety is always a cultic phenomenon. Owing to this reappropriation of the Reformers' ecclesiocentrism, Schleiermacher was able to break through the rationalistic and atomistic *loci* method of Orthodox (Melanchthonian) theology, and to articulate for the first time since the sixteenth century an authentic *Church* dogmatics which "views and judges every part of the system from the standpoint of the redeemed community of Christ." [12]

Yet Schleiermacher, like Kant, did not remain consistently faithful to the Reformation principle. Among other weaknesses he inclined to subjectivism, deriving theological statements from an analysis of the redeemed community's present religious consciousness, rather than following the

[10] For these latter criticisms, see esp. J. & R. I, 401-10, 415-16.

[11] *Ibid.*, p. 450. Cf. p. 451: "To the theological discernment, redemption, the Redeemer, and the community that is the subject of redemption, stand in inescapable relation to one another. Hereby for our scientific knowledge is again fixed that which I have already pointed out to be the culminating point of the religious and practical consciousness of the Reformers [p. 157]."

[12] J. & R. III, 5. Cf. J. & R. I, 452: "If, then, the consciousness of community belongs to the fundamental conditions of religion, and religion cannot be rightly apprehended or practiced apart therefrom, then German Protestantism in which this consciousness has been obscured ever since the time of Melanchthon, and as good as lost by means of the Illumination, owes a debt of gratitude to the independent, scientific discernment of Schleiermacher, for having opened up to the religious contents of Christianity the path of a richer development than that which it had found in the entire course of Lutheran theology up to his time."

Reformers in their attempts to ground Church doctrine on the total life course of the historical Jesus attested in the apostolic kerygma. Ritschl's critique of Schleiermacher on this point is aptly summarized by Daniel Deegan:

> Ritschl's acknowledgment of indebtedness to Schleiermacher should not . . . lead us to underestimate the difference between the two figures. Kattenbusch in his comparison between Schleiermacher and Ritschl finds the distinctive feature of the latter's system in the fact that he takes his departure, not from the religious consciousness, but from the historical events of the Gospel which serve as the norm for the unfolding of all faith within the Christian community. Kattenbusch rightly indicates how Ritschl's definition of the essence of Christianity is bound up with his conception of Jesus Christ attested in the New Testament, and experienced in the community founded by Him as the unique and sufficient revelation of God. . . . Ritschl's effort to state the essence of Christianity is expressed in his reference to the standard and historical ground of faith as contained in the whole course of Christ's life, especially His sufferings unto death.[13]

Ritschl also censured Schleiermacher for representing "Christ's influence upon men not directly as ethical but rather as aesthetic." [14] That is to say, Schleiermacher expounded a quasi-Abelardian view of redemption through Christ "by means of aesthetic attractiveness, by means of the

[13] Daniel Deegan, "The Ritschlian School, the Essence of Christianity and Karl Barth," *Scottish Journal of Theology* 16 (1963): 394-95. Deegan's reference to F. Kattenbusch is to the latter's work, *Die deutsche evangelische Theologie seit Schleiermacher* (Giessen, 1926). See also the highly interesting remarks of Wilhelm Herrmann in his rectoral address of 1890 at Marburg, *"Der evangelische Glaube und die Theologie Albrecht Ritschls"* (Eng. trans., "Faith as Ritschl Defined It," in *Faith and Morals,* London, 1904, pp. 33-34): While the religious liberals of the school of Schleiermacher share in Ritschl's rejection of *fides auctoritatis,* they seek to put in its place "not Christian faith, but a religiousness which, in their view, is rooted in the nature of the human soul. They do not understand that Christian faith is unconditional submission to the power which a Christian distinguishes from his own inner life—that is, to the Revelation of God. Of the two propositions—Faith saves a man, and, Faith is a submission to the authority of a revelation—they are willing to hold only the former. Ritschl maintained both. That made him incomprehensible to most of his contemporaries; but it also puts him in the front rank of those who have wanted to rescue and preserve the work of Luther from forms that are falling to pieces." Cf. also p. 58: "Founding on Holy Scripture Luther has made clear the faith we have described as the spiritual experience in which, according to God's ordinance, a person is made humble yet strong, conscious of his misery, yet saved. Ritschl has carried forward this work of Luther. And seeing that we, his pupils, follow him in this matter, we do not yield ourselves to the delusion that because we are members of a university we must make it our business to establish this faith by scientific means."

[14] J. & R. I, 474.

impression of beauty that Christ's life produces," to the neglect of the concrete historical lineaments of Christ's mediatorial activity.[15] Deegan again states Ritschl's case succinctly:

Schleiermacher has shunned the historical determination of Christ's influence as Founder, neglecting reference to the sayings of Jesus and failing to take His Passion into consideration, finding in it no "primary element" for his ideas. He has failed to express the relation of Christ to His community because he does not portray adequately the work of Christ in His historical life in word and action. Schleiermacher aims at giving expression to the intention of the Reformation theology, yet here he fails, for the fundamental thought of the Reformation is that the Christian becomes conscious of his acceptance by God only "in virtue of the perfect obedience of Christ" as the ground of salvation.[16]

It would not be germane to the task at hand to assess the validity of Ritschl's interpretation and critique of Kant and Schleiermacher. The point is that he expressly called them both to account before the bar of Reformation theology, doing so in a far from superficial fashion. Ritschl's procedure in this matter demonstrates that his "continuity with the intention of the Reformers" must not be depreciated, as heretofore has largely been the case, through an almost exclusive concentration on his nineteenth-century forebears. In the first place, then, the significance of Ritschl's Luther interpretation lies in its corrective value. It calls into question all rash attempts to portray Ritschl as the great betrayer of Protestantism to Enlightenment rationalism or, as is more often the case, to explicate his thought solely in terms of his reputed Kantian moralism and supposed relapse into the subjectivism of Schleiermacher. His reputation as a theologian has suffered unduly and unfairly from such stereotyped judgments and hasty generalizations.[17] In treating Ritschl, historians of

[15] *Ibid.*, p. 472. Cf. J. & R. III, 406: "If the Godhead of Christ, or His lordship over the world in His present state of exaltation, is to be a postulate of the Christian faith, an integral part of the Christian view of the world, then it must be demonstrated to us in Christ's influence upon ourselves. But *every form of influence exerted by Christ must find its criterion in the historical figure presented by his life*" (italics added).

[16] Deegan, "The Ritschlian School," pp. 395-96.

[17] A particularly extreme instance of such critical one-sidedness is James Richmond's discussion of Ritschl in *Faith and Philosophy* (New York, 1966). Richmond compares Ritschl's interpretation of Christianity with Kant's in *Religion Within the Limits of Reason Alone*. While conceding that "Ritschl's account is much broader, fuller and richer, and very much more biblical"—and also that "Ritschl places a greater emphasis on grace, on the divine condescension to an imperfect humanity, and thus on liberation and redemption"—Richmond finds nevertheless that "fundamental similarities remain. Among these is the definition of God almost wholly in ethical terms. Within

modern religious thought have been distressingly prone to apply misleading descriptive labels ("neo-Kantian") or to subsume the individual under the general ("nineteenth-century liberal Protestantism"), rather than undertaking a patient, laborious investigation of the particular details of his thought in all their complexity and ambiguity and in the intricacy

Ritschlian as within Kantian Christianity it is hard to say anything more about God—indeed, we are forbidden to say anything more—than that he performs a moral *function*. He prevents man from sinking without trace into the abyss of mechanical nature. Ritschl's conception of Jesus, not unlike Kant's, concerns almost wholly his moral obedience and his *function* as moral ideal and archetype. Ritschl's conception of the Church is curiously rather like that of Kant—a society or community with a moral function to perform; to assist men in their struggle against nature, and thus to achieve their true moral selves. In Ritschl as in Kant there is a rather disconcerting moral grimness and sternness which is disconcerting [*sic*]. . . . Most fundamental and obvious of all, there is a similarity in the unequivocally anthropological, humanistic, moral approach of them both. From that anthropological (or, better still, anthropocentric) standpoint of Ritschl stem most of the criticisms that have subsequently been brought against his theological system" (pp. 84-85; italics in original). One is astonished to find no mention of Ritschl's critique of Kant for confusing religion with ethics, nor of Ritschl's own paramount emphasis on God's free forgiveness as the foundation stone of Christianity, on Jesus as the revealer of divine *agape* and the mediator of forgiveness to his disciples, on the believing community as the sphere of divine worship, and of the Christian's realized lordship over the world through trust, patience, humility, and prayer (each of these being a *religious* activity), etc. Richmond's truncated portrait of Ritschl is untenable but, unfortunately, typical of much of the secondary literature. Cf. John Macquarrie's treatment of Ritschl in his *Twentieth Century Religious Thought* (New York, 1963)—a work to which Richmond is indebted. Macquarrie approves the "harsh verdict" of Guido de Ruggiero that " 'the God of Harnack, like the God of Ritschl, cannot be worshipped, loved or feared, but only criticized as a logical error,' " and further argues that, contra Ritschl and the Ritschlians, "we must beware of the danger of making our conception of God *exclusively* ethical, or he then becomes an abstraction. A God who can be exhaustively characterized in moral terms is a humanized God, lacking those elements of mystery and majesty for which the deeper aspirations of worship seek" (pp. 92-93; italics in original). One may share Professor Macquarrie's protest against Ritschl's virtual elimination of the "idea of the Holy," but certainly Ritschl did not offer an *exclusively ethical* conception of God or of the Christian religion. Cf. J. & R. III, 12-13: "For when good action towards our fellowmen is subsumed under the conception of the Kingdom of God [which, as founded by Jesus, is no less a 'religious community' than 'the organization of humanity through action inspired by love'], this whole province is placed under the rule and standard of religion. And so, were we to determine the unique quality of Christianity merely by its teleological element, namely, its relation to the moral Kingdom of God, we should do injustice to its character as a religion." Again and again Ritschl's many critics fail to comprehend that practically every Ritschlian category—justification, reconciliation, Christian perfection, the kingdom of God, etc.—is framed in such a way as to take into account *both* its moral *and* its religious dimensions. There are *two* foci in the Ritschlian ellipse, and even if one were to conclude that "activity in the Kingdom" ultimately receives greater stress than "redemption through Jesus," this conclusion is warranted only *after* one has come to terms with Ritschl's repeated emphasis on divine pardon as the heart of the Christian religion and on the religious no less than the moral virtues of Christianity.

of their interconnections. Only by virtue of this latter pursuit, however, does historical knowledge become worthy of the name.

In summary, I maintain that the theme "Ritschl and Luther" (or, more broadly stated, "Ritschl and the Reformation") has as much heuristic value as the more frequent theme "Ritschl and Idealism." One could speak of both themes as ideal types in the Weberian sense: preliminary concepts which suggest certain fruitful questions and working hypotheses to guide research. Each theme, however, must be allowed its own integrity while remaining open to possible correction as well as completion by the other. Certainly my own investigation has been but a first step on the way to delineating Ritschl's total relationship to the Reformation, since (among others) Calvin is accorded a place of honor alongside Luther as a preeminent teacher of justification by faith and a churchly theologian. Furthermore, I have been particularly intent on sketching the broader features, one might say the macroscopic dimensions, of Ritschl's encounter with Luther's theology, limiting my detailed analysis to a comparison of Ritschl and Luther on justification. As a result several important topics have been put aside, e.g., Ritschl's attempt to construct a Christology "from below upward" in the name of Luther's dynamic, existential Christology (wherein, according to Ritschl, deity is predicated of Jesus owing to his "vocation" or actual historical work—since the Son performs the same redemptive deeds as the Father; and owing to the "value" of Jesus for faith—since to confess him "my Lord" is to acknowledge him to be nothing less than God *pro me*).[18] Nevertheless, I believe that this inquiry, in spite of such limitations, has been of sufficient amplitude to cast new light on Ritschl's comprehensive theological undertaking.

Ritschl and Twentieth-Century Luther Research (Karl Holl)

The significance of Ritschl's Luther interpretation resides not only in its value as a counterweight to one-dimensional readings of Ritschl's theology, but also in its positive impact on modern Luther research—an impact, however, which frequently has been slighted or simply forgotten. It is a commonplace of historical scholarship that the so-called Luther renaissance of the twentieth century is to be traced directly to the influence of Karl Holl's masterful Luther studies, in tandem with the contemporaneous rise of dialectical theology. It is not my intention to reject this *opinio communis*, but to refine it. Certainly Holl's great Luther vol-

[18] See J. & R. III, 391-92; 416-17.

ume of 1921 was a magnificent achievement and marked a watershed in Luther research, but Holl's work did not transpire in a historical vacuum. It is quite definitely related to earlier Luther scholarship, in particular to Ritschl's *Lutherdeutung*. In general, one can say that Ritschl's Luther interpretation entered into the fabric of Holl's research by posing certain outstanding problems for further investigation, by suggesting the proper methodological procedure, and not least by providing substantive judgments which Holl made his own.[19]

One of the foremost problems to which Holl devoted his scholarly energies was that of the paradoxical relationship between God's wrath and love in Luther's theology.[20] This same problem, however, was precisely a major point of contention between Ritschl and Theodosius Harnack in their respective Luther interpretations.[21] Ritschl rejected the notion of God's wrath as fundamentally at odds with Luther's anti-juristic outlook, and thus saw it as a relapse into an Anselmic mode of thinking. Of far greater moment, according to Ritschl, this notion served to undercut Luther's christocentric theology of revelation (for to speak of a God of wrath is to speak of an arbitrary, inscrutable *Deus absconditus* who exists apart from the *Deus revelatus*). Harnack, on the contrary, insisted on the objective ("metaphysical") reality of God's wrath and so defended Luther against Ritschl's polemic, primarily in the name of an Anselmic and Melanchthonian theory of vicarious satisfaction. Harnack, however, was unable to maintain Luther's tensive correlation between God's wrath and love, and ended up with a stark dualism. Thus Holl inherited this issue in the specific form which it had assumed in the controversy between Ritschl and Harnack. Holl's achievement is that he was able to resolve

[19] W. von Loewenich particularly emphasizes the continuity between Ritschl and Holl insofar as the latter, like Ritschl before him, made Luther's theology of direct and inescapable significance for Protestant systematic theology. Cf. *Luther und der Neuprotestantismus*, p. 280: "What has been called the 'Luther renaissance' of our day—to use a scarcely attractive term—can be traced to the work of Karl Holl. This [term] signifies not only that Luther research since Holl's time has become an important discipline within Evangelical theology and that an immense number of specialized studies in Luther's theology have since appeared; but it means above all that on the Evangelical side one can no longer conceive of any serious theological undertaking of a comprehensive sort which does not attach itself to Luther and make positive use of his basic religious views. Owing to Holl, Luther's theology has been removed from the province of purely historical investigation and has become an object of systematic theology. Therewith Holl, in his own way, continues the tradition of Albrecht Ritschl."

[20] Throughout this section on Ritschl and Holl I am particularly indebted to Walter Bodenstein's recent book, *Die Theologie Karl Holls im Spiegel des antiken und reformatorischen Christentums* (Berlin, 1968).

[21] See below, p. 185, n. 86.

the problem through an intensive study of critically sifted primary sources. His solution favors Ritschl's dominant emphasis on God's love, in opposition to Harnack's "legalism." At the same time, Holl overcame the superficiality of the Ritschlian position, namely, Ritschl's failure to comprehend Luther's *theologia crucis* (for, as is supremely evident in the cross of Christ, God's love is hidden under his wrath over sin, and thus God performs his "strange work" of judgment for the sake of his "proper work" of mercy).[22]

A no less pressing problem which occupied Holl's attention had to do with the organic relationship of justification to sanctification in Protestant dogmatics and particularly in the theology of Luther. I have indicated in Chapter IV that this very issue was one to which Ritschl devoted massive attention. In fact one can rightly say that this was the problem par excellence in Ritschl's doctrinal system no less than in his Luther interpretation. It was in their specific capacity as Luther scholars, therefore, that both Holl and Ritschl took up virtually identical questions: Why, that is, to what end, does God justify the sinner? What specific difference does divine forgiveness make for the present life of the believer? Or, in Ritschl's characteristic terminology, what is the *teleological* relationship of justification to renewal? These were questions forced on Evangelical theology by the failure of the traditional dogmatics to hold together faith and ethics (the forensic and effective sides of the Reformation teaching on justification). The purely forensic doctrine of justification espoused by Melanchthonian Orthodoxy lacked any convincing demonstration of how and why faith is active in love. It so focused on the external and objective reference of Christ's atoning work to the justice and wrath of God that it obscured the reference of this work to the subjective activity of the believer under the lordship of Christ. In short, Orthodox dogmatics separated Christ from the Holy Spirit because it could show no genuine inner connection between past satisfaction and present sanctification. Ritschl observed that the Roman Catholic doctrine of justification as a real making righteous appeared to be far more persuasive than the Evangelical doctrine, precisely because the former was framed in such a way as to answer both to man's quest for blessedness and to God's demand that the divine law

---

[22] Cf. Holl's essay, "Was verstand Luther unter Religion?" in *Gesammelte Aufsätze zur Kirchengeschichte*, I: *Luther* (Tübingen, 1921), 33: "In God wrath and love do not stand on the same level. Love is his 'proper' work, wrath his alien [*uneigentliches*] work. Wrath is the mask behind which 'God' hides himself. God's own nature is such that he also reveals himself in his contrary. Yet he does this not from caprice, but according to a definite plan. God uses wrath in order to attain his goal: to remove those hindrances which obstruct the pure realization of the highest good."

be fulfilled.[23] And Holl was directly confronted by the stinging taunts
of the Dominican theologian Denifle that Luther's and Protestantism's
doctrine of justification actually made a hypocrite of God, since God presumably declares that person righteous who in reality is still nothing but
a sinner.[24]

I shall not here repeat either Ritschl's critique of Luther on this point
or Ritschl's own systematic position; nor shall I examine Holl's findings,
except to note that he recovered and reemphasized Luther's doctrine of
the *Christus efficax* which Ritschl had hastily dismissed as "Christ mysticism." [25] I wish only to underscore the point that Holl the Luther scholar
took up in a concentrated fashion a concrete problem which had already
been sharply posed by Ritschl the Luther scholar; and, furthermore, that
Holl was impelled to consider this issue because of those serious defects
in the traditional doctrinal systems which had already been specified in a
rigorous manner by Ritschl the critic of Melanchthonian Orthodoxy.[26]

Perhaps Holl's outstanding attainment as a Luther scholar, certainly
as a critical historian, was his mastery of the primary sources in concert
with a penetrating use of the genetic method. He carefully employed the

[23] J. & R. I, 172.

[24] In his *Luther und Luthertum in der ersten Entwicklung quellenmässig dargestellt*,
Vol. I, Part 1 (1904), p. 267, Heinrich Denifle wrote: "Luther makes God into a hypocrite of the worst sort: outwardly Luther's God is utterly indifferent to, even winks at,
what he hates according to his innermost being." Cited by Bodenstein, *Die Theologie
Karl Holls*, p. 115.

[25] On Ritschl, see above, Chapter IV, pp. 127 ff. On Holl, see his essay, "Die Rechtfertigungslehre in Luthers Vorlesung über den Römerbrief," in *Gesammelte Aufsätze*
I, 100-101: "Already in the Psalms lectures [1513-15] one finds that Luther has given
currency to the Pauline thought that the believer *enters into an inner union with
Christ* and that Christ thereupon works in him as a living power. On this view Christ's
dwelling in the believer is identical for Luther to the bestowal of the Spirit or the
communication of grace. . . . Correspondingly, however, it must be observed that in
this context Christ and the relationship to him appear only as gift, as God's own instrumentality. The standpoint that God alone creates righteousness in men is thereby
strongly preserved" (italics in original).

[26] Attention should also be given to the striking fact that Theodosius Harnack
in his *Luthers Theologie*—a work in two volumes totaling some 1100 pages—devoted
only a relatively brief *concluding* chapter to the topic of "Justification, Its Nature and
Its Fruits" (cf. II, 407-72). I should like to suggest in passing that a major reason why
Harnack's estimable work failed to win greater influence in its own day was precisely
this lack of attention to the pressing issue of the viability and "practicality" of the
doctrine of justification by faith alone. On this score Ritschl's Luther interpretation is
distinguished by its massive attention to the problem of "verifying" justification as
the *sine qua non* of Christian faith and praxis. Ritschl, in short, used his Luther research in a much more creative and compelling way for his theological contemporaries
than did Harnack.

categories of development and change in his reading of the sources, according particular attention to the emergence of the new and original in Luther's world of thought. That is, he attempted to pinpoint those decisive turning points in Luther's theological development where the specifically Reformation motifs first came to light in contrast to various traditional thought patterns (e.g., Luther's evangelical break with Augustinianism, Nominalism, Humanism, mysticism, etc.). Of course this procedure led Holl to investigate the nature of Luther's continuity, as well as discontinuity, with the theological tradition, and to consider the internal coherence and consistency of Luther's total thought. Holl was favorably placed to undertake this demanding kind of historical-critical inquiry because of his superior philological equipment and his previous experience as an editor of the Greek church fathers, but especially because he had at his disposal the first truly critical edition of Luther's works, the *Weimarer Lutherausgabe* of 1883 ff. As Walter Bodenstein has remarked, "one could say that [Holl] was the first person to become accomplished in the use of the Weimar edition." [27] Holl also put to fruitful use Johannes Ficker's independent critical edition in 1908 of Luther's *Romans Lectures* (1515-1516), together with Hans von Schubert's edition in 1918 of Luther's *Galatians Lectures* (1516-1517). Thus Holl also provided the first intensive, comprehensive, and critically established study of the young Luther.

Yet Holl was not the first scholar to employ the genetic method in Luther research, although he was perhaps the first to do so in a satisfactory manner. The pioneering efforts of Ritschl along this same line should not be overlooked. Whereas Theodosius Harnack treated Luther's theology as one homogeneous whole, without directing significant attention to the problem of change in Luther's outlook or of possible differences between the young and the mature Luther, Ritschl posited a severe discontinuity between the earlier and the later Luther. Hence Ritschl was literally compelled to consider the nature and locus of the dramatic alterations in Luther's original perspective on such matters as justification, the Church, God, Christian freedom, etc. This procedure meant that Ritschl, no less than Holl, operated with the categories of development and change, and thereby Ritschl became the first scholar to transcend the traditional systematic approach to Luther's theology. As has been noted previously, however, Ritschl's Luther study was vitiated by his uncritical hypothesis of a radical break in Luther's theological development, inasmuch as Ritschl did not actually *establish* discontinuity by means of

[27] Bodenstein, *Die Theologie Karl Holls*, p. 109.

genetic analysis but simply assumed and asserted such discontinuity, employing a genetic method strictly in support of this assumption. One could say, therefore, that Ritschl's use of genetic analysis was not prompted by an overriding concern to clarify Luther's theological development, but by the insistent need to disengage the authentic Luther from the scholastic and Melanchthonian Luther of Orthodoxy. He assumed, but did not prove, that the mature Luther and the Orthodox Luther were identical, that the original Luther had ultimately regressed into Scholasticism along with, and owing to the direct influence of, Melanchthon. He did not question the legitimacy of Orthodoxy's claim to the later Luther. He devoted himself solely to rescuing the real—original—Reformation Luther from the toils of Melanchthonianism. In sum, Ritschl carried out his study of the young Luther not for the sake of pure scholarship but in the interest of contemporary polemics.

Ritschl was right, of course, in sharply distinguishing between Luther and Melanchthonian Orthodoxy, and Holl took over this distinction and established it on much firmer ground.[28] Yet Holl also showed that the *mature* Luther was decidedly not a Melanchthonian and did not depart radically from his earlier insights, in spite of certain changes in emphasis in new historical situations. Where Ritschl, therefore, was bent on disclosing Luther's disastrous "regress" into outmoded and previously rejected scholastic viewpoints—Luther's partial return to "Catholicism"; Holl, and the entire twentieth-century *Lutherforschung* after him, consistently endeavored to identify the nature and occasion of Luther's decisive "emergence" from his scholastic heritage—the appearance of the "evangelical" Luther. It is owing to this dramatic change in perspective that Ritschl's Luther scholarship has been most pointedly outdated by the newer Luther research.

The relationship of Holl's Luther interpretation to Ritschl's was con-

---

[28] Holl was in a position to establish this distinction because he could show on textual grounds that a number of Luther's later writings—particularly the important *Genesis Lectures* (1535-1545)—had been "edited" by students in a consistently "Melanchthonian" fashion, i.e., in conformity to the orthodoxy of second-generation Lutheranism. Holl established his own critical canon of authentic Luther texts, distinguishing sharply between those writings which came directly from Luther (e.g., as autographs, or transcripts of his lectures by demonstrably reliable scribes, or writings prepared for publication by Luther himself) and those which had been extensively reworked by his editors. Ritschl made no such distinctions; apparently the possibility of textual corruptions did not suggest itself to him, or at least he did not pursue such a possibility. In addition, as was noted previously, Ritschl lacked a fully critical edition of Luther's works and had no working knowledge of Luther's earliest biblical lectures. Thus Ritschl's equation of the mature Luther with Melanchthonian Orthodoxy can in part be explained by the then existing state of textual unreliability and incompleteness.

siderably more direct, however, than the previous remarks would suggest. One can also point to numerous instances of Holl's material indebtedness to characteristic viewpoints of Ritschl on both Luther and the Reformation. In fact Holl has frequently been labeled a "Ritschlian" by various critics owing to his reputed ethicizing of Luther's theology. In 1940 Wilhelm Pauck noted that Holl had recently been "subjected to rather heavy criticism" on the grounds that, among other things, "he had interpreted Luther's religion in terms of Kantian and Ritschlian moralism." [29] John Dillenberger has gone so far as to claim that "although Holl was dissatisfied with the work of Ritschl, he emphasizes the central place of morality in the gospel of salvation more than Ritschl does. . . . It is as if the elliptical character of Ritschl's thought had been transformed into a circle of which the center is a single point in which grace is determined by morality." [30] Dillenberger's judgment is overly severe, but it does underscore Holl's indebtedness to Ritschl insofar as Holl, like Ritschl, was preeminently concerned to unfold Luther's "ethic of justification," namely, to show how for Luther God's free forgiveness entailed nothing less than a far-reaching "reconstruction of morality." [31]

Furthermore, following Ritschl, Holl attempted to demonstrate that modern civilization, and particularly German culture, were as decisively shaped by the spirit of the Reformation as by the Renaissance and the Enlightenment. Holl's rejoinder to Ernst Troeltsch in his famous essay, *Die Kulturbedeutung der Reformation* (1911), contains many echoes of, and direct parallels to, Ritschl's less known *Festrede* of 1883 (in which Ritschl was responding to Paul de Lagarde, who was a teacher of Troeltsch and favorably regarded by the latter).[32] According to Holl, Luther—by virtue of his new understanding of the gospel—"threw two major ideas as active forces into the stream of culture: a new concept of personality and a new concept of community." [33] It was precisely both these concepts,

[29] Pauck, "The Historiography of the German Reformation During the Past Twenty Years," *Church History* 9 (1940): 311.

[30] Dillenberger, *God Hidden and Revealed*, p. 25.

[31] Cf. Holl, "Der Neubau der Sittlichkeit," in *Gesammelte Aufsätze* I, 133-244.

[32] On Ritschl and Lagarde, see below, pp. 163 ff.

[33] Holl, *The Cultural Significance of the Reformation* (Eng. trans. of *Die Kulturbedeutung der Reformation*, New York, 1959), p. 30. This essay dates from 1911, was revised by Holl in 1918 and published in *Gesammelte Aufsätze* I in 1921. In it Holl refers only to an article by Troeltsch on natural law, but in the background stand Troeltsch's *Die Bedeutung des Protestantismus für die Entstehung der modernen Welt* (Munich and Berlin, 1906, 2nd ed., 1911; Eng. trans., *Protestantism and Progress*, New York, 1912), and his *Die Soziallehren der christlichen Kirchen und Grup-*

however, which Ritschl originally emphasized in his delineation of the Reformation principle, namely, in his exposition of the religious self- and Church understanding according to which the believer through forgiveness attains to a new awareness of his personal relationship to God and of his complete dependence on the religious fellowship. For Holl, then, even as for Ritschl before him, Luther's idea of justification by faith had the practical significance that the believer, through experiencing God's unconditional pardon, gains a heightened sense of individual freedom, unconstrained by legal requirements, and simultaneously subordinates himself to the religious community as the sphere where such freedom expresses itself in loving service to the world. Holl also exhibited specific dependence upon Ritschl in his discussion of the centrality of the kingdom of God and of work (the Christian "calling"), as well as in his stress on Luther's displacement of Roman Catholic asceticism.[34]

If one maintains, therefore, that Karl Holl's Luther study marked a turning point in the history of Luther scholarship, one must not abstract this study from its considerable indebtedness to Ritschl's Luther interpretation (and also to the Luther scholarship of such Ritschlians as Ferdinand

---

pen (Tübingen, 1912; Eng. trans., *The Social Teaching of the Christian Churches*, New York, 1931).

[34] Cf. *The Cultural Significance of the Reformation*, pp. 29, 33-39, 46-47, 126-32, 151. Attention should also be directed to Holl's correspondence with Adolf Schlatter during the years 1897-1925, edited by Robert Stupperich in the *Zeitschrift für Theologie und Kirche* 64 (1967): 169-240, particularly the letter to Schlatter dated January 8, 1920, pp. 227-28. In response to Schlatter's commemorative article, "Die Entstehung der Beiträge zur Förderung christlicher Theologie und ihr Zusammenhang mit meiner theologischen Arbeit," in *Beiträge zur Förderung christlicher Theologie* 25 (1920): 7-89, Holl remarked that in this essay (cf. p. 74) Schlatter had certainly been unfair to Ritschl, and proceeded to explain: "What Ritschl *intended* was not as far removed from your own concerns as you suppose. . . . When I consider that Ritschl intended to put Christ in the center even as you do, that he battled against perfection out of commitment to the doctrine of justification, that he comprehended and always emphasized the significance of the will in religion, that [he insisted that] all religious benefits [*Güter*] are bound up with the religious community: then I note here numerous points of contact between you. Yet with Ritschl everything came out sounding so excessively formal and intentionally reserved, giving evidence of an underlying imperious will, that many persons were repelled from the outset. But in any event Ritschl's theology—during the time when it seemed to afford me a solution—did not hinder me from taking Christianity seriously. In addition to Schleiermacher and Biedermann, Ritschl's theology proved to be for many . . . the very bridge by which they recovered their Christian faith. Still there remained something in this [theology] which continued to nag me like a bad conscience; only I didn't quite know how to put my finger on the real error. Subsequently I discovered it to reside in Ritschl's way of approaching everything from the perspective of 'goods' [*Güterbetrachtung*, i.e., in light of the concept of the highest good and the virtues and values related to it]. Permit me to add at this time that I primarily have you to thank if I have advanced beyond this point."

Loofs and Adolf von Harnack). Modern Luther research owes more to Ritschl than it has usually cared to remember. It is a curious fact that when Ritschl set out to take up Luther's leading motifs into his own theological system—being the *first* nineteenth-century dogmatician to do so in such concentrated fashion—he actually put into motion a scholarly enterprise which was destined to overshadow that system and which, more remarkably still, was to result in a widespread ignorance of Ritschl the earnest student of Luther's theology. For this reason alone, if for no other, a fresh perspective on Ritschl's theological goals and accomplishments is imperative.

2. THE CONTEXTUAL SIGNIFICANCE OF RITSCHL'S LUTHER INTERPRETATION

In 1913, almost twenty-five years after Ritschl's death, Arthur Titius penned a substantial article setting forth his views on Ritschl's significance for contemporary theology. In the process he made the following noteworthy analysis of the essence of the Ritschlian system:

If out of the multitude of valuable stimuli which Ritschl brought to the theology of his time, one attempts to expound the decisively central impulse, then—according to Ritschl's own testimony—this must be construed as follows: the new factor was not formed by isolated theological propositions of a systematic or historical sort, but rather by Ritschl's belief that amidst later excrescences he had newly discovered the original type of Christian, i.e., biblical-Reformation piety, and had given it new currency as a solution to the religious problems even of his own day. When in the course of his Reformation studies the awareness first ripened that the authentic essence of the Reformation becomes evident in Luther's Christianity, not in the doctrinal formulations of the later confessions;—and when this Christianity of Luther's flowed together with that of Paul and the New Testament to comprise one homogeneous magnitude: then for the first time there developed in Ritschl that imposing self-awareness which characterized him, that conviction that he was able to give something new to the theology and the religious life of his age, something normative and definitive.[35]

This statement might well have served as a prefatory motto for this entire investigation since it admirably expresses my basic point of view and, *in nuce* at least, touches on my primary findings. Like Titius I have located the central, unifying dynamic of Ritschl's theology in his self-conscious

[35] A. Titius, "Albrecht Ritschl und die Gegenwart. Ein Vortrag," *Theologische Studien und Kritiken* 86 (1913): 67.

return to biblical-Reformation Christianity and his projected recovery of such piety from its subsequent deformations—a lifetime's endeavor involving both historical criticism and systematic restatement and ultimately directed to the re-formation of contemporary Protestantism.

Yet it remains to consider in what specific respects, if any, Ritschl may have imparted something normative and definitive to the religious life of his day. Did his theological program achieve palpable results in his own ecclesiastical and cultural setting, or were his labors fruitless? Given the severity of my judgment on his Luther interpretation, one might readily conclude that the latter had little real significance in its own time. Or one might rashly assume that he already knows what Ritschl achieved in his day: nothing less than the selling out of Protestant theology to the modern mind! The truth, however, is that Ritschl's adherence to Luther and Reformation theology, notwithstanding its limitations, takes on fully positive, indeed new dimensions when examined in its historical context. In what follows I shall treat two major respects in which Ritschl's Luther interpretation was of fundamental importance in his day and age.

The Vindication of Protestantism

Ritschl's long-term, intensive involvement with Reformation theology represented an explicit assertion of classical Protestantism's *contemporary viability* in answer to its numerous cultured despisers throughout the nineteenth century (as well as its traditional Roman Catholic antagonists). Such contemporaries of Ritschl as Paul de Lagarde and Jacob Burckhardt, not to speak of Friedrich Nietzsche, made no effort to conceal their unrelieved scorn for the paltry legacy of the Reformation in matters of both doctrine and life. In Burckhardt's eyes the Protestant Reformation had been at root a movement of negation, a violent and senseless rejection of that Catholic asceticism which had ever been the fertile ground of Christianity's most valuable cultural contributions. "The accomplishments of a thousand years, the vessel of a religion, the correlate of a thoroughly formed popular culture had been stolen from [the Catholics] and thoroughly destroyed. And in Germany this had not even happened in tragic battle, but with a sudden appeal to general undisciplined action beside which the positive new 'faith' meant little." [36]

[36] Burckhardt, *On History and Historians* (New York, 1965), p. 117. Cf. p. 106: "How different was the effect of Christianity on people in its beginning: repentance, surrender of property at the feet of the apostles—and now, by contrast, '*nos evangelistes de taverne*'! The worst elements of the population rose to the top. In the time of transition, brutal acts of violence against priests and the like occurred. . . . This was

The Reformation, in short, was an act of unrestrained destruction perpetrated against everything sanctioned by age and authority. The Reformers themselves were not courageous restorers of primitive Christianity and its stern ethic, but grasping confiscators of church properties, endowments, etc.—the ecclesiastical counterparts, one might say, of the Spanish conquistadors. "Few people would want to know of them today," concluded Burckhardt, apart from their current esteem as "battering rams against the greatest and thus, by implication, any authority." [37]

Still more vitriolic in his assault on Protestantism was Paul de Lagarde—the textual critic and editor of the Septuagint, founder of the *religionsgeschichtliche Schule*, advocate of a new Germanic religion, and a colleague of Ritschl on the Göttingen theological faculty. Fritz Stern has supplied an incisive sketch of Lagarde's views:

Lagarde's attack on Protestantism, in which scholarship was peppered by polemics, was bent on proving that the faith of the Reformation had been a misbegotten child of Catholicism, that its development had been the gradual unfolding of ineffectuality, interrupted by brief moments of pernicious power. In matters of dogma the Reformation had retained most of the Catholic tradition, itself fraudulently evolved, but had repudiated the apostolic authority which hitherto had protected the unity of faith and dogma. Lagarde ridiculed the Protestant claim to have ensconced the Bible and the individual conscience as the new sources of authority. The major dogmas of Christianity, after all, could not be justified by any interpretation of the Gospel, however liberal. As for the only distinctly Protestant belief—justification by faith—Lagarde argued that faith had so completely disappeared from contemporary life as to make it a mockery.

The creative impulse of the Reformation had withered almost at once: "If Luther was ever valid, his validity ceased in 1546," when he died. If Protestantism was ever a live force, it ceased to be one in 1648, "for when it received the solemn permission to live, it had lost its last excuse for existence." Its historic consequences had been lamentable: Protestantism had perpetuated

---

done only out of hatred of the church, not out of love of the gospel; otherwise they [i.e., the plunderers] would have started their reform with themselves. (The Reformation made its great strides not through its positive teachings, but as a negation of something that had existed up to that time; without this negation the masses would not have been won over.)" *On History and Historians* is a translation by H. Zohn of Burckhardt's *Historische Fragmente*—lecture notes prepared for his history courses at the University of Basel from 1865 to 1885, selected by Emil Dürr and first published in 1929 as Vol. VII in Burckhardt's Collected Works. To the best of my knowledge Ritschl was not acquainted with the writings of Burckhardt and certainly did not respond directly to the latter's treatment of the Reformation. But Burckhardt is representative of a climate of cultured opinion in the latter nineteenth century, and his viewpoint serves to put Ritschl's Luther interpretation into its proper perspective.
    [37] *Ibid.*, pp. 104-5.

German disunity; "by sanctioning the princes' rebellion and by thus introducing caesaropapism," it had surrendered Germany to barbarism. . . .

Nor were the cultural achievements of German Protestantism more impressive. The most cherished possession of the Protestants, the Luther Bible,
Lagarde sought to scrap as obsolete. After 1648 Protestant theology had dried
up and by the nineteenth century "pietism and rationalism [had] devoured
Luther's Protestantism." Its one beneficent consequence had been achieved
by its very ineffectuality: it had been so weak that it was unable to thwart
the intellectual and artistic life of the peoples under its control and thus,
indirectly, it promoted the resurgence of German culture. On the other hand,
its utter insignificance was attested by its failure to mold or affect this resurgence. . . .[38]

For critics such as Burckhardt and Lagarde, then, Protestantism had no
positive significance of its own; indeed the Protestant Reformation simply
marked the beginning of the dissolution of ancient Christianity. Furthermore, the doctrine of justification by faith—the venerable *articulus stantis
et cadentis ecclesiae*—was especially subjected to ridicule. Burckhardt
maintained that this "new dogma"—this "innovation vis-à-vis the entire
church up to that time"—was in fact "a more impressive burden than
Catholicism had been previously," although in practice this teaching
meant that "the Reformation is the faith of all those who would like not
to have to do something any more." [39] Burckhardt particularly dwelled on
the antinomian and quietistic consequences of Reformation theology:
"Through the problems of justification, good works, predestination, and
the like, *all of ethics got out into the high seas*." [40] Indeed "the decisive
thing about Luther was the fact that in addition to indulgences he also
abhorred good works in the widest sense." [41] Perhaps the Basel historian
found some solace in his conclusion that "the doctrine of justification
through faith, in Luther's version, now has been abandoned by all prominent Protestant theologians." [42] Once again it was Lagarde, however, who

[38] Fritz Stern, *The Politics of Cultural Despair: A Study in the Rise of the Germanic
Ideology* (New York, 1965), pp. 70-72. On p. 40 Stern makes some brief remarks
on Lagarde's strained relations with Ritschl (whom, curiously enough, Stern refers
to as "Alois" Ritschl).

[39] Burckhardt, *On History and Historians*, pp. 101, 107-8, 98. Cf. pp. 105-6: "A
large proportion of the population certainly was quick to join [the Reformation]. It was
pleasant to skip confession and penance immediately, to break fast, to be rid of vows
and indulgences, and, as was thought, not to be paying tithes any longer (of these the
peasants were nowhere relieved). The Reformation must have had an enormous at-
traction for all *those who enjoy not having to do something any longer*" (italics in
original).

[40] *Ibid.*, p. 107 (italics in original).

[41] *Ibid.*, p. 100.

[42] *Ibid.*, p. 103.

uttered the most uncompromising denunciation of this doctrine, finding its Jewish legalism incompatible with the gospel and even denying its centrality for the Reformers:

The doctrine of justification is not the gospel, but a minor Pauline discovery, born out of Paul's Jewish spirit. And for Paul himself it was not the unique or even the most profound method of resolving the problem of man's guilty condition, while today it is altogether dead in the Protestant churches—and rightly so! For the doctrines of justification and reconciliation are mythological constructs, valid only for those who take seriously the Early Church's trinitarian doctrine—which today is scarcely true of anyone.[43]

The central thrust in Lagarde's denigration of justification, it should be noted, was nothing original to him. It was basically a reiteration of Fichte's earlier contention that the Pauline doctrine of justification simply marked a relapse into Judaism, to be accounted for by Paul's Pharisaic background.[44] Fichte himself could make sense of justification only as a spiritual truth already self-evident, indeed connate to *homo naturalis*: "Every man, by the very fact that he has been born a man and bears man's countenance, is able to enter the kingdom of heaven, and God is prepared to enliven and enrapture him; for precisely this is man's reason for being and solely on this condition is he truly a man." Likewise, according to Fichte, "the true Christian knows of no covenant or mediation with God, but only that old, eternal and immutable relationship: that in him we live and move and have our being." [45] At the close of the cen-

---

[43] Cited by Karl Holl in his informative article, "Die Rechtfertigungslehre im Licht der Geschichte des Protestantismus," *Gesammelte Aufsätze zur Kirchengeschichte*, III: *Der Westen* (Tübingen, 1928), 525. Holl locates this statement in Lagarde's book, *Ueber einige Berliner Theologen und was von ihnen zu lernen ist* (Göttingen, 1890)—written in the year following Ritschl's death. Holl, however, gives no page reference and, in spite of a close examination of Lagarde's work itself, I have been unable to verify this citation. But cf. the following closely related passage in Lagarde's treatise, where Ritschl is directly attacked by name: "I find it incomprehensible that people in an age which prides itself on its discernment could ever take seriously a man who has managed to make 'the Christian doctrines of justification and reconciliation' central to a theology, in the way Ritschl has done. These doctrines are mythological constructs, nothing more. In fact they only serve to pose a problem which they are powerless to resolve, except at most for those who continue to adhere to the ancient church's trinitarian doctrine—a group that includes neither Ritschl nor our clergy and laity" (p. 105). Lagarde concludes: "Accordingly, I can only regard the foundation of Ritschl's theology as worthless, and therefore I cannot concede that this theology will revitalize Protestantism" (pp. 109-10). See Lothar Schmid, *Paul de Lagardes Kritik an Kirche, Theologie und Christentum* (Stuttgart, 1935); pp. 58-62 pertain to Lagarde and Ritschl. Cf. also Robert W. Lougee, *Paul de Lagarde* (1827-1891): A *Study of Radical Conservatism in Germany* (Cambridge, Mass., 1962).

[44] Holl, *Gesammelte Aufsätze* III, 550.

[45] Cited by Holl, *ibid.*

tury Wilhelm Dilthey pursued a related line of thought. Like Lagarde, he asserted that "the doctrine of justification stands only so long as its dogmatic presuppositions (the incarnation and vicarious satisfaction of Christ) hold good." Unlike Lagarde, however, Dilthey evidenced a positive regard for Luther and his Reformation, while his strictures on the doctrine of justification were of little moment to him since (here again like Lagarde) he could write: "I completely deny that the essence of Reformation spirituality is located in the renewal of the Pauline doctrine of justification by faith." [46]

One could profitably read Ritschl's total Reformation studies, and particularly his Luther interpretation, as an almost point-for-point refutation of these absolutistic charges leveled so remorselessly by Burckhardt, Lagarde, *et al.* In the course of this essay, albeit in various contexts, I have repeatedly touched upon the most salient features of Ritschl's counter-proposals. Ritschl constantly insisted, for example, that Luther's doctrine of Christian freedom had nothing to do with petulant opposition to any and all authority, nor did it simply rationalize the moral laxity of the self-indulgent masses. Luther taught an inner being-set-free from sin, guilt, and earthly evils, and so preached the Christian's God-given freedom for loving service to the world in obedience to his Lord. Likewise Ritschl completely denied the oft-repeated assertion that Catholicism alone, owing to its self-abnegating, ascetic character, had been a positive historical force. The truth, rather, is that precisely this ascetic Catholicism has been at root a movement of negation, because of its monastic *Weltflucht*, its mystical and acosmic spirit, its ethically dangerous distinction between clerical and lay morality, its inculcation of a *timor filialis* which frequently paralyzes the believer's moral will, its spurious pretensions to political overlordship, etc. And where Burckhardt discerned the Reformation's "essential spirit" in the reputed anarchistic tendencies of Anabaptism, Ritschl argued that the latter movement was in fact a recrudescence on Evangelical soil of that late medieval sectarian phenomenon, Spiritual Franciscanism.[47]

Ritschl was especially intent on disproving the familiar charge that the Reformation doctrine of justification by faith was a complete innovation. The Reformers may have broken with Roman Catholic monasticism, mysticism, papal-caesarism, hierarchism, etc., but their leading principle

[46] Cited by Holl, *ibid.*, pp. 525-26.

[47] Cf. Burchkhardt, *On History and Historians*, p. 106; and Ritschl's article "Wiedertäufer und Franciscaner," *Zeitschrift für Kirchengeschichte* 6 (1883): 499-502.

of *sola gratia* was a recovery of the Western (and Primitive) Church's profoundest piety. Nor was their idea of justification a mere dogmatic formula or intellectual proposition which must be accepted on ecclesiastical authority; it denoted a simple experience of forgiveness, a new self-understanding grounded on God's mercy in Christ. This consciousness of free forgiveness is not predicated on assent to certain dogmatic hypotheses because it is strictly a practical experience of the believer within the community of faith, predicated on the actual historical vocation of the Church's Lord—a vocation which, on the warrant of the Reformers themselves, can be comprehended in terms other than such theoretical constructs as the dogma of Christ's two natures or the legalistic notion of vicarious satisfaction.

For the moment I shall forego a consideration of Ritschl's emphasis on the practical relevance of the doctrine of justification, as well as his denial of the supposedly quietistic implications of this doctrine. Here one may briefly note his insistence on the positive cultural significance of the Reformation, as outlined in his *Festrede* of 1883.[48] On the occasion of this academic address Ritschl particularly had in view Lagarde's sweeping assertions concerning the Reformation's total sterility in the cultural realm. Lagarde claimed that the rise of Protestantism resulted in the fragmentation and stunted growth of the German state. Ritschl replied that Luther's purely religious idea of Christian freedom, as distinct from Rome's hierocratic principle, actually allowed the state to be the state for the first time, since the Christian rules as a king over the world solely in a spiritual, not a material, sense. Thus for Protestants the Church is not a type of state, a *Rechtsordnung* in competition with the secular authority, but exists only to equip God's reconciled children for spiritual world dominion through the gift of forgiveness. Ritschl then proceeded to argue that a necessary condition of cultural development is the positive evaluation of labor, and here he reminded his listeners of Luther's doctrine of the *Beruf* based on the Christian's freedom to serve his neighbor. Luther recognized all labor for the public good, however humble or lofty, as constituting one's ordinary service to God, and he likewise attributed a priestly quality to fidelity in one's calling. Of no less significance, Luther's message of Christian lordship over the world is the implicit presupposition of natural science. By announcing human mastery over the world as God's gift to his spiritual creation, this teaching effectively removes the veil which medieval superstition had cast over nature and so opens up the

[48] For what follows, see esp. pp. 15-17 of the *Festrede*.

entire natural world to scientific inquiry. Ritschl contended that only a *religious* motive could ultimately demythologize that heathenish sacralization of nature which had found expression in the medieval cosmology.

The cogency and value of these various arguments are open to debate.[49] What must be underscored, however, is that Ritschl did not argue for the modernity of the Reformation as something already self-evident to the bourgeois mentality of Bismarck's Germany, as something which the proverbial schoolboy already knew. On the contrary, he strove mightily to unfold the epoch-making cultural implications resident within that much maligned doctrine of justification by faith and its practical correlate of Christian liberty. While Protestantism, therefore, may ultimately be linked with cultural progress, the latter is not inevitable because, on Ritschl's view, it presupposes continuing trust and confidence in the Lord of history. Thus Ritschl did not simply put Luther's (and the Bible's) seal of approval on the status quo. He attempted, rather, to show that the specifically Christian *Welt- und Lebensanschauung*—grounded on trust in God's fatherly guidance of historical life, and on patience, humility, and prayer—was no inconsequential ghetto theology but a perspective which literally opened up the heart of reality to the eyes of faith, laying bare the inner nature of things. Paul de Lagarde and others of similar persuasion might dismiss the Reformation doctrine of justification as an outmoded remnant of dogmatic traditionalism and a mythical fabrication demanding a *sacrificium intellectus*. Ritschl, however, as I shall show in greater detail in the next section, contended that this teaching actually made possible a theology of genuine secularity, because it directly connected God's grace with man's ethical vocation in the world.

[49] I have already called attention, however, to Holl's indebtedness to several of Ritschl's leading themes (see above, pp. 159-60). So also the influence of Ritschl on Wilhelm Dilthey is discernible in the latter's famous essay, *Auffassung und Analyse des Menschen im 15. und 16. Jahrhundert,* in *Gesammelte Schriften,* Vol. II (Stuttgart, 1940). A partial translation of this essay is to be found in Lewis W. Spitz, ed., *The Reformation: Material or Spiritual?* (Boston, 1962), pp. 8-16. Dilthey specifically calls attention to "Ritschl's significant presentation" of Luther's theology (in the *Festrede*), and Ritschl's hand is clearly evident in Dilthey's description of Luther's position on justification: "The justification through the faith, which Luther experienced, was the personal experience of the believer standing in the continuity of the Christian community, who experienced in the personal event of faith the trust in the grace of God through the appropriation of the performance of Christ, brought about by the personal election of grace" (Spitz, p. 12). Unlike Ritschl, however, Dilthey rejected Luther's doctrine of justification as a remnant of "dogmatic Christianity" and found Luther's "fundamental thought" to be "the autocracy of the believing person" (p. 14). Thus it is the Enlightenment's *Lutherbild,* not Ritschl's, which again comes to expression in Dilthey's presentation. In this light Ritschl's viewpoint appears decidedly "un-modern."

Thus in his own historical setting, which here has been rapidly sketched in broad strokes, Ritschl's Luther interpretation had the immediate significance of being a vindication of Protestantism and especially of its cardinal teaching. Certainly Ritschl was going against the stream of much contemporary opinion when he forthrightly claimed that justification is "the foundation-stone of the Christian religion." [50] And, more importantly, he did not rest content with bald assertion, but directed his impressive scholarly energies to demonstrating in a coordinated, constructive fashion the central Reformation truth that God's unmerited forgiveness of the sinner is "the key to the whole domain of Christian life." [51] In sum, Ritschl defended the Protestant principle on biblical and historical grounds and unfolded it, in all its richness of detail and implication, in his carefully worked-out doctrinal system. Of course Ritschl himself maintained that contemporary Protestantism and the original piety of the Reformation were two quite different realities. What current critics were taking for the essence of Reformation spiritually was often little more than its disposable husks, presently embodied in a deformed Protestantism. The true Reformation had been so disfigured by later rationalism, moralism, mysticism, sectarianism, etc., that the genuine article could scarcely be distinguished any longer from its counterfeit. When Ritschl, therefore, put himself forward as a reformer of Protestantism he did so not out of an inordinate sense of self-worth, but because reformation was imperative in the face of widespread popular and learned ignorance about the true meaning of Protestantism.[52]

But Ritschl also knew that more than historical ignorance was at work in the contemporary animus against the Reformation and Protestantism. To the modern mind the very notion of justification and reconciliation was increasingly anathema, since it presumably threatened personal freedom and seemed to undercut the need for a moral reordering of society. Furthermore, to speak of God's creative act of grace as the *conditio sine qua non* of the God-man relationship was to deny the possi-

---

[50] J. & R. III, 141.

[51] *Ibid.*, p. 113.

[52] Cf. Ritschl's revealing "apology" in the *Festrede*, p. 8: "Since I am attempting to characterize Luther's leading religious thoughts—in order to adduce from them his general influence on modern culture—I certainly see myself standing in opposition to widely circulated misinterpretations of his Reformation, which from the outset must be corrected. Whoever intends to explain Luther's achievement in a genuinely historical fashion, and in accord with Luther's own intention, must put himself forward to a certain degree as a reformer vis-à-vis misunderstandings which obscure the actual situation and render it unintelligible."

169

bility of a purely natural religion based on divine and human reasonableness. Although Ritschl himself spoke disparagingly of apologetic theology, his major work can properly be read as a massive defense of the biblical-Reformation doctrine of divine forgiveness for Christ's sake as the fundament of Christian faith and life, in answer to all who proclaimed a relationship with God on some presumed "higher ground" than that of a unique historical event and in some locus other than the Christian Church. It is a supreme irony that Ritschlianism has become virtually synonymous with modernism—with a tepid theology of culture, characterized by servile capitulation to the *Zeitgeist*—when Ritschl devoted almost his entire career to investigating, expounding and defending a doctrine that the *moderni* regarded as a dead issue.

The Overcoming of History by History

"To overcome history by history" is a programmatic theme usually associated with the thought of Ernst Troeltsch, but, properly understood, it is no less applicable to Ritschl's comprehensive theological enterprise. Through his proposed critical reappropriation of Luther's original Reformation theology—which itself was a recovery of the earliest and purest Christianity—Ritschl intended to overcome all historical deformations of this great tradition: Roman Catholic world negation, mystical ahistoricism, Orthodox scholasticism, pietistic sectarianism, Enlightenment individualism, and Romantic (Hegelian) speculation. Ritschl's conviction that he had something new to give to the Evangelical Church of his day arose out of, and found concrete expression in, this resolve to purge the Reformation heritage of all foreign growths, all alien patterns of thought and life. Heretofore I have primarily measured the adequacy of his Luther interpretation by reference to *Luther's theology itself*, with a view to answering my basic question: "Did Ritschl in fact apprehend the 'authentic' Luther, as he claimed to have done?" But such adequacy must also be measured by taking into account the possible ways in which Ritschl's Luther studies had their *intended effect*, i.e., succeeded in overcoming or breaking through various deformations of the Reformation principle. Put otherwise, Ritschl may not have recovered the integral Luther, but he may well have recovered a Luther who was significantly new on the scene of late nineteenth-century theology—a Luther whom he could invoke specifically against those churchmen who prided themselves on their faithfulness to the Reformer's understanding of the gospel.

I have already shown on previous pages how Ritschl called into question and corrected the widely held Enlightenment portrait of Luther as the outspoken apostle of an autonomous religion of the conscience and of private biblical interpretation. (It was this portrait, incidentally, which Paul de Lagarde accepted as accurate only to repudiate as pernicious, thereby linking the "demagogic" Luther with the "Pharisaic" Paul as a perverter of true religion.) But undoubtedly Ritschl's foremost accomplishment as a Luther interpreter is to be found in his rigorous attack on the nineteenth-century Orthodox view of Luther, which posited an a priori continuity between Luther and Melanchthon and so between Luther and seventeenth-century Lutheran dogmatics. In fact it was Ritschl who, along with J. C. K. von Hofmann, first sensed the magnitude of Melanchthon's divergence from Luther and sought forthwith to disengage Luther's theology from its encapsulation in Melanchthonian thought forms. Ritschl undertook this task at a time when Theodosius Harnack, Hofmann's colleague at Erlangen, was no less earnestly striving to maintain the unbroken continuity between Luther, Melanchthon, and Orthodox dogmatics. In order to assay the merit of Ritschl's Luther-based critique of Melanchthonian Orthodoxy, it is first necessary to examine more closely the leading features of this critique.[53]

Ritschl especially scored Orthodoxy for its wholesale juristic bias, its patent legalism. It establishes the law, in the form of an immutable legal code or *lex aeterna*, as the permanently valid ground of the God-man relationship. Starting out from this premise of an all-encompassing legal world order, patterned on the role of civil law in the state, Orthodoxy explicates the whole of Christian doctrine in a consistently deductive fashion. The doctrines of God (as Lawgiver and Judge), sin (as lawlessness), salvation (as predicated on obedient fulfillment of the law, if not by man himself then by his Substitute), atonement (as vicarious satisfaction), justification (as a courtroom procedure wherein the guilty is declared just) are all placed within a comprehensive juridical framework and interpreted according to the standard of legal necessity.

Combined with this pervasive legalism, indeed growing directly out of it, is Orthodoxy's sterile objectivism, in which Christian faith becomes essentially a cognitive phenomenon: the right knowledge of saving truths (*Rechtglaübigkeit*) rather than the personal trust of the heart in the God who freely forgives. The primary function of the gospel is to convey authoritative information about the permanent validity of Christ's past,

---

[53] For Ritschl's critique of Orthodoxy, see J. & R. I, 234-89; J. & R. III, *passim* (esp. pp. 245-84); and *Theologie und Metaphysik* (Bonn, 1881; 2nd ed., 1887). Also see above, pp. 81-82.

objective reconciliation of God with man (and of God with himself). This notion of reconciliation is further elaborated in dogmatic formulations (e.g., Christ's two natures, *unio personalis, communicatio idiomatum, satisfactio sufficiens*, etc.) to which assent must be given if personal salvation is to be realized. Thus faith itself is intellectualized in a quasi-legal fashion. It becomes a theoretical knowing about the divine plan of salvation and a bare holding for true of a past atonement comprehended in doctrinal terms, rather than a personal, contemporary meeting with the Savior himself. As a result the *present* reality of salvation becomes problematic because the personal activity of the believer—the conformity of his will to God's will revealed in Christ, his personal love for God in response to God's love for him—is given little or no scope. In fact, since justification is purely forensic (*pura reputatio*), any sustained talk of human activity, or of reciprocity between God's redemptive acting and the Christian's faithful response, would bear the taint of Pelagianism. Justification and reconciliation are complete in themselves and admit of no reference to the believing subject, except of course to his faith; but even faith is pure passivity.

Finally, as is already more than plain, according to Ritschl Orthodoxy is deformed by its thoroughgoing rationalism, its scholastic character. Although the young Melanchthon, in full agreement with Luther's faith principle, had rightly asserted: "This is what it means to know Christ, namely, to know his benefits," he subsequently regressed into vapid speculation on God's eternal being in himself, Christ's preexistence and two natures, etc. In this neo-scholastic quest for a self-subsistent, timeless essence behind its given historical actuality, a Platonic epistemology was introduced into Evangelical theology, and history was literally overcome by metahistory, namely, by dogma. In the process the positive Reformation theology of revelation, Luther's christocentrism, was obscured, if not supplanted, by a rationalistic natural theology.

A careful reading of the third volume of *Justification and Reconciliation* will show that time and again Ritschl directly appealed to Luther's theology in seeking to countermand Orthodoxy's legalism, objectivism, and rationalism. And there can be little question that on many such occasions he truly had Luther on his side. With keen insight Ritschl grasped what is perhaps Luther's most significant ideational divergence from Orthodoxy: his refusal to ground the fundamental relationship between God and man on an objective, rational, permanently valid *lex aeterna*.[54] As Ritschl rightly

[54] The crucial difference between Luther and Melanchthon (Orthodoxy) in their respective interpretations of the divine law is clearly brought out by Lauri Haikola,

observed, "Luther does not consider the relation of the first man to God as ordered by law; for him it consists in the reciprocation of Divine goodness and human gratitude." [55] Thus it was Luther the theologian of divine love whose authority Ritschl claimed when he declared: "If the religion of reconciliation is derived from God, it must be based upon a different conception of God's relation to man from that on which stress has been laid hitherto, namely, upon his *grace*." [56]

Certainly it is true that for Luther God's relationship to his creation is ever one of self-giving love and ineffable mercy, while man lets God be God precisely through acknowledging his fatherly goodness in prayer, praise, and thanksgiving. It is no less true that Luther, unlike Melanchthon, never allowed the possibility of salvation being predicated on obedience to the law *under any condition,* even in the pristine state of man.[57] Hence for Luther the fundamental conception of Christianity could not be identified with what Ritschl took to be the dominant idea of Orthodoxy: "that God must requite the diverse actions of men in one of two ways (i.e., by reward or punishment)"—an idea "based upon the Hellenic juridical conception of Divine justice." [58] One does not have to concur

---

"Melanchthons und Luthers Lehre von der Rechtfertigung: Ein Vergleich," in *Luther and Melanchthon*, ed. V. Vajta, pp. 89-103. Cf. pp. 97-98: "In his doctrine of justification Luther proceeds from an altogether different view of the law than does Melanchthon. For this reason Christ's work of reconciliation and justification also appears in a different light than in Melanchthon's theology. Luther does not know of a *lex aeterna* that represents an eternal and objective order of things, from which one could derive substantive norms for every righteous act of God and man. The content of the law cannot be expressed in a variety of universally valid and eternal rules. God's claim on men can never be exhaustively described by human rules, in a way that Melanchthon regards as possible."

[55] J. & R. III, 170. As noted previously, however, according to Luther God enters into relationship with man by placing upon him an absolute and unlimited claim for his total faith and love (see above, pp. 97 ff). This divine claim cannot be explicated in terms of some immutable legal code precisely because it is unlimited, i.e., it cannot be fixed once and for all but requires unconditional trust in God in every life situation. Thus for Luther man at no time has a "free will" vis-à-vis the divine will—which would presuppose that man knows exactly what is required of him in every situation—but must go about his work "blindly" in confidence that God's work will be done through him. See Haikola, in *Luther and Melanchthon*, p. 100. Ritschl rightly polemicized against orthodoxist legalism in Luther's name, but he did not actually recover Luther's own standpoint.

[56] J. & R. III, 263 (italics in original).

[57] Cf. Paul Althaus, *The Theology of Martin Luther*, pp. 121-22: "God wills that under no circumstances is the relationship between himself and men to be determined by the law but solely and absolutely by his free grace received through faith. . . . Fulfilling the law avails as little for justification before God as the failure to fulfill it. God simply does not wish to deal with men in this way."

[58] J. & R. III, 259, 262.

with Ritschl's every censure of Orthodoxy, and must not wrongly assume that Luther and Orthodoxy were wholly incompatible, but it cannot be gainsaid that Luther has a significantly different understanding of the law than Melanchthonian Orthodoxy—a difference which Ritschl clearly recognized and applied with great effectiveness in his fight against nomistic religion.

Ritschl also rightly perceived that Luther held together God's righteousness and his love in a way that would render untenable Orthodoxy's disjunction between these divine attributes (a disjunction of a metaphysical character, rooted as it were in the very essence of God). Satisfaction of God's offended honor is not required as a prior condition of his mercy. Grace is not subordinated to legal requirement. Rather God's righteousness *is* his powerful, creative, self-emptying love. His grace does not come alongside of, and in opposition to, his righteousness, but he is the Righteous One precisely in his will-to-save. Out of pure fatherly goodness he resolves to forgive the sinner, to break down the walls of separation and so bring about community with himself. On Luther's authority, then, as well as on scriptural grounds (primarily Old Testament exegesis), Ritschl defined God's righteousness as his "self-consistent saving purpose" identical to his love or grace revealed in Christ.[59] He expressed astonishment, therefore, "that the Orthodox theologians, in spite of their endeavors to reproduce the ideas of Holy Scripture, have been entirely oblivious to the fact that Jesus explicitly connected this [saving] operation of God with his *attribute as Father*." [60] These theologians related forgiveness primarily to God's role as Lawgiver and Judge, in analogy to a head of state who punishes and pardons on the basis of civil law. Ritschl, by contrast, sought to articulate a theology of reconciliation based on God's trust-inspiring fatherhood, in analogy to the loving head of a family who orders all things in the best interests of his children. Ritschl was persuaded that through this enterprise of systematic reconstruction he was not only restoring to its rightful place the Reformation teaching on God's free favor and mercy for Christ's sake, but also organizing the totality of Christian doctrine around Luther's theological first principle: "the abiding revelation of love as the essence of God in Christ." [61]

[59] *Ibid.*, pp. 93-94. It is to Ritschl's lasting credit that he saw clearly how, on the orthodoxist model, God's grace is subordinated to his law, his mercy to his justice; but, again, Ritschl failed to do justice to Luther's understanding of God's holy love (see above, pp. 98 ff.).

[60] *Ibid.*, p. 93 (italics in original).

[61] J. & R. I, 159. See above, pp. 40-42.

Because God's relationship to persons is rooted in love rather than law, the true meaning of sin is to be determined by religious rather than moral criteria. Ritschl was quite correct in maintaining that Luther "finds the chief evil of original sin in the perversion of man's original reverence for God." [62] Sin is not merely the transgression of a legal code (*anomia*) or illicit desire (*concupiscentia*), as defined in the theologies of old and new Scholasticism, but above all unfaith and irreverence toward God, indeed enmity against God. [63] "In his treatment of this point Luther is epoch-making," concluded Ritschl, "for he distinguishes between the irreligious and the immoral aspects of sin, and subordinates the latter to the former." [64] Since Christianity is first and foremost a religion, not a system of morals, a genuinely Christian theology must show how the very love of God which men scorn actually takes the field in the person and work of Jesus Christ to encounter and overcome their unbelief, transforming it into complete trust and confidence in their heavenly Father and placing them within the redeemed community of which Christ is Head, where they now enjoy the blessed liberty of the adopted sons of God. [65] Of course man's sin must not be minimized lest God's grace be seen as self-evident in some purely rationalistic fashion. Sin is nothing less than active contradiction to God evidenced in the awareness of guilt, and real separation from God evidenced in mistrust. The heart of Christian theology, therefore, is God's justification and reconciliation of the sinner based on the redemptive doing and suffering of Jesus Christ. "For justification removes the guilt, and reconciliation the enmity, of sin towards God." [66] Hence the entire Christian life, as Martin Luther so powerfully

[62] J. & R. III, 170-71.

[63] *Ibid.*, pp. 342 ff.

[64] *Ibid.*, p. 171.

[65] I take this sentence to be an accurate summation of an absolutely basic motif in Ritschl's systematic theology—an avowedly "religious" motif which must be accorded its full weight before one speaks of Ritschl's supposed moralization of the Christian religion.

[66] J. & R. I, 8-9. Frequently Ritschl's critics have decried his trivialization of the doctrine of sin as demonstrated in his well-known statement that "sin is estimated by God . . . as ignorance" (J. & R. III, 384). These critics often overlook Ritschl's qualification that sin is regarded as ignorance strictly *from God's viewpoint* because it does not pose an insuperable barrier to his love, i.e., it is only because men are truly the objects of divine redemption and reconciliation that their sin is not seen to be "final and thoroughgoing opposition to the good" (III, 378). In addition, sin for Ritschl is real *contradiction* of God because God is the author of the moral law which men fail to fulfill (see III, 57-59). I find the primary defect of Ritschl's concept of sin to reside in his failure to deepen the *consciousness* of guilt into the phenomenon of the guilty *conscience*, i.e., Ritschl lacks an understanding of man as radically question-

taught, is comprehended in God's "pure, fatherly, and divine goodness and mercy," that is, in the unmerited forgiveness of sins.[67]

Luther also proved to be a potent ally in Ritschl's assault on orthodoxist objectivism or depersonalization. Justification treats of no mere intellectual knowledge directed to a past event of universal reconciliation, whereby God's justice and mercy were forever reconciled and owing to which forgiveness could be legally forthcoming for all future time—an event which has only to be known, assented to, and believed in, to become efficacious at any given moment. The paramount meaning of forgiveness, rather, is that it provides for a wholly practical understanding of one's daily life in the Church and the world. It bestows a self-understanding which is at once geared to present action and stands open to the future—for through forgiveness the believer is led to exercise religious dominion over the world and, by his incorporation into the believing community, becomes a co-worker in the kingdom of God, thus knowing his own self-end to be one with God's final purpose for the world. Hence the Christian's dependence on God by no means nullifies his own religious and moral activity through which the present reality of forgiveness is verified:

For the operation of God, which is called justification, works a change in the person concerned. That this change has taken place, that the Divine cause has produced its effect, has its evidence only in the faith *excited* by God's pardon, and in those various relationships which faith embraces. . . . For however ear-

---

able and answerable *coram Deo* (a perspective which Karl Holl recovered). In Luther the bad conscience is deepened into a state of absolute despair which can only be conquered from "above" the moral realm through the miracle of divine love (what Tillich describes as the appearance of the transmoral conscience). Perhaps one could say that Ritschl too quickly psychologized the concept of sin (as the consciousness of guilt and the feeling of pain at having left the moral law unfulfilled), whereas Luther consistently theologized it (as the actual robbery of God's glory as a result of which one stands under the divine wrath).

[67] Small Catechism, II, 2, in BC, p. 345. In 1909 the Swedish Luther scholar Einar Billing wrote as follows in his highly regarded tract *Our Calling* (Eng. trans., 1955): "Anyone wishing to study Luther would indeed be in no peril of going astray were he to follow this rule: never believe that you have a correct understanding of a thought of Luther before you have succeeded in reducing it to a simple corollary of the thought of the forgiveness of sins" (p. 7). Undoubtedly this rule is questionable because it is overly reductionistic, but certainly it advocates an authentically Ritschlian approach to Luther. Edgar Carlson states in his survey of modern Swedish Luther scholarship, *The Reinterpretation of Luther* (Philadelphia, 1948), that "Ritschlianism, in a modified form, had an able representative [at the University of Lund] in Pehr Eklund, the leading theological figure in the latter half of the [nineteenth] century. The Luther renaissance may be said to begin with him. Wilhelm Herrmann left a deep impression on Einar Billing, perhaps the ablest Swedish theologian of all time" (p. 26). In these remarks the intimate connection between Ritschlianism and the Luther renaissance finds further attestation.

nestly we may strive to bring out man's passivity in this respect, yet we can never get over the fact that he receives and apprehends the unconditioned operation of God. And that means that he is spiritually active. . . ."[68]

"Theology," said Ritschl, "has to do not with natural objects, but with states and movements of man's spiritual life." It must explain, therefore, "how the changing functions of the spirit, its feeling, knowing, and willing, take on throughout a religious character, and become active in the service of God." [69] Such a theology is, in Ritschl's language (following Schleiermacher), thoroughly ethical: it has to do with "the province of personal and social Christian life under the form of *personal activity.* [70] But an ethical theology, or what today could properly be called an existential theology, is not complete in itself, since the ground of personal activity is the redemptive activity of God. Accordingly ethics must always be correlated with dogmatics, which "comprises all the presuppositions of Christianity under the form of *Divine operation.*" [71] The praxis of faith

[68] J. & R. III, 173-74 (italics in original).

[69] *Ibid.,* p. 20.

[70] *Ibid.,* p. 14 (italics in original).

[71] *Ibid.* (italics in original). Cf. III, 34 for a fuller statement of these two viewpoints: "Dogmatics comprehends all religious processes in man under the category of Divine grace, that is, it looks at them from the standpoint of God. But it is, of course, impossible so thoroughly to maintain this standpoint in our experience, as thereby to obtain complete knowledge of the operations of grace. . . . If what is wanted is to write theology on the plan not merely of a narrative of the great deeds done by God, but of a system representing the salvation He has wrought out, then we must exhibit the operations of God—justification, regeneration, the communication of the Holy Spirit, the bestowal of blessedness in the *summum bonum*—in such a way as shall involve an analysis of the corresponding voluntary activities in which man appropriates the operations of God. This method has been already adopted by Schleiermacher." In short, then, there are two necessary and inextricably related perspectives on all the phenomena of the Christian religion: that perspective which proceeds from personal experience in the form of the inner or outer activity of the believing subject; and that which proceeds from the divine standpoint, from the believer's understanding that his entire life and experience are dependent upon God's grace and thus are worked by God. The ethical (*ethisch*) viewpoint is necessary if theology is not to lose hold on reality, and thus lose itself in arid speculation, by operating solely from an objective perspective. Theological rationalism—whether of the Hegelian or orthodoxist variety—is controlled by this speculative impulse in which the individual person and his experience forfeit their rightful place. Yet the self-experience of the believer is never something autonomous but serves rather as the epistemological ground for recognizing the gracious operations of God; hence the religious (*religiös*) or dogmatic (*dogmatisch*) viewpoint is required lest theology fall prey to subjectivism. For Ritschl this latter perspective turns on God's own self-revelation in the person and work of Jesus Christ, i.e., it involves a transsubjective disclosure on the plane of history of God's will and ways. The specific meaning of a divine operation is to be determined by the constant reference to the historical life course of Christ: "In Christianity, revelation through

is not independent of grace; it presupposes forgiveness, the new relationship with God which is God's own gift in Christ. But neither can divine pardon be spoken of apart from the corresponding activity of faith, if the former is not to appear a mere legal fiction and a purely impersonal phenomenon. Certainly the regenerate life is one empowered by the Holy Spirit, but theology must give up all idle attempts to answer the insoluble question of *how* a person is grasped by the Spirit; instead it must verify life *in* the Spirit "by showing that believers know God's gracious gifts, that they call on God as their Father, that they act with love and joy, with meekness and self-control, that they are on their guard above all against party spirit, and cherish rather a spirit of union. In these statements the Holy Spirit is not denied, but recognized and understood." [72]

Ritschl regarded his ethical standpoint as a contemporary revalidation and reworking of Luther's original practical theology. Frequently this conviction has been questioned in the name of Luther's uncompromising polemic against work-righteousness, particularly against the Roman teaching on faith formed by love. Certainly the Lutheran theologians of repristination in Ritschl's time were quick to condemn his "Pelagianizing" tendencies. Other critics have traced this conviction directly to Ritschl's "neo-Kantian" epistemology, mediated through R. H. Lotze, according to which a thing (e.g., forgiveness) is known only in its effects (e.g., religious and moral conduct); in other words, presumably we are here encountering a foremost example of Ristchl's "Kantianism." Yet Ritschl's explicit appeal to Luther, while not unproblematical, is not without considerable weight and warrant. Because Luther had completely repudiated the law as a way to salvation, he could also speak of the believer's good works in a fully positive manner without any connotations of synergism. Blessedness is to be found in the unity of man's will with God's will, in man's total surrender to God's total claim on his trust and love expressed in the First Commandment. "Since the absolute unity of will with God in faith and love amidst all the circumstances of life constitutes the intention and fulfilment of the law, God's work and man's work cannot be isolated from each other or opposed to one another as competing

---

God's Son is the *punctum stans* of all knowledge and religious conduct" (III, 202). On Ritschl's view, as I have repeatedly noted, Schleiermacher and his successors did not accord sufficient weight to this historical revelation and so tended toward subjectivism.

[72] J. & R. III, 22-23. For a penetrating discussion of Ritschl's two methodological viewpoints, see Rolf Schäfer, *Ritschl*, pp. 66-70. I am much indebted to Schäfer's clarification of Ritschl's somewhat confusing terminology.

factors." [73] God's claim, according to Luther, cannot be fulfilled apart from man's response of faith and love; indeed God's work makes possible for the first time the true fulfilling of the First Commandment.[74]

In Melanchthonian Orthodoxy, however, owing to its doctrine of Christ's infinite satisfaction and of forensic justification, the meaning and specific nature of the believer's activity posed an acutely difficult problem. If satisfaction for sin has been completely accomplished and God's law has been perfectly fulfilled for all times, and if the sinner is declared righteous solely on the basis of Christ's alien righteousness imputed to him, then the most that can be attributed to the believer is a purely *receptive* faith. The entire legal process takes place outside man, and so the believer's participation must be reduced to a minimum. Otherwise God's judgment might appear to be predicated on something in man and thus not be a purely gracious judgment. Furthermore, if faith were to be spoken of as really active, as in any sense a work, then the Catholic notion of merit would again be at hand because the sole sufficiency of Christ's satisfaction would implicitly be called into question. Divine monergism would then be threatened by synergism. Given these premises, Melanchthon and his successors constantly wrestled with the crucial problem of showing how faith can be active in love without thereby suggesting that justifying faith per se is other than purely receptive. This issue is a complex one, involving subtle nuances and fine distinctions. Suffice it to say that Luther, as has been indicated, was largely spared such difficulties because he did not interpret God's grace and man's faith from a predominantly juridical, rationalistic perspective. And it is a true measure of Ritschl's greatness that he attempted to overcome the Melanchthonian "captivity" of Protestant theology by restoring Luther's original, anti-legalistic view of the full reciprocity between grace and faith. One might say, in brief, that Ritschl was seeking to reunite ethics and dogmatics, doing so primarily on Luther's authority (not simply Kant's!).[75]

---

[73] Haikola, in *Luther and Melanchthon*, p. 99.

[74] In a famous passage in the 1535 Galatians lectures Luther even asserts that faith "consummates the Deity; and, if I may put it this way, it is the creator of the Deity, not in the substance of God but in us. For without faith God loses His glory, wisdom, righteousness, truthfulness, mercy, etc., in us; in short, God has none of His majesty or divinity where faith is absent" (LW 26, 227).

[75] A noteworthy treatment of Luther's teaching on the correlation between grace and faith, God's action and the believer's response, is K. O. Nilsson's book, *Simul: Das Miteinander von Göttlichem und Menschlichem in Luthers Theologie* (Göttingen, 1966).

When Ritschl, therefore, wrote the following sentence—"A man does not experience the fact of his justification so much in a contemplative act which presents to his mind justification or Divine pardon in an isolated way, but rather in trust in God, which embraces likewise the believer's situation in the world"—he was not attacking orthodoxist intellectualism in a uniquely Ritschlian fashion but was expressing a specifically Lutheran sentiment.[76] In fact one does not go too far in claiming that this sentence admirably sums up the heart of Ritschl's Luther interpretation and of his own constructive theology. For both his Luther study and his total system can appropriately be subsumed under the rubric, "the ethic of justification," insofar as both are focused on the issue of the personal activity of faith as evoked by the divine saving operation of forgiveness.[77] Certainly Christianity is a religion of redemption, and Christian theology must never obscure the truth that God in Christ is the sole agent of salvation. But Christianity is also a religion of faith and obedience before God, and Christian theology must never diminish the truth that man is the locus of salvation. Hence theology must speak of both the living God who justifies and the living person who is reconciled. Yet Ritschl's historical-critical investigations disclosed that

theology, especially within the Evangelical Confessions, has laid very unequal emphasis on these two principal characteristics of Christianity. It makes everything which concerns the redemptive character of Christianity an object of the most solicitous reflection. Accordingly it finds the central point of all Christian knowledge and practice in redemption through Christ, while injustice is done to the ethical interpretation of Christianity through the idea of the Kingdom of God.[78]

In order to restore the balance, therefore, and especially in view of contemporary attacks on the continuing validity and vitality of Protestantism, the ethical dimension of Christianity—the concrete praxis of the believing community in its exercise of positive world dominion and its service in the kingdom of God—must again be accorded due weight.

[76] J. & R. III, 174.
[77] Otto Wolff summarizes the central points in Ritschl's Luther interpretation in a section entitled "The Ethic of the Justified Life" (*Die Haupttypen*, pp. 181-97). Cf. p. 183: "For Ritschl also ethical issues are of decisive centrality, or expressed otherwise: *God's justification of the sinner and the life based thereon.* Here flows the lifeblood of this system: in the exposition of the Christian ethic issuing out of justification and reconciliation. Here we confront most clearly Ritschl's *de facto* appropriation of Luther, namely, in the systematic assimilation of a number of Luther's fundamental ethical concepts" (italics in original).
[78] J. & R. III, 10-11.

And this must be done in a fully personalistic fashion, carefully specifying the ways in which justification or forgiveness regulates the believer's total religious and moral conduct, and showing that precisely through such activity forgiveness is verified as a present, transforming power which holds the key to the riddle of human life in the world. Ritschl's foremost ally in this twofold task of rectifying the traditional one-sidedness of Protestant theology, and vindicating the contemporary worth of the Reformation's chief doctrine, was the young Luther. Following Luther's lead, Ritschl set out to delineate and defend justifying faith as a truly existential phenomenon. If the God who reveals himself in Christ as pure love is God *pro me*, then this means that God's salvific action has immediate bearing on the believer's total life conduct (*Lebensführung*). Ritschl thus bored in, as it were, on the Lutheran "for me" and consistently explicated that "me" in personal-existential terms. The person who is spoken of in theology is the believing self who overcomes the world through trust in God, patience, humility, prayer; and who participates in God's ongoing realization of lordship over the nations through steadfastness in his vocation and love to his neighbor. In dependence on Luther, then, and in opposition to the regnant theological tradition, Ritschl was intent on taking up both self and world into all God talk, for God and his saving activity cannot be rightly comprehended apart from real encounter with man in his actual historical existence.

Perhaps Ritschl's outstanding achievement as a Luther interpreter was his recovery of Luther's so-called faith principle in opposition to Orthodoxy's rationalistic aberrations:

Luther admits no "disinterested" knowledge of God, but recognizes as a religious datum only such knowledge of Him as takes the form of unconditional trust. This knowledge, however, is so exclusively bound up with Christ, that whatever knowledge of God exists alongside of it does not, as the Scholastics suppose, arrive at a neutral idea of God, but issues solely in contempt of or hatred of Him. This line of thought is to be found not only in Luther's Large Catechism, but also in the Augsburg Confession, XX, 24. In 1543 Melanchthon merely echoes in a feeble way the principle that God is knowable only through the mediation of Christ, a principle which in the *Loci* of 1535 he had recognized with a certain emphasis. The while, he builds Christian doctrine on a foundation of natural theology, after the model of the Scholastics. All this is a result of his return to Aristotle. Not only does the close affinity between Humanism and Scholasticism betray itself here, but Melanchthon abandons the task of constructing theology according to Luther's principle.[79]

[79] *Ibid.*, pp. 6-7. Ritschl continues: "That task I essay in the full confidence that my action is justified and rendered imperative by the standard writings of the Reformation."

In these ringing words Ritschl not only accurately described the incursion of natural theology into later Lutheranism, but also implicitly prescribed Evangelical theology's self-conscious return to the Reformation's *principium cognoscendi*: God is to be spoken of in a true and saving way only from the point of view of positive faith in him. If theology's proper subject is the God who has revealed himself in Christ, *Deus in Christo*, then its proper method is one which construes every part of the theological system from the standpoint of the believing community. Only through this strict correlation of revelation with faith can theology establish and preserve its independence of all purely philosophical or theoretical (and so value-less) statements about God. Such statements are not merely disinterested or neutral, but, as Luther knew so well, direct expressions of unbelief—not preliminary steps on the way to perfect understanding, but fateful stages on the way to an abysmal ignorance of God. The so-called natural knowledge of God is nothing other than the actual breakdown of all knowledge of God, for what does it mean to have a God—as opposed to an *Abgott*—save to call him Father, to repose absolute trust and confidence in him, and to expect from him every good? But "we could never come to recognize the Father's favor and grace were it not for the Lord Christ, who is a mirror of the Father's heart." [80]

Ritschl's critique of Melanchthonian Orthodoxy on this point was telling indeed. In the Apology Melanchthon had listed ignorance of God as an effect of original sin, for God can be known through his Word alone. But in his later period Melanchthon offered rational demonstrations of the existence of God, the immortality of the soul, the congruence between philosophical morality and the divine law, etc. And, as Werner Elert has noted, "once Melanchthon—like medieval dogmatics—had returned to the path of natural theology, there was no longer any stopping." [81] It now became possible to ascribe to natural reason a knowledge (even if obscure) of God's truthfulness and beneficence—something which for Luther, and Ritschl after him, was totally unthinkable apart from the forgiveness of sins. Hence there is real force to Ritschl's contention that later Lutheran theology, in deviating from Luther's christocentrism and ecclesiocentrism, had in effect surrendered "the most practical ideas of the Reformation." [82] This fateful development can be seen most plainly in Johann Gerhard's assigning faith in God's providence to natural theology. "The fidelity of this Orthodox divine to the Augsburg Confession," observed Ritschl,

[80] Large Catechism, Second Part: The Creed, 65, in BC, p. 419.
[81] Elert, *The Structure of Lutheranism*, I (St. Louis, 1962), 53.
[82] J. & R. III, 181.

"is such that he declares possible to the natural, that is, sinful man, the very trust in God which the chief standard of the Church expressly denies to him!" [83]

Surely one of Ritschl's foremost services to Evangelical theology was his relentless critique of such rationalism, combined with his no less rigorous effort to ground faith in providence solely on the Christian experience of reconciliation with God through Christ in the Church. According to Otto Wolff, Ritschl engineered an "impressive restructuring of Christian faith in providence":

The certainty which expresses itself in such faith was not for him, as it was in Orthodoxy, a rational participation in God's foreknowledge, nor was it a pietistically narrowed belief in the guidance of the soul. And by no means did faith in providence signify "an element of natural religion" [J. & R. III, 625] or "a law of phenomena discovered inductively" [III, 618], as in the Enlightenment. Even so at no time was it some kind of anthropocentrically grounded assurance, since faith is never "a self-contained activity of the individual" [III, 623]. What was specifically "Lutheran"—and that in an epoch-making way—in Ritschl's taking up of faith in providence is primarily this: that he was able to interpret it as the authentic expression of practical saving faith in a far more convincing way than was previously the case, and so established it directly—as the specific form of personal saving faith—on that faith which springs out of justification. Providence was again comprehended unequivocally as God's loving care and provision [*Vorsorge und Fürsorge*] and the indissoluble bond between such certainty and justification was systematically demonstrated. [84]

---

[83] *Ibid.* Cf. Elert, *The Structure of Lutheranism*, p. 55: "In the doctrinal tradition established by Johann Gerhard the clear-cut break between man's natural relationship to God and his faith relationship to Him, as it existed in Luther, is constantly weakened more and more, yes, obliterated." Ritschl, one should note, did find in the *devotional literature and hymnody* of the Lutheran Church various authentic expressions of Luther's *Vorsehungsglaube*. Cf. J. & R. III, 184-85: "[Paul] Gerhardt gives repeated expression to that special faith in Providence which brings every experience of joy and sorrow under the goodness of God. . . . Who can deny that these hymns form the classical expression of the practical faith which takes its stand upon justification and reconciliation through Christ?" Just as the *sola gratia* piety of the Medieval Church was superior to its doctrinal theology of justification, so the piety or public worship of later Lutheranism often proved superior to its public teaching. Theology and religion are two different magnitudes, and Ritschl the critical historian always sought to do justice to an underlying "continuity" in piety from age to age even where he saw only "discontinuity" in the sphere of doctrine. It is not so strange, therefore, that Ritschl at one time should have requested that the last two stanzas of Paul Gerhardt's famous hymn, "O Haupt voll Blut und Wunden," be sung at his death-bed—even though Ritschl explicitly rejected the doctrine of vicarious satisfaction which informs the theological background of this hymn. (The circumstances of Ritschl's death did not permit his request to be carried out. See *Leben*, II, 524.)

[84] Wolff, *Die Haupttypen*, p. 186. Cf. J. & R. III, 625: "But the confidence

Ritschl, in short, succeeded in regaining the true Reformation standpoint which made justifying faith the epistemological ground of trust in God's providence. If nowhere else, the caricature of "Ritschl the rationalist"— his portrait as the nineteenth-century's chief representative of the "perfected Enlightenment"—falls completely to the ground when faced with such considerations.[85]

It is quite evident, therefore, that Ritschl's intense polemic against Melanchthonian Orthodoxy had a legitimate base in Luther's theology. There is a demonstrable congruity between many of Ritschl's central arguments and Luther's seminal insights, especially with respect to Luther's anti-legalistic and anti-rationalistic outlook. Certainly Ritschl did succeed in rendering untenable the traditional assumption of unbroken continuity between Luther and Orthodox (Melanchthonian) dogmatics. And in this process he also prepared the way for subsequent scholarship by indicating the general path to be followed in rightly distinguishing between Luther and later Lutheranism. At the same time, however, one cannot assert that Ritschl truly *overcame* Orthodoxy through a successful reappropriation of Luther's practical motifs. The most one can say is that he *broke through* various facets of the Orthodox Luther interpretation without actually recovering the authentic Luther. He shattered some stereotypes but did not restore the prototype. In Chapter IV I noted several major points

---

with which, whether in favorable or adverse positions in life, men cast themselves on the guidance and help of God, regarding themselves as enjoined by Him to seek the one highest good, dominion over the world in the fellowship of the Kingdom of God, is in reality a product of the Christian religion. For the God Who is the Lord over the world and our Father, Who cherishes no envy and wrath against His children, gives them the assurance that all things serve for their good. And this truth stands firm only when based upon our reconciliation with God."

[85] It is quite remarkable that Karl Barth should say little or nothing in his survey of nineteenth-century theology about Ritschl's rejection of natural theology and Ritschl's christocentrism. H. Richard Niebuhr, by contrast, in his brief treatment of Ritschl in *The Meaning of Revelation* (New York, 1960), is much fairer in his appraisal of Ritschl's achievement—even though Niebuhr is certainly no less critical of Ritschl's "anthropocentrism" than Barth. Cf. pp. 23, 26-27: "The great empirical theology of the nineteenth century was at least partly based on the renewal of [Luther's] understanding [of the correlation between revelation and faith]. Both Schleiermacher and Ritschl owed no small part of their success to their observance of the limitation of theology to the point of view of faith in the God of Jesus Christ. . . . The renewal of the faith method in theology had . . . important consequences: it gave impetus to the historical examination of Christian faith, since scholarship was encouraged to seek the bases of that faith in Christian life itself rather than in idealistic or other philosophic dogma; it re-enforced the interest of Christians in the historic Jesus and in his religious faith; it provided strength for the growing social gospel and invigorated the moral life of the church. The fruits which this faith-theology produced gave some evidence of the correctness of its method."

at which both Ritschl and Orthodoxy went wide of Luther's own position, e.g., in their mutual failure to comprehend the full dynamic of Luther's theology of the Word and his concept of the *fides Christi*. A full-scale appraisal of Ritschl's critique of both Orthodox dogmatics and Orthodoxy's view of Luther would have to take into account several other striking instances in which both Ritschl and his Orthodox opponents occupied virtually the same standpoint in their misinterpretation of Luther.[86]

[86] It is particularly noteworthy that both Ritschl and Orthodoxy failed to grasp Luther's profound doctrine of God in which the divine love and wrath were held together in dialectical tension. Ritschl simply dismissed the notion of God's wrath as incompatible with the theological procedure which comprehends God from the perspective of eternity, i.e., in the light of God's Kingdom as the final end of the world the idea of God's love alone has validity since the redemption of sinners can be traced only to the divine favor. The idea of God's wrath is due to the believer's mistaken transposition of a subjective feeling occurring in time to the divine being and world order which can be rightly comprehended only *sub specie aeternitatis*. In other words, the concept of God's wrath arises because the believer confuses his "individual religious thinking," conditioned by his existence in time, with "the theological conception of the whole from the viewpoint of eternity" (J. & R. III, 322-23). While Ritschl thus *eliminated* the idea of God's wrath as a subjective illusion, Theodosius Harnack—the foremost Orthodox Luther interpreter of the nineteenth century— *relativized* this idea. Harnack, to be sure, sought to defend Luther's concept of divine wrath, especially because the orthodoxist doctrine of vicarious satisfaction required a sharp dualism between God's justice and his mercy, his wrath and his love. But Harnack could only make sense of Luther's teaching by breaking apart Luther's dialectic, i.e., by rigidly distinguishing between wrath and love as two different modes of God's being corresponding to two different modes of knowing God. Wrath pertains solely to God's existence *ausser Christo* and so to that knowledge of God which is derived from the law. But this view of God is ultimately less valid than that knowledge of him derived strictly from the gospel, which pertains solely to God's being as pure love *in Christo*. In a wooden fashion Harnack fitted Luther's distinctions between wrath and love, law and gospel, sin and grace, etc., into this overarching distinction between God as he is known outside Christ and God as he is known in Christ. This procedure means in effect, however, that the one type of knowledge must finally be *less true* than the other, and so God's wrath is only relatively true while his love is absolutely true. From such considerations it is apparent not only that both Ritschl and his Orthodox counterpart Harnack abandoned Luther's perspective, but also that both in effect *intellectualized* Luther's view of God's wrath. For Harnack God's wrath is relativized by the true knowledge of God in Christ, namely, by the saving knowledge of Christ's objective satisfaction of the law which makes God's wrath of no account. For Ritschl Luther's view of God's wrath rests on a misunderstanding, a confusion of the religious with the theological mode of cognition; hence Luther's view must be corrected by that proper understanding which occupies "God's standpoint" (III, 324). Thus in spite of Ritschl's denunciation of Orthodox intellectualism one can see that here the thesis still lives on in the antithesis! One could indeed ask whether Ritschl's introduction of God's standpoint—not in the sense of God's historical self-disclosure but of his being-in-eternity—does not mark Ritschl's own reversion to theological speculation. Certainly by denying the significance of the Christian's experience of

Yet such critical reservations cannot diminish the signal service which Ritschl performed in his own day by dissolving the supposedly indissoluble connection between Luther's theology and the traditional dogmatic systems. Modern Luther scholarship simply takes for granted this disjunction between Luther and later Lutheran Orthodoxy, but in Ritschl's time it was definitely not axiomatic. In fact this viewpoint has become a commonplace today largely because we have appropriated the fruits of Ritschl's (and the Ritschlian school's) Luther study, although we seldom pause to give Ritschl his due, largely because we no longer remember Ritschl the Luther scholar. It has been my intention throughout this investigation—and indeed by means of this investigation—to bring about just such a remembrance of things past.

God's wrath, Ritschl traversed his own strictures on the necessary *correlation* of the experiential and the dogmatic viewpoints.

APPENDIX

ALBRECHT RITSCHL

Festival Address
On the Four-Hundredth Anniversary of the Birth of
Martin Luther

November 10, 1883 [1]

in an Academic Celebration of the University of Göttingen

Translated by David W. Lotz

Honorable Assembly!

Almost eighty years ago a man who was later affiliated with our university as a professor, Charles Villers, a Frenchman and a Catholic, published a work entitled: "Essay on the Spirit and Influence of Luther's Reformation." This book received the prize in a competition on that topic conducted by the United Academies of the French Institute. The recognition accorded by the author to the German Reformer obviously had found the approval of that highest scientific authority of the French people. Yet the change of perspective between then and now, from which Luther's historical significance is assessed, cannot be seen any more clearly than from the way Villers set about delimiting his subject. He simply takes it for granted that in his own age—the period when the French Revolution is drawing to a close—no more than mediate, indirect effects of Luther's Reformation can be recognized. Paying no attention whatever to the formation of a new Church under Luther's impact, he limits himself to showing the influences of Luther's Reformation on the spheres of politics and science. In the political realm he credits Luther's view of the state with having brought about the development among the European nations of the modern state, characterized by independence from the Church, a mutuality of interests obtaining between rulers and subjects, the struggle for a balance of power among the various national groups, and the development of international law. On the other hand he calls attention to the

---

[1] "Festrede am vierten Seculartage der Geburt Martin Luthers, 10, November, 1883," in *Drei akademische Reden* (Bonn, 1887), pp. 5-29. For stylistic reasons, the paragraphing in the original German text has been slightly altered in the translation.

freedom which Luther gained for scientific work in the areas of religion, ethics, and history, in order to give him credit for the entire Enlightenment of the last century. On this view, strangely enough, Luther's most genuine activity—his religious thought which he used in the service of the Church—has been left out of account. But this defect is characteristic of the position taken by Villers at the beginning of this century, against the backdrop of the scarcely concluded French Revolution. Today even a political historian, dealing with that subject, could not overlook the fact that during the course of the last four centuries the Western Churches—regardless of their diversity in political influence—have by no means become as insignificant for the culture and the historical status of the nations, especially for the state of affairs inside our own country, as it might have appeared in Villers' time. Taking this latter proviso for granted, one will discover in Luther's efforts on behalf of the renovation of the Christian religion and Church the key to his indirect influence on the formation of the states and the general intellectual life.

Certainly these correlations of the Reformation also require the attention of the theologican who, as a member of a German university on the occasion of its gathering for the four-hundredth anniversary of Luther's birth, has been accorded the honor of commemorating that man whose historic greatness is confirmed even by the enduring enmity and ever-repeated calumnies of ecclesiastical adversaries. But please do not expect me to yield to these latter provocations, which again are the order of the day and which, owing to the smoothness and subtlety of their presentation, also find a foothold in impressionable Protestant souls. Given his heroic character, Luther also had the flaws which usually attend such a character; and if passion, stubbornness, and inflexibility in certain matters are especially conspicuous in him, the explanation lies in his early monastic life which left him deficient in training in social intercourse and in the acquisition of requisite self-control. Our evaluation of his person and his accomplishments need not take these flaws into account, because we are not dealing with his personality and all its individual traits but rather with the valuable service he rendered in having pointed out the way to Christianity's original *Weltanschauung* and attitude toward life. Only if Luther were to be viewed as the founder of a religion would his adherents have to account for his personal failings. But he has rejected precisely this role, and rightly so. For as the Reformer of the Church he has become the signpost to that interpretation of redemption and its effects which not only shines forth in the New Testament documents but can also be shown to be the sound fundamental idea of Western Catholicism. If this is what really matters in Luther's Reformation of the Church, then it is of little moment that in a great many ways he was also subject to the prevailing mentality of his age, in the sense, for example, that his understanding of natural phenomena was given over to that superstition which dominated the sixteenth-century populace. Nor is it incumbent upon us to inquire about the authority in whose name Luther undertook his Church reformation, inasmuch as he was neither a pope nor, strictly speaking, a prophet. This question about the guaranties for truth, a regnant concern in the Roman system, must not be pursued—as has been so long done by the Lutherans when they reply that Luther was in fact the Third Elijah who was obliged to restore the Church before the end of the world. This claim could only be established through an analogy, but not by a direct promise of a divine sort. Luther's right to reform the Church is legitimated even before his Roman opponents by the fact that his interpretation of Christianity represents the logical development of Latin Catholicism's basic formula, which had been covered over and deprived of its salvific efficacy by all the accretions of a ritualistic and political ecclesiasticism.

Since I am attempting to characterize Luther's leading religious thoughts, in order to adduce from them his more general influence on modern culture, I certainly see myself confronted with widespread misinterpretations of his Reformation which must be corrected at the outset. Whoever intends to explain Luther's achievements in a genuinely historical fashion, and in accord with Luther's own intention, must put himself forward to a certain degree as a reformer in opposition to misunderstandings which obscure the actual situation and render it unintelligible. How widepread still is the opinion of the Illuminati, represented by Villers, that Luther brought into the world the principle of religious and intellectual liberty, resting solely with the individual, or the idea of release from all authority; particularly that he vindicated the freedom of scientific research, first in reference to the Scriptures and then with respect to all objects of knowledge; and that he himself forced the way open to this freedom. What is true in this assumption is that Luther did call for the civic toleration of divergent religious views and rejected the idea that they were punishable—an idea which both Melanchthon and Calvin continued to uphold in accord with the law of the Christian Roman Empire. But Luther never entertained the notion that this demand could properly entail such an unrestricted use of individual freedom as would shatter the religious and moral fiber of society. If the situation were otherwise, the Roman bishop would be right who just recently attempted once again to hold Luther's Reformation responsible for every revolution in church and state. The truth, rather, is that in the sixteenth century the Reformation worked precisely toward strengthening the power of the state; that it directly supported the transformation of the German territorial powers [*Territorialgewalten*] into the authoritarian state [*Staatsgewalten*]; and that it actually put an end to the revolutionary condition of society at the close of the Middle Ages. So too the extremist movements in the religious arena of that time—the Anabaptists and the Socinians—do not have their origin in any of Luther's principles but rather in certain impulses coming from monasticism and Scholasticism, both of which had been in a state of dissolution long before Luther. And, as is well known, the political revolution of the more recent period of history has come into fashion among nations which were kept in obedience to the Papal See by the strongest forms of coercion. Likewise, it was Thomas Aquinas, the Roman Church's theologian par excellence, who put forward that conception of the state which includes the right of the people to overthrow the established government. Finally, the enlightened indifference toward everything churchly is for the most part the [continuing] reaction of certain elements in the theological system of the medieval Church against the religious wars that had been instigated and sanctioned by no one more than the popes themselves. The ecclesiastical and political revolution, therefore, must directly and indirectly be debited to the Roman Church and not to Luther's Reformation. Furthermore, the characteristic ideas of the socialist revolution, which made its appearance already before Luther, can quite definitely be traced to the influence of the mendicant orders upon the people, since these ideas are completely foreign to the perspective of the Reformer.

The freedom which Luther has caused to shine forth brightly, namely, Christian freedom, does not at all involve a religious independence from communal norms and considerations—as was the case with the young Goethe when he derived from Gottfried Arnold's *Kirchen- und Ketzer-Historie* the right to form his own religion, something which he believed everyone was free to do. Indeed this very authority invoked by Goethe is in substance diametrically opposed to Luther's discernible intention, being rooted in purely Catholic motifs of religious formation. Luther intended Christian freedom— which he derived from that teaching for which he ever battled, namely, the doctrine of justification by faith—to be the content of a communal, churchly Christianity, which he proposed to win back from the system prevailing up to that time. Nor did this teaching at all signify that a man could meet with approval before God through the independent resolve of his belief and disposition, which takes precedence over the multitude of prescribed deeds and accomplishments. Such an evaluation of the spontaneous religious and moral resolution would be nothing new or original. For even in the Catholic system this Christian attitude holds good as the basis on which all moral and ceremonial work are regarded as merits, which God will reward by granting salvation. But the freedom which Luther derives from the justification or reconciliation of the sinner with God through Christ attains a far higher plane.

What really is the realm within which every religion moves and wherein Christianity proves itself the highest and most perfect form of religion? It is the position occupied by man as a spiritual being, according to which, on the one hand, he claims to be worth more than the whole universal order [*Naturzusammenhang*], but, on the other, finds himself limited and hemmed in by, or subject to, that natural order of things. Regardless of the form it has taken, religion has at all times been the endeavor—with the support of higher spiritual powers—to resolve that contradiction in which one finds himself vis-à-vis the world in favor of a position of power over the world. This actually transpires in all the religions, which form a hierarchy according as individual goods or a highest good are striven after; according as the latter is filled with various contents; according as the higher powers are taken to be several or one and are relatively or absolutely distinguished from the world. But Christianity excels all religions in perfection and provides the key to understanding all the others, because it supplies the conditions under which the spiritual life really achieves power over the world in a spiritual manner. The religions of those peoples who have made the preeminent contributions to world history and cultural history—the Hebrews, Greeks, and Romans—have accorded the rank of highest good, even in a religious sense, to the state, as well as to the political unification and domination of all national groups living within their horizon. These religions have been surpassed by Christianity because this sort of world dominion is not the highest good, but must rather give place to a community of mankind that is to be realized according to the law of universal charity [*Nächstenliebe*] and in which, as Luther maintains, every member has the dignity of king and priest. On this view every Christian—by exercising his priestly authority before God, by reposing his trust in God as God's child, by giving thanks to God and seeking his aid, by practicing intercessory prayer in order to take up all other men into his concern before God—establishes through God's help that dominion over the world which is the content of the kingly office. In the Christian religion trust in God is decisively informed by the idea that the aim or purpose of the world is the association of men in the kingdom of God; that the order and course of the world are subordinated by God to that purpose; and that, as Paul says, with those who love God and are loved by God all things work together for good, even the very restraints and limitations attendant on the course of life in the world. This confidence in God, to which the Christian religion entitles us and for which it equips us, is the power whereby we rise above the world and subdue it—in all of life's commonplace as well as momentous affairs. It is also the power wherein we experience our own value, the value of a spiritual existence—something which to a certain degree men lay claim to in every religion. As little as any other man is the Christian so freed from the world as to be spared those evils which are caused by the natural order and by the position of other men in it. But through his trust in God, patience, and thankfulness, he transmutes all the evils which befall and impede him into the means for his spiritual freedom and independence.

It may be granted that this display of patience in the face of suffering, and of a discipline that generally renders us indifferent toward evils which are most perturbing to the untrained, might allow virtually no distinction between its Stoic and Christian forms; in fact some of the earliest Church's foremost teachers did confuse them. But if it is true that spiritual attainments are to be distinguished by their motives, so that acts which externally appear to be quite similar are intrinsically of quite different value, then there is a marked difference between the Stoic who attains imperturbable patience and serenity by submitting or adjusting himself to the unchangeable law of nature, and the Christian who—in accord with the clear and prominent thought of his Savior—is aware of ruling patiently over the whole combined weight of the world which makes itself felt in every moment of suffering, even the most trifling one. If in accord with this view we know that we are both summoned and empowered to exercise patience, then our thankfulness before the God who sends us suffering in order to test and strengthen us imprints a character on our patience which is lacking to the Stoic. He may claim that his virtuous submission to the inescapable laws of the universe is true humility. He may be convinced that he is thus exercising self-denial in a superior way, namely, by renouncing the value of his own personal independence from the world. Nevertheless he deceives himself, because he misjudges both the world and himself. For one can properly display humility only in response to the spiritual power and beneficent purpose of the revealed God, whereas the Stoic, in spite of all his formal self-denial, actually goes on maintaining his inalienable self-value owing to his defiant and haughty attitude. The lordship over the world which the Christian attains, and in which he experiences his salvation, exalts him above the common human weakness of dependence on and limitation by the world, of misery and despair, because he has grounded his claim to life on a much different attitude toward the world.

Dependence on the world, however, is twofold. It is partly undeserved, partly deserved; in part the general weakness of the individual creature, in part the will's bondage through an inordinate desire for worldly goods that countermands the nature and destiny of the will to be free of such impulses to individual or corporate selfishness. This distorted relationship to the world, in which Christianity finds mankind, is thus not merely a natural weakness but also sin and guilt, the perversion of what the will and character were meant to be, threatening to lay waste man's original title to lordship over the world. For the worthlessness of sin for the sinner himself is perceptible, in the first instance, in that it cripples and runs at cross-purposes to the positive valuation and destiny of man not only for life in community but also for his position before the world. Yet the highest standard for what is to be regarded as sin and guilt is God, the world's creator and ruler, who has destined man for lordship over the world and who guarantees it. This is not only the case when we acknowledge the moral law, the order of man's communal life, as the divine order, but already in the preceding form of relation, namely, that we are committed to respecting God's rulership over all human life and to trusting in his beneficent purpose for us. And even as we Christians, according to Luther, attain mastery over the world by trusting in God's goodness, so also our bondage to illicit motivations deriving from the world or our sin is at bottom nothing but indifference, lack of trust, mistrust of the God who is due our reverence and confidence. This spiritual attitude is not only the presupposition or substance of any actual transgression of the moral law in social intercourse; but such lack of trust and indifference toward God are for us quite generally, and especially in our experience of evil, the real expression of sin and guilt which separate man from God and alienate him from his destined lordship over the world. This is the double misery in which man constantly finds himself vis-à-vis the world: the aimless oscillation between hubris and timidity, between resignation which rejects the value of life and a hollow defiance.

From this above all one sees that sin—which is indifferent to, or mistrustful of, God's help or even dissociates itself altogether from the thought of God in hatred and contempt—is a reproach for any people. Now if mankind is to be raised out of this condition to a position of spiritual dominion over the world, thus attaining harmony between its own proper destiny and God's purpose for the world, then the religion which makes this possible must first of all be founded on the forgiveness of sins by God, and this blessing must be the fundamental promise which God has given mankind. The forgiveness of sins, that pardon by which God does away with the alienating effect of guilt on sinners, is well known and highly esteemed by the religions of the civilizations antedating Christianity. Yet there its function and interpretation are different. For the Greeks, Romans, and Hebrews it is always required only in individual cases; but for Christians it is the revealed, all-encompassing ground of their religious and moral life. Furthermore, these other peoples expect that the evil of which they are guilty will be blotted out by the forgiveness of sins, whereas Christians expect to experience God's pardon in that their mistrust and doubt will be replaced by trust in God; and, in line with this inner reversal of their relationship to God, they take evil upon themselves, whether it was caused by them or not, as a punishment which serves their education rather than their condemnation. Therefore Luther says with respect to dominion over the world in the Christian sense: where there is forgiveness of sins, there is life and salvation.

I must refrain from any attempt to verify this statement from the Small Catechism through showing its necessary connection with what Christ has done for men, for sinners, in his world-conquering life and suffering. Only one condition must be added, however. Since every religion is a communal matter, it follows from the communal character of divine grace, as vouchsafed by Christ, that the forgiveness of sins is the fundamental endowment of the Christian community. Therefore Luther insists that it is within this Christendom that God forgives the individual his sins daily and abundantly. Just as it is a communal concern that the gospel of the forgiveness of sins be carried on, so also the appropriation of this blessing and of the others following from it has no scope or activity of its own which would not be encompassed by this religious sense of community. This is also the reason why the community of Christ, in the course of its spread through time and space, was obliged to attach itself to various civil institutions, and why one must attend to the defects in the Church with patience. The freedom of conscience, which Luther brought about, is the freedom of the conscience from guilt before God; and the recognition of its value and its communal conditions does not provide for anything like that position at which Goethe arrived, actually starting from quite different presuppositions, namely, that he like anyone else could establish his own private religion. Such a formula can only erroneously be brought into connection with Luther. This is obvious at least from the observation that the moral order of society, in which, as Luther says, everyone is a dutiful servant to the other, would have no validity within Christianity unless religion and the religious interpretation of man's relation to the world were also an affair of community.

Luther's interpretation of Christianity, directed to the end of spiritual lordship over the world, surpasses the other basic conception which proposes flight from the world as the goal of life. His understanding of the Church as the religious community, in which legal ordinances are only subordinate means, abolishes the Catholic assumption that the Church is preeminently a legal order, a kind of state, namely, the spiritual universal-state. In this way Luther has been able to make the state, considered as the legal form of any national group, including the Christian ones, independent of the encroaching claims of the Roman papacy. His doctrine of the state leaves behind the theories of medieval men like Dante and Occam who, while they pursued similar goals, ultimately did not have anything else to say than that the state, though independent as far as God's will is concerned, must serve the Church's purposes. Certainly Luther does acknowledge the legal order—the community of civil justice—as an important presupposition of, or an educational means toward, the religious and moral life in the Christian sense; but from this does not follow the state's subordination to the Church as a legal institution. Rather the legal aspect of the Church's existence is dependent on the order maintained by the state. This idea of Luther's has become operative not only among the nations which accepted his Reformation, but also the Catholic states have organized their relationship with the Roman Church according to this criterion.

In the realm of culture the state holds pride of place. Accordingly Luther's understanding of religious freedom, this purely religious idea, is the key to the direction taken by the world-historical nations during the past three centuries as bearers of their own distinct cultures. The second condition of all culture is the positive valuation of labor. Here also Luther has provided the criterion, by recognizing that any type of work which serves the commonweal—however lofty or menial that task might be—is the very substance of one's ordinary service to God, and by attributing a priestly quality to fidelity in one's calling. It is no less true that the Christian liberty which Luther proclaimed is the fundament of the autonomy and rich diffusion of all forms of inquiry. Whoever has become independent of nature and of the restrictions inherent in society, by virtue of religious lordship over the world, is also in this way equipped to gain insight into the interaction of freedom and necessity—the counter-effects of the energies and intentions of individual men and of the forces of society: all of which is overlooked with indifference by those who conduct themselves, in line with the standards of medieval culture, solely as models of submission to that church which bases its claims upon unhistorical presuppositions. Fundamentally, religious lordship over the world also removes that awe before the natural world which dominated the medieval mind as an aftereffect of certain pagan life forces and prevented the exact observation and investigation of nature. Granted that Luther himself did not draw these conclusions; that the superstition in which he shared continued to control several generations of Protestants after him; that the unconstrained investigation of nature had also to be wrested arduously from the Protestant churches; that, finally, the success of natural science during the current century has not been accompanied by an awareness of its connection with Luther's leading practical idea: all this cannot fairly be held against our argument. For where else can one find already prepared the basic premise of all scientific research—that the human mind has power over the world and is of higher value than the world—save in Luther's religious idea of the freedom of a Christian? If, however, the dread of nature which persisted among the medieval people is an aftereffect of pagan religion, it can ultimately be overcome only by a religious motive of an opposite sort.

Luther's Reformation did not issue from the womb of the medieval Church in the same way as Athena sprang in full panoply from the head of Zeus. As a simultaneously patriotic and religious deed, it stirred up a long-lasting excitement among both the German people and, directly or indirectly, many other European nations. Yet these effects deriving from the powerful spiritual impulse generated by Luther stand in striking contrast with the fact that the ruling idea within the practical context outlined above did not remain as highly esteemed and as clearly formulated as one would have expected. Although one could grant that Luther himself did not articulate all the possible implications of the Christian freedom pointed out by him, one would certainly expect that the norm of original Christianity discovered by the Reformer would always have been clearly present in his mind and could be exhibited as the thought which permeates all his writings. This, however, is not the case. One cannot, of course, understand Luther's Catechisms as a coherent whole without having clearly in view the sequence of thoughts delineated above; yet these writings only hint at a number of such thoughts rather than clearly stating them. And thus a mass of theological reflections is deposited in Luther's writings wherein the practical apex or the new Reformation ideal of life is left out of consideration. Similar observations can be made apropos of the theology of Melanchthon, Luther's co-worker. He achieved a penetrating expression of Luther's leading ideas in the Augsburg Confession and its Apology, but he never exhaustively investigated the value of reconciliation with God for life in the Church. In his theological textbook he was at no time able to formulate the practical proof of reconciliation or justification as he had successfully done in the Apology to the Augsburg Confession. To be sure, in a general way Melanchthon understood and repeated Luther's significant suggestions for a new, positive form of theology which would surpass its medieval stage; yet he failed to pursue that course. Instead he allowed the whole of theology to remain in that form which lay at the root of medieval Scholasticism. In this Melanchthonian theology—whose design and scope have been considered normative up to the present day—Luther's reformatory series of thoughts has found no place, and his fundamental assertions relative to theological method no application. Thus the genuine ideas of the Reformation were more concealed than disclosed in the theological works of Luther and Melanchthon.

As a result one could even entertain doubts about whether this sequence of thoughts, obscured in this way, can really be considered the heart of the matter. I reject such doubt most assuredly. If one were in fact required to regard Melanchthon's textbook as the authentic and exhaustive document of the Reformation, then one should no longer speak of the Reformation of the Church but rather of the founding of a theological school alongside the Church, a school of meager productivity incapable of sustaining the community that had been formed in connection with it. This atrophy of Luther's Reformation, transpiring in the very hour of its birth, has been the chief reason for the limitation of its effects. This fact is to be explained by reference to the state of controversy into which Luther's undertaking was inextricably drawn from its inception. Whoever is required to defend his position against opponents who cannot attain to his newly inaugurated mental horizon runs the risk of abridging and dislocating it. The controversial situation in which the Reformers found themselves was marked not only by opposition from the Catholic side, but soon also by competition from a movement which disputed those doctrines concerning which Luther and Melanchthon could and would not give up agreement with the Catholic Church. Hemmed in by this attack from both sides and concerned to maintain the legal ground of the Roman Empire— upon which the Reformation put itself in motion and sought to secure its permanence, the Reformers brought their cause under the roof of a theology which must necessarily overshadow the practical motifs and implications of Luther's ideas.

But this was not the only trait of weakness with which Luther's Reformation was born. Another relates to the new ecclesiastical organization in which the Reformation made its appearance, and which was fragmented because the traditional organs of the Church—the pope, the bishops, and the Roman emperor—rejected the reform of the Church. Therefore the implementation of reform devolved upon those princes and city authorities who decided in favor of it. The majority of these, however, had a more or less restricted range of power. Yet this phenomenon [of princely reform]—which appears even more striking if contrasted with the subsequent concentration of authority in the papal church—is only the continuation of a combination of events which took place in the fifteenth century. When the bishops at the councils of Constance and Basel failed to gain power over the papacy, the popes steadily allied themselves with the princes against the bishops in order to limit or hinder episcopal authority. In the place of the bishops a number of German princes during the fifteenth century exercised the right of reformation in the Church by reforming monasteries, i.e., by recalling the monks to a strict observance of their rules in reaction to a growing laxity. In consequence of this right yielded to them by the pope, the princes were now prepared [in the sixteenth century] to put into effect the more comprehensive reforms of Luther, in line with their duty to be solicitous of all the needs of their subjects. Thus the disintegration of the Church's constitution, brought about by the fifteenth-century popes, is the reason for the [reformatory] involvement of the princes. If the imperial power had been ready to make common cause with Luther and at the same time to transform the Empire into a national monarchy, a state of equilibrium would have been established between the ecclesiastical reality of the Reformation and the authority previously granted to the state. But since the Spanish Hapsburg emperor could not take this course for personal and political reasons, the new church structure, forced upon the Reformation, came into existence in a state of fragmentation which damaged its importance and influence from the very beginning.

The ultimate goal that Luther intended to attain through his reform of doctrine and worship was the elevation of morality according to the norm which had ever been valid in Christianity. During the second half of the Middle Ages many attempts had already been made to reform the Church in this direction. Ever since St. Francis of Assisi had imposed upon the whole Christian community, and not merely upon the members of his own order, the evangelical law of nonresistance to injustice, of reconciliation, of goodness and amicability, of poverty and self-denial, this task [of moral renovation] had been pursued in the most manifold ways. Particularly during the fifteenth century, preaching and devotional literature continued to attune the people to these legalistic demands of Christian perfection. Luther indeed pursued the same goal, albeit purged of the monastic elements, precisely by following a way different from that of preaching the law. His basic concern is that by religious edification and well-rounded education a formation of character can be achieved which will make it possible to reach the highest ideal of fulfilling one's duties toward one's fellowmen. The differences between his method and the legalistic method of the medieval reformers might perhaps be likened to that between two possible directives on how to jump over a bar. The medieval reforms of morality appear like the demand to jump from the spot, with the feet together. Luther's instruction instead is like saying that the jump will succeed only if one takes a long run. This means that first there has to be a personal training in faith and in the disposition of love before the goal of moral perfection can be approached. In this respect the Reformation could not show any quick results; it had to disappoint the expectations cherished by many contemporaries who espoused the traditional standards of reform of the Christian life. And when the violent movements within the nation, which were triggered off only incidentally by the Reformation, intensified the already prevalent decay of public morality, Luther's impact upon many who initially had placed their hopes in him faded away again, and his very principles were held responsible for the growth of moral disorder.

From the outset, however, nothing deformed the Reformation more than the contentiousness which was exercised in its very midst among the various groups. It is a peculiar phenomenon that Church reform in the sixteenth century emerged simultaneously in two closely related branches at different places, and that Luther and Zwingli were forthwith joined by Calvin as the third. In spite of the close relationship among them they differ in significant respects. But it was a misfortune, for which those involved must bear the blame, that the differences were judged with mutual mistrust and impatience and burdened with exaggerations. Yet such actions were not alone responsible for the quarrels among the Protestants; but the minor theological differences among the Lutherans themselves were so blown up by their spokesmen, in the face of the enemy, that a single generation after its beginning the German Reformation, protected by the imperial peace, could almost have passed from the scene. It is possible to explain this fateful development. The Reformation, in its beginnings, was not favored with theologians who had been raised in its spirit and who were endowed with a moral character suitable to its purpose. Most of its protagonists, particularly the outstanding ones, were—in spite of their Lutheran appelation—monks: obstinate, vehement, and incapable of distinguishing between trivial and momentous matters. Owing to them it was necessary to summarize Reformation doctrine in the rigidly dogmatic Formula of Concord—a work respectable enough among its kind, yet one which no longer permits the spirit and practical goals characteristic of Luther's Reformation to be immediately recognized. It may be that under the prevailing circumstances this theoretical encapsulation of Luther's Reformation worked to its advantage. But that this was not universally the case is evident from the fact that this doctrinal formulation failed to afford sufficient nourishment for piety. Even before the end of the sixteenth century the Lutherans seized upon certain elements of Catholic piety in order to satisfy their devotional needs. Mysticism—which by that time was being channeled into the Lutheran Church in a broad stream, and Pietism—which somewhat later opposed the growing rigidity and torpor of the Christian life by emphasizing its inwardness and practical orientation, are both methods which are directly or indirectly shaped by the monastic, that is, Catholic tradition.

Under the conditions which prevailed in the Protestant sector of Germany after the Peace of Westphalia these methods of piety engendered an indifference toward churchly Christianity by preparing for the emergence of the so-called Enlightenment. Up to the present this movement has held its own among large sectors of the Protestant population, offering a tenacious if passive resistance to the counterblows of an orthodoxy that has been reestablished upon a new pietistic base. The historically perceptive observer who understands the connections between these successive movements of German Protestantism will not join with those who simply condemn the Enlightenment as a fundamental lapse from Christianity. The religious motivation with which it emerged one hundred and fifty years ago also entails a positive relation to Luther's basic idea. Furthermore, the Enlightenment still endures among many today who have no intention to accept a form of the church that remains incomprehensible to them, mainly because of the strangeness of its pietistic foundation. But there are also many for whom the prevailing aesthetic education, as well as the demand for political liberalism deriving from the Enlightenment, have given reason to assume that nineteenth-century culture no longer has anything in common with the Christian religion or even with the Protestant Church. The same antipathy is found among the masses, who in their economic struggle for existence and their unrealizable demand that the state should protect them against it seem to have dropped below the level on which religion has any validity.

So it is that for the past forty years Ultramontane voices have presumed to announce the self-dissolution of Protestantism, and more recently within this camp there is an ever-increasing delight in the anticipated return of Protestants into the womb of the one church which alone bestows salvation. In that camp scornful looks and words also attend the celebration of Luther's birthday, as if there were no real reason for it anymore and it were nothing but a palpable self-deception. As I near the end of this address I invite you to examine this opinion of the opponents. It is based on two considerations: the continuing disagreement among Protestants concerning the conditions of their unity; and the presumably increasing indifference of many Protestants toward their church. One would like to ask what possible interest Catholics might have in admitting this heterogeneous mass of aspirations for freedom into their seemingly well-ordered fellowship. Do they want to admit all this confusion into their midst in order gradually to overcome it with the spiritual means which are supposedly at their disposal? Several of its representatives have already indicated that this is not the official Roman Catholic view. Rather one reckons on the possibility that once all Protestants have turned Catholic, and thus all national governments have also returned to the obedience of the Roman See, then sword and fire will stand ready at hand to effect the desired peace of the cemetery. Such is the goal of the loving solicitude for our salvation. I believe I am able to prove that here one of the greatest weaknesses of the Roman Church comes to the fore; yet I deem it inappropriate to judge the others. Rather I intend to use their judgment on Protestantism for the purpose of our self-correction and the strengthening of our self-esteem.

It is true that Protestantism from the beginning has suffered severely from its disunity. Limiting myself to the German situation, I can only note that the fighting has grown more bitter on account of that party which for thirty years now has claimed Luther's name for itself alone; which identifies itself with the Evangelical Church; and which, by constantly judging the speck in the eye of others, provides the principal reason for the Ultramontane belief in the decline and fall of Protestantism. I do not doubt for a moment that the adherents of this party intend to serve the cause of evangelical truth. Yet the Pietism which they foster in their circles is Catholic in content and origin, and whoever thinks that he can and must dominate the Church always leans upon a Catholic concept of the Church. Luther counts the cross and suffering among the marks of the true Church, through which one allows himself to be trained in patience; but they wish to see the Church shine forth in glory and legislative influence. This tendency, along with their shortsighted attempts to implement ecclesiastical uniformity, puts them on the same track as the Ultramontanes and seduces them into aiding the cause of the Roman pope in the sphere of the state. By following the example of this power in aiming at the separation of church and state, they disturb the order of the established churches [*Landeskirchen*] and invite the English and American sects to snatch away from the Church those circles which are nothing but pietistic. These men consider themselves Lutherans, but their theology is solely that of Melanchthon; they constantly appeal to the Lutheran Symbols, but have only a very imprecise knowledge of them. Otherwise they would realize that they are less orthodox than they think, just as they—contrary to their intentions—share in the blame for the widespread indifference shown to the Evangelical Church. On the one hand many who want to participate in the life of the Church are embittered by them; while on the other many seize upon the virtually watertight excuse that they simply are not interested in a community which frustrates their expectation of Christian forbearance, patience, gentleness, and peacefulness. For thirty years now religious instruction in our high schools has been dependent on instructional materials which come closest to the standards of current orthodoxy. From years of observation I have concluded that in most cases this kind of instruction makes no impact on the students or even instills in them a resentment against the subject. Here and now I wish to testify publicly to this fact; for it shows most conspicuously that this current orthodoxy does not suffice to insure the future of Protestantism.

The Ultramontanes, who for this and other reasons expect the imminent dissolution of Protestantism and the return of the Protestants into the Roman Church, are simply victims of wishful thinking. Led astray by one-sided developments in the Evangelical churches and by accounts in certain newspapers, they overlook those forces which guarantee the future of Protestantism. Owing to their narrowminded conclusions they fail to reckon with the power of resistance inherent in a historical community which, after all, has developed its own characteristic culture—one which is by no means inferior to Catholic culture. Or if they think that party disunity and the indifference of others will insure the ruin of Protestantism, they are dogmatists pure and simple, wholly ignorant of the laws of history. According to the accounts of Eusebius, the third-century Church went through a period in which bishops fought against bishops and churches against churches, because Christians—carrying their freedom to extremes—had slipped so deeply into indifference and laxity, hypocrisy and loss of a spirit of community, that they no longer trusted even in God's providence, while the bishops excelled one another solely in their love of power. And during the Middle Ages the Latin Church repeatedly went through similar crises in which the papacy, through the fault of its own representatives, was deeply humiliated and rendered incapable of providing the Church that continuity which supposedly it alone could bestow. And if the papacy has been spared such crises for the past three hundred years, no other reason can be adduced than the existence of Protestantism. The latter has taken upon itself the defects which had previously plagued the undivided Church. If in the foreseeable future the desire of the hostile Ultramontanes for a return of the Protestants into the haven of their church should actually be fulfilled, then the Roman Church would again suffer from the disunity of which the medieval period was replete, and her glory, which she has enjoyed only for the last three hundred years, would vanish. Then perhaps it might again transpire that two or three popes would simultaneously struggle for primacy in the church.

The difficulties, however, with which Protestantism has had to contend since its inception can be judged correctly only by comparing the conditions under which Protestantism itself, Western Catholicism and, by contrast with the latter, Eastern Catholicism came into being. These three stages in the formation of Christianity must be taken into account if the legitimacy and prospects of Protestantism are to be made plausible. The branching-off of Latin Catholicism from the common Catholic Church dominated by the Greeks was favored by the development of the two churches in geographically separate areas. It still took from the fifth to the twelfth century, from Augustine to St. Bernard, until the new stage—in all its characteristic forms of doctrine, piety, and church government—was fully developed and the influences of the Greek Catholic stage had been definitely overcome. This process took so long, of course, because of the intervention and consequences of the tribal migrations and the replacement of the Roman Empire by the Germanic and Romanic nations. Yet one may conclude from this single case that a few centuries more or less are not decisive for a development within Christianity.

The development of Protestantism has been rendered more difficult because it took place among the same nations, and on the same geographical scene, where the Roman Church also continued to assert herself—and she has sorely beset her rival with great power and much cunning. Apart from the restrictions imposed by this adversary and the concomitant narrowing of doctrinal development, Protestantism from the outset has been obliged to suffer from, and to struggle with, the progressive political fragmentation of the Holy Roman Empire, the constellations of European politics in general, and an entanglement with diverse aspirations in the cultural realm. The latter, having their origin in the disintegration of medieval culture, pushed into the foreground the antihistorical elements of medieval learning, namely, natural law and natural religion, upon which the claims of all modern philosophies are built. If we further recall the Catholic character of pietistic piety—voluntarily renewed because the practical goal of Protestant piety had become blurred—along with other forms of rapprochement with the adversary, then the three hundred and fifty years of Protestantism to date are far too brief a period, measured against these obstacles, to warrant any despair about its future. Until now the practical root idea of Luther's Reformation has not yet been employed in all clarity and vigor for the regulation of Protestantism's many tasks, i.e., it has still not been directed to the ordering of theology and its demarcation from all useless forms. Therefore Protestantism has been forced to rely on instruments of thought which are alien to its character, and to pursue an uncertain course that cannot be circumvented by reliance on foreign support so long as an independent sense of direction is lacking. I should like to advance the thesis that to date Protestantism has not yet emerged from its age of teething problems, but that its independent course will begin when— on the basis of a thoroughgoing comprehension of its practical root ideas— it reforms theology, fructifies churchly instruction, shores up the moral sense of community, and achieves political resoluteness for the actualization of those spiritual riches which one of her greatest sons once acquired for our nation. To this end we do not have recourse to any instruments of coercion, but we may and must have confidence in the power of the truth we have come to know and in the divine assistance which has been promised to the upright. Or is there perchance in this matter some form of support more certain than God's help?

We are inspired to trust [in this divine aid] and to conduct ourselves accordingly precisely by Luther's own personal conduct. Throughout his entire public life there runs a characteristic trait which coincides with that practical proof of Christianity expounded by him: confidence in God for the legitimacy and durability of his affair, in defiance of appearances and political probabilities. It is striking that Luther repeatedly had to struggle for the certainty of his salvation against adverse medieval ideas, which in general he recognized as erroneous. These internal conflicts [*Anfechtungen*] show how difficult it was for the Reformer to sever his emotional ties to these norms, which indeed were no longer valid for him. But his confidence in God in everything touching his reformatory work rendered him indifferent even to the support of political power if such ran contrary to existing public law. When in 1530 at the Diet of Augsburg the toleration of Protestantism by the emperor and Empire was dependent upon the attempts at theological agreement between the two parties, and Melanchthon, as negotiator, was for good reason most vitally concerned about the result but was also, in keeping with his nature, quite overwhelmed by this anxiety, Luther wrote him from the Coburg:[2] "You are torturing yourself about the end and outcome of the cause because you cannot comprehend them. If you could comprehend them, I should not like to be a participant, much less the author, of this cause. God has subsumed it under a certain basic concept which you do not have in your rhetoric or your philosophy. This is faith. And in this faith are comprehended all the things that are not seen and do not appear. If somebody tries to make this visible, apparent and comprehensible, as you do, he may reap anxiety and tears as the fruit of his labor, as you do, while all of us vainly cry out against it. The Lord said that he would dwell in thick darkness, and he made darkness his secret place. Let him who

---

[2] The original text of this excerpt from Luther's letter to Melanchthon, dated June 29, 1530, is located in WA-Br 5, 406, 54–407, 56. The English translation is based on that in *Luther: Letters of Spiritual Counsel*, ed. and trans. Theodore G. Tappert (Vol. XVIII in the Library of Christian Classics, Philadelphia, 1955), pp. 150-51. The present rendering adheres to certain minor editorial changes and omissions introduced by Ritschl in his address.

will do otherwise. May the Lord increase your faith and the faith of all of us. If we have faith, what can Satan accomplish even with the whole world? But if we do not have faith, why do we not at least strengthen ourselves with the faith of others? For there are bound to be others who have faith in our stead unless there is no longer a Church in the world and unless Christ has ceased to be with us. If Christ be not with us, where, pray, is he in all the world? If we are not the Church or part of it, where is the Church? If we do not have the Word of God, who has it? If, then, God be for us, who can be against us? We are sinners and ingrates, but this does not make him a liar. Yet we cannot be sinners in this holy cause of God which we are serving, even if we be wicked in our own ways of life."

One does not understand Luther at all if he does not share in this fundamental confession of Luther's life. Without this kernel all confessions of evangelical faith are but empty shells lacking in substance. They possess value only if they serve this personal trust in God. The lordship over the world which springs from reconciliation with God through Christ assumes concrete form in this freedom of confidence in God. Viewed in this context trust in God—against all the evidence—is the test of genuine Protestantism. In this sign Protestantism will conquer.

BIBLIOGRAPHY

I. Primary Sources

A. *Ritschl's Major Works* (listed chronologically):

[For a complete listing of A. Ritschl's writings, see Otto Ritschl, *Albrecht Ritschls Leben*: Vol. I, 1822-1864 (Freiburg i. B., 1892), pp. 438-47; Vol. II, 1864-1889 (Freiburg i. B. and Leipzig, 1896), pp. 526-32.]

Die Entstehung der altkatholischen Kirche. Bonn, 1st ed., 1850, 2nd ed., 1857.

De Ira Dei. Bonn, *1859*.

Die christliche Lehre von der Rechtfertigung und Versöhnung.
> Vol. I: *Die Geschichte der Lehre*. Bonn, 1st ed., 1870, 2nd ed., 1882, (= 3rd ed., 1889). E. T. from the first edition by John S. Black, *A Critical History of the Christian Doctrine of Justification and Reconciliation*. Edinburgh, 1872.
> Vol. II: *Der biblische Stoff der Lehre*. Bonn, 1st ed., 1874, 2nd ed., 1882, 3rd ed., 1889.
> Vol. III: *Die positive Entwickelung der Lehre*. Bonn, 1st ed., 1874, 2nd ed., 1883, 3rd ed., 1888 (= 4th ed., 1895). E.T. from the third edition by H. R. Mackintosh and A. B. Macaulay, *The Christian Doctrine of Justification and Reconciliation: The Positive Development of the Doctrine*. Edinburgh, 1900. (Reprinted, Clifton, N. J., 1966.)

Die christliche Vollkommenheit. Ein Vortrag. Göttingen, 1st ed., 1874, 2nd ed., 1889. E.T. from the first edition by E. Craigmile and A. Duff, Jr., *Christian Perfection*, in *Bibliotheca Sacra* 35 (1878) : 656-80.

Schleiermachers Reden über die Religion und ihre Nachwirkungen auf die evangelische Kirche Deutschlands. Bonn, 1874.

Unterricht in der christlichen Religion. Bonn, 1st ed., 1875, 2nd ed., 1881, 3rd ed., 1886 (= 4th ed., 1890 = 5th ed., 1895). E.T. from the fourth edition by Alice Mead Swing, *Instruction in the Christian Religion*, printed in Albert T. Swing, *The Theology of Albrecht Ritschl* (New York, 1901), pp. 171-286.

[Fabricius, Cajus, ed. *Kritische Ausgabe: Die christliche Vollkommenheit. Ein Vortrag. Unterricht in der christlichen Religion*. Leipzig, 1924.]

Geschichte des Pietismus, 3 vols. Bonn, 1880-1886.
> Vol. I: *Geschichte des Pietismus in der reformierten Kirche*. Bonn, 1880.

Vol. II: *Geschichte des Pietismus in der lutherischen Kirche des 17. und 18. Jahrhunderts.* Erste Abteilung. Bonn, 1884.

Vol. III: *Geschichte des Pietismus in der lutherischen Kirche des 17. und 18. Jahrhunderts.* Zweite Abteilung. Bonn, 1886.

Theologie und Metaphysik. Zur Verständigung und Abwehr. Bonn, 1st ed., 1881, 2nd ed., 1887.

Drei akademische Reden. Bonn, 1887. [Includes *Festrede am vierten Seculartage der Geburt Martin Luthers,* 10. November, 1883. *Festrede über Reformation in der lateinischen Kirche des Mittelalters,* zur akademischen Preisvertheilung 8. Juni, 1887. *Festrede zur Feier des 150-jährigen Bestehens der Georg-Augusts-Universität,* 8. August, 1887.]

Fides implicita. Eine Untersuchung über Köhlerglauben, Wissen und Glauben, Glauben und Kirche. Bonn, 1890.

Gesammelte Aufsätze, ed. Otto Ritschl. Freiburg i. B., 1893. Neue Folge, Freiburg i. B., 1896.

B. *Luther's Works:*

D. *Martin Luthers Werke.* Kritische Gesamtausgabe. Weimar, 1883-   .

Pauck, Wilhelm, ed. and trans. *Luther: Lectures on Romans.* Vol. XV in the Library of Christian Classics. Philadelphia, 1961.

Pelikan, Jaroslav, and Lehmann, Helmut T., gen. eds. *Luther's Works.* American Edition. St. Louis and Philadelphia, 1955-   .

Tappert, Theodore G., *et al.,* ed. and trans. *The Book of Concord: The Confessions of the Evangelical Lutheran Church.* Philadelphia, 1959.

II. Recent Secondary Works on Ritschl

Barth, Karl. "Ritschl," Chapter XI in *Protestant Thought: From Rousseau to Ritschl,* trans. Brian Cozens (New York, 1959), pp. 390-97.

Berndt, Bruno. "Die Bedeutung der Person und Verkündigung Jesu für die Vorstellung vom Reiche Gottes bei Albrecht Ritschl." Unpublished dissertation: Tübingen, 1959.

Deegan, Daniel L. "Albrecht Ritschl as Critical Empiricist," *Journal of Religion* 44 (1964): 149-60. [Also appeared in *The Scottish Journal of Theology* 18 (1965): 40-56.]

————. "Albrecht Ritschl on the Historical Jesus," *The Scottish Journal of Theology* 15 (1962): 133-50.

————. "The Ritschlian School, the Essence of Christianity and Karl Barth," *The Scottish Journal of Theology* 16 (1963): 390-414.

Foley, Grover. "Ritschls Urteil über Zinzendorfs Christozentrismus," *Evangelische Theologie* 20 (1960): 314-26.

Forde, Gerhard O. "Albrecht Ritschl," Chapter VII in *The Law-Gospel Debate: An Interpretation of Its Historical Development* (Minneapolis, 1969), pp. 96-119.

Foster, A. Durwood. "Albrecht Ritschl," in *A Handbook of Christian Theologians,* ed. Martin E. Marty and Dean G. Peerman (Cleveland, 1965), pp. 49-67.

Graby, James K. "The Problem of Ritschl's Relationship to Schleiermacher," *The Scottish Journal of Theology* 19 (1966): 257-68.

Guthrie, George P. "Kant and Ritschl: A Study in the Relation Between Philosophy and Theology." Unpublished dissertation: University of Chicago, 1962.

Haenchen, Ernst. "Albrecht Ritschl als Systematiker," in *Gott und Mensch: Gesammelte Aufsätze* (Tübingen, 1965), pp. 409-75.

Hammer, Karl. "Albrecht Ritschls Lutherbild," *Theologische Zeitschrift* 26 (1970): 109-22.

Hefner, Philip. "Albrecht Ritschl and His Current Critics," *The Lutheran Quarterly* 13 (1961): 103-12.

————. "The Role of Church History in the Theology of Albrecht Ritschl," *Church History* 33 (1964): 338-55.

————. *Faith and the Vitalities of History: A Theological Study Based on the Work of Albrecht Ritschl.* New York, 1966.

Hök, Gösta. *Die elliptische Theologie Albrecht Ritschls nach Ursprung und innerem Zusammenhang.* Uppsala, 1942.

Jersild, Paul. "The Holiness, Righteousness and Wrath of God in the Theologies of Albrecht Ritschl and Karl Barth." Unpublished dissertation: Münster, 1962.

————. "Natural Theology and the Doctrine of God in Albrecht Ritschl and Karl Barth," *The Lutheran Quarterly* 14 (1962): 239-57.

————. "Judgment of God in Albrecht Ritschl and Karl Barth," *The Lutheran Quarterly* 14 (1962): 328-46.

Jodock, Darrell. "F. C. Baur and Albrecht Ritschl on Historical Theology." Unpublished dissertation: Yale University, 1969.

Klaas, Walter. "Ritschls 'Unterricht in der christlichen Religion' und Karl Barths Abrisse der Dogmatik. Ein Vergleich," in *Antwort: Karl Barth zum siebzigsten Geburtstag am 10 Mai, 1956* (Zollikon, 1956), pp. 388-98.

Koenig, Emil. "The Use of the Bible in Ritschl's Theology." Unpublished dissertation: University of Chicago, 1953.

Metzler, Norman. "The Ethics of the Kingdom." Unpublished dissertation: Munich, 1971.

Mueller, David L. *An Introduction to the Theology of Albrecht Ritschl.* Philadelphia, 1969.

Ryan, Michael. "The Function of the Discipline of History in the Theological Interpretation of Albrecht Ritschl." Unpublished dissertation: Drew University, 1966.

Schäfer, Rolf. "Das Reich Gottes bei Albrecht Ritschl und Johannes Weiss," *Zeitschrift für Theologie und Kirche* 61 (1964): 68-88.

————. "Die Rechtfertigungslehre bei Ritschl und Kähler," *Zeitschrift für Theologie und Kirche* 62 (1965): 66-85.

————. *Ritschl: Grundlinien eines fast verschollenen dogmatischen Systems.* Tübingen, 1968.

Schlosser, Walter. "Orthodoxe Tradition und kritischer Neuansatz in der Gotteslehre Albrecht Ritschls." Unpublished dissertation: Göttingen, 1962.

Schütte, Walter. "Die Ausscheidung der Lehre vom Zorn Gottes in der Theologie Schleiermachers und Ritschls," *Neue Zeitschrift für systematische Theologie und Religionsphilosophie* 10 (1968): 387-97.

Senft, Christoph. "Ritschl: Der Glaube als Gabe und Tat," Chapter IV in *Wahrhaftigkeit und Wahrheit: Die Theologie des 19. Jahrhunderts zwischen Orthodoxie und Aufklärung* (Tübingen, 1956), pp. 124-66.

Timm, Hermann. *Theorie und Praxis in der Theologie Albrecht Ritschls und Wilhelm Herrmanns. Ein Beitrag zur Entwicklungsgeschichte des Kulturprotestantismus.* Gütersloh, 1967.

Vorster, Hans. "Werkzeug oder Täter? Zur Methodik der Christologie Albrecht Ritschls," *Zeitschrift für Theologie und Kirche* 62 (1965): 46-65.

Walther, Christian. "Der Reich Gottes Begriff in der Theologie Richard Rothes und Albrecht Ritschls," *Kerygma und Dogma* 2 (1956): 115-38.

―――. *Typen des Reich-Gottes-Verständnisses. Studien zur Eschatologie und Ethik im 19. Jahrhundert.* Munich, 1961.

Werner, Martin. "Die Theologie Albrecht Ritschls," in *Der protestantische Weg des Glaubens*, Vol. I (Berne, 1955), pp. 799-813.

Wölber, Hans-Otto. *Dogma und Ethos. Christentum und Humanismus von Ritschl bis Troeltsch.* Göttingen, 1950.

Wrzecionko, Paul. "Der Einfluss der Philosophie Kants auf die Theologie Albrecht Ritschls." Unpublished dissertation: Münster, 1953.

―――. "Der geistesgeschichtliche Horizont der Theologie Albrecht Ritschls," *Neue Zeitschrift für systematische Theologie und Religionsphilosophie* 5 (1963): 214-34.

―――. *Die philosophischen Wurzeln der Theologie Albrecht Ritschls. Ein Beitrag zum Problem des Verhältnisses von Theologie und Philosophie im 19. Jahrhundert.* Berlin, 1964.

III. Older Secondary Works on Ritschl

[For an extensive bibliography of literature on Ritschl from *ca.* 1880 to 1940, see Gösta Hök, *Die elliptische Theologie Albrecht Ritschls* (Uppsala, 1942), pp. xiii-xxxiv. See also E. C. Richardson, *Alphabetical Subject Index and Encyclopaedia to Periodical Articles on Religion, 1890-1899* (New York, 1907) pp. 939-40 for Ritschl literature.]

Akers, Samuel. *Some British Reactions to Ritschlianism.* Yale Studies in Religion, No. 8. Scottdale (Pa.), 1934.

Bornemann, W. "Die Theologie Albrecht Ritschls," *Die christliche Welt* 3 (1889): 337-41; 354-59.

Brown, William Adams. *The Essence of Christianity.* New York, 1913. [Chapter on Ritschl contains extensive bibliography.]

Denney, J. *Studies in Theology*, rev. ed. London, 1895.

Dieckmann, A. "Die christliche Lehre vom Zorne Gottes nebst Kritik der betreffenden Lehre A. Ritschls," *Zeitschrift für wissenschaftliche Theologie* 36 (1893): 321-77.

Eck, S. "Die theologische Entwicklung Albrecht Ritschls im Zusammenhang mit frühern Richtungen der evangelischen Theologie," *Die christliche Welt* 7 (1893): 756-60; 779-87.

Ecke, G. *Die theologische Schule Albrecht Ritschls und die evangelische Kirche der Gegenwart,* 2 vols. Berlin, 1897-1904.

Esslinger, R. *Zur Erkenntnistheorie Ritschls. Eine Studie.* Zürich, 1891.

Fabricius, Cajus. *Die Entwicklung in Albrecht Ritschls Theologie von 1874 bis 1889 nach den verschiedenen Auflagen seiner Hauptwerke dargestellt und beurteilt.* Tübingen, 1909.

Flew, R. Newton. "Ritschl," Chapter XXI in *The Idea of Perfection in Christian Theology: An Historical Study of the Christian Ideal for the Present Life* (Oxford, 1934), pp. 374-93.

Flügel, O. A. *Ritschls philosophische und theologische Ansichten,* 3rd ed. Langensalza, 1895.

Frank, F. H. R. *Zur Theologie Albrecht Ritschls,* 3rd ed. Leipzig, 1891.

Garvie, A. E. *The Ritschlian Theology, Critical and Constructive: An Exposition and an Estimate.* Edinburgh, 1st ed., 1899, 2nd ed., 1902.

———. "Ritschlianism," article in *Encyclopaedia of Religon and Ethics,* ed. James Hastings, Vol. X (New York, 1918), pp. 812-20.

Girgensohn, K. "Zu Albrecht Ritschls hundertjährigem Geburtstag," *Neue kirchliche Zeitschrift* 33 (1922): 168-99.

Goguel, M. *La théologie d'Albert Ritschl.* Paris, 1905.

Günther, E. "Albrecht Ritschls spätere theologische Entwicklung," *Theologische Studien und Kritiken* 95 (1922): 195-229.

Häring, Th. "In welchem Sinn dürfen wir uns immer noch 'Göttinger' heissen? Albrecht Ritschls Bedeutung für die Gegenwart," *Zeitschrift für Theologie und Kirche* 20 (1910): 165-96.

Halliday, G. *Facts and Values: A Study of the Ritschlian Method.* London, 1914.

Harnack, A. "Ritschl und seine Schule," *Reden und Aufsätze,* Vol. II, 2nd ed. (Giessen, 1906), pp. 345-68. [Review of G. Ecke's work.]

———. "Albrecht Ritschl: Rede zum hundertsten Geburtstag am 30. April 1922 in Bonn gehalten," *Reden und Aufsätze,* Neue Folge, Vol. IV (Giessen, 1923), pp. 327-45.

Haug, L. *Darstellung und Beurteilung der Theologie Ritschls, zur Orientierung dargeboten,* 3rd ed. Stuttgart, 1895.

Herrmann, Wilhelm. *Der evangelische Glaube und die Theologie Albrecht Ritschls,* 2nd ed. Marburg, 1896. E.T. by R. W. Stewart, "Faith as Ritschl Defined It," in *Faith and Morals* (New York, 1904), pp. 7-62.

———. "Albrecht Ritschl: Seine Grösse und seine Schranke," *Festgabe von Fachgenossen und Freunden A. von Harnack, zum siebzigsten Geburtstag dargebracht,* ed. Karl Holl (Tübingen, 1921), pp. 405-6.

Kügelgen, C. W. von. *Grundriss der Ritschlschen Dogmatik,* 2nd rev. ed. Leipzig, 1903. [1st ed. entitled, *Die Dogmatik Albrecht Ritschls.* Leipzig, 1898.]

Lechler, P. "Zur Theodicee. Eine Anmerkung zu A. Ritschls Theologie," *Theologische Studien und Kritiken* 67 (1894): 161-70.

Lehmann, Paul. *Forgiveness: Decisive Issue in Protestant Thought*. New York, 1940.

Lipsius, R. A. "Die Ritschlsche Theologie," *Jahrbücher für Protestantische Theologie* 14 (1888): 1-28.

Luthardt, Chr. E. "Zur Beurtheilung der Ritschlschen Theologie. Eine Entgegnung," *Zeitschrift für kirchliche Wissenschaft und kirchliches Leben* 2 (1881): 617-58.

————. "Zur Kontroverse über die Ritschlsche Theologie," *Zeitschrift für kirchliche Wissenschaft und kirchliches Leben* 7 (1886): 632-58.

Lyman, Eugene W. "Ritschl's Theory of Value-Judgments," *Journal of Religion* 5 (1925): 500-518.

Mackintosh, Hugh Ross. "The Theology of Moral Values: Albrecht Ritschl," Chapter V in *Types of Modern Theology* (London, 1937), pp. 138-80.

Mackintosh, Robert. *Albrecht Ritschl and His School*. London, 1915.

Mozley, J. K. *Ritschlianism: An Essay*. London, 1909.

Nippold, F. *Die theologische Einzelschule im Verhältnis zur evangelischen Kirche, mit besonderer Rücksicht auf die jung-Ritschlsche Schule und die Streitigkeiten über das liturgische Bekenntnis*. Brunswick, 1893.

Orr, James. *The Ritschlian Theology and the Evangelical Faith*. London, 1897.

————. *Ritschlianism: Expository and Critical Essays*. London, 1903.

Pfleiderer, O. *Die Ritschlsche Theologie, kritisch beleuchtet*. Brunswick, 1891.

Rade, M. "Unkonfessionalistisches Luthertum. Erinnerung an die Luther-freude in der Ritschlschen Theologie," *Zeitschrift für Theologie und Kirche* 45, Neue Folge 18 (1937): 131-51.

Ritschl, Otto. "Ritschl, Albrecht," article in *Realencyclopädie für protestantische Theologie und Kirche*, 3rd ed. (1906), Vol. XVII, pp. 22-34.

————. "Ritschl, Albrecht," article in *The New Schaff-Herzog Encyclopedia of Religious Knowledge*, ed. S. M. Jackson (New York, 1911), Vol. X, pp. 43-46.

————. "Albrecht Ritschls Theologie und ihre bisherigen Schicksale," *Zeitschrift für Theologie und Kirche* 16 (1935): 43-61.

Schmidt, H. "Ritschls Lehre von der Sünde," *Zeitschrift für kirchliche Wissenschaft und kirchliches Leben* 5 (1884): 489-96; 545-60; 569-81.

Staehlin, L. *Kant, Lotze and Ritschl*. Edinburgh, 1889.

Stange, C. *Der dogmatische Ertrag der Ritschlschen Theologie nach Julius Kaftan*. Leipzig, 1906.

————. *Albrecht Ritschl: Die geschichtliche Stellung seiner Theologie*. Leipzig, 1922.

Stephan, H. "Albrecht Ritschl und die Gegenwart," *Zeitschrift für Theologie und Kirche* 16 (1935): 21-43.

Sulze, E. "Zum Gedächtnis Albrecht Ritschls," *Protestantische Kirchen-zeitung* 36 (1889): 480-87.

Swing, A. T. *The Theology of Albrecht Ritschl*. New York, 1901.

Thikötter, J. *Darstellung und Beurtheilung der Theologie Albrecht Ritschls*, 2nd ed. Bonn, 1887.

Tillich, Paul. "Albrecht Ritschl, zu seinem hundertsten Geburtstag," *Theologische Blätter* 1 (1922): 49-54.

Titius, A. "Albrecht Ritschl und die Gegenwart. Ein Vortrag," *Theologische Studien und Kritiken* 86 (1913): 64-92.

Traub, F. "Ritschls Erkenntnistheorie," *Zeitschrift für Theologie und Kirche* 4 (1894): 91-129.

————. "Die Beurteilung der Ritschlschen Theologie in Theobald Zieglers Werk, 'Die geistigen und sozialen Strömungen des Neunzehnten Jahrhunderts,'" *Zeitschrift für Theologie und Kirche* 12 (1902): 497-548.

————. "Zur Interpretation Ritschls," *Zeitschrift für Theologie und Kirche* 35, Neue Folge 8 (1927): 269-73.

Vischer, E. *Albrecht Ritschls Anschauungen von evangelischem Glauben und Leben.* Tübingen, 1900. (*Sammlung gemeinverständlicher Vorträge*, No. 18.)

————. "Albrecht Ritschl, zu seinem hundertsten Geburtstag," *Sammlung gemeinverständlicher Vorträge*, No. 103. Tübingen, 1922.

Wehrung, G. "Die Haupttypen theologischen Denkens in der neueren Theologie," *Zeitschrift für systematische Theologie* 2 (1924/25): 75-145.

Wendland, J. *Albrecht Ritschl und seine Schüler im Verhältnis zur Theologie, zur Philosophie und zur Frömmigkeit unserer Zeit dargestellt und beurteilt.* Berlin, 1899.

Wendt, H. H. "Albrecht Ritschls theologische Bedeutung. Zu seinem hundertsten Geburtstag (25 März, 1822): *Zeitschrift für Theologie und Kirche* 30, Neue Folge 3 (1922): 3-48.

Wobbermin, Georg. "Der Ertrag der Ritschlschen Theologie bei Carl Stange," *Zeitschrift für Theologie und Kirche* 17 (1907): 53-59.

————. "The Theology of Albrecht Ritschl and Its Significance for the Present Day," *Yale Divinity Quarterly* 4 (1907): 85-99.

————. *Schleiermacher und Ritschl in ihrer Bedeutung für die heutige theologische Lage und Aufgabe.* Tübingen, 1927. (*Sammlung gemeinverständlicher Vorträge*, No. 125.)

IV. Other Literature Cited in Text

Althaus, Paul. *The Theology of Martin Luther*, trans. Robert C. Schultz. Philadelphia, 1966.

Billing, Einar. *Our Calling*, trans. Conrad Bergendoff. Rock Island (Ill.), 1955.

Bodenstein, Walter. *Die Theologie Karl Holls im Spiegel des antiken und reformatorischen Christentums.* Berlin, 1968.

Boehmer, Heinrich. *Martin Luther: Road to Reformation*, trans. John W. Doberstein and Theodore G. Tappert. New York, 1959.

Bornkamm, Heinrich. *Luther und das Alte Testament.* Tübingen, 1948.

————. *Luther im Spiegel der deutschen Geistesgeschichte.* Heidelberg, 1955.

Burckhardt, Jacob. *On History and Historians*, trans. Harry Zohn. New York, 1965.

Carlson, Edgar. *The Reinterpretation of Luther.* Philadelphia, 1948.

Cauthen, Kenneth. *The Impact of American Religious Liberalism*. New York, 1962.

Dillenberger, John. *God Hidden and Revealed*. Philadelphia, 1953.

Ebeling, Gerhard. *Evangelische Evangelienauslegung: Eine Untersuchung zu Luthers Hermeneutik*. Munich, 1942.

———. "The New Hermeneutics and the Early Luther," *Theology Today* 26 (1964): 34-46.

———. *Luther: Einführung in sein Denken*. Tübingen, 1964. E.T. by R. A. Wilson, *Luther: An Introduction to His Thought*. Philadelphia, 1970.

———. *The Word of God and Tradition*, trans. S. H. Hooke. Philadelphia, 1968.

Elert, Werner. *The Structure of Lutheranism*, Vol. I, trans. Walter Hansen. St. Louis, 1962.

Greschat, Martin. *Melanchthon neben Luther: Studien zur Gestalt der Rechtfertigungslehre zwischen 1528 und 1537*. Witten, 1965.

Haikola, Lauri. "Melanchthons und Luthers Lehre von der Rechtfertigung: Ein Vergleich," *Luther and Melanchthon*, ed. Vilmos Vajta (Philadelphia, 1961), pp. 89-103.

Harnack, Adolf von. "Zur gegenwärtigen Lage des Protestantismus," *Reden und Aufsätze*, Vol. II. Giessen, 1906.

Harnack, Theodosius. *Luthers Theologie mit besonderer Beziehung auf seine Versöhnungs- und Erlösungslehre*, 2 vols. Erlangen, 1862, 1886; 2nd ed., 1927.

Holl, Karl. *Gesammelte Aufsätze zur Kirchengeschichte*. Vol. I: *Luther*, 2nd and 3rd rev. ed. Tübingen, 1923. Vol. III: *Der Westen*. Tübingen, 1928.

Josefson, Ruben, "Christus und die Heilige Schrift," *Lutherforschung heute*, ed. Vilmos Vajta (Berlin, 1958), pp. 57-63.

Kantzenbach, F. W. "Lutherverständnis zwischen Erweckung und Idealismus," *Luther* (Zeitschrift der Luther-Gesellschaft) 36 (1965): 9-30.

Lagarde, Paul de. *Ueber einige Berliner Theologen und was von ihnen zu lernen ist*. Göttingen, 1890.

Loewenich, Walther von. *Luther als Ausleger der Synoptiker*. Munich, 1954.

———. *Luther und der Neuprotestantismus*. Witten, 1963.

———. "Wandlungen des Evangelischen Lutherbildes im 19. und 20. Jahrhundert," *Wandlungen des Lutherbildes: Studien und Berichte der Katholischen Akademie in Bayern*, ed. Karl Forster, Vol. 36. Würzburg, 1966.

Lohse, Bernhard, ed. *Der Durchbruch der reformatorischen Erkenntnis bei Luther*. Darmstadt, 1968.

Lougee, Robert W. *Paul de Lagarde (1827-1891): A Study of Radical Conservatism in Germany*. Cambridge (Mass.), 1962.

Macquarrie, John. *Twentieth Century Religious Thought*. New York, 1963.

Niebuhr, H. Richard. *The Meaning of Revelation*. New York, 1960.

Nilsson, K. O. *Simul: Das Miteinander von Göttlichem und Menschlichem in Luthers Theologie*. Göttingen, 1966.

Oberman, Heiko A. " 'Iustitia Christi' and 'Iustitia Dei'; Luther and the Scholastic Doctrines of Justification," *Harvard Theological Review* 59 (1966): 1-26.

Ostergaard-Nielsen, H. *Scriptura sacra et viva vox*. Munich, 1957.

Pauck, Wilhelm. "Luther and Melanchthon," in *Luther and Melanchthon*, ed. Vilmos Vajta (Philadelphia, 1961), pp. 13-31.

————. "The Historiography of the German Reformation During the Past Twenty Years," *Church History* 9 (1940): 305-40.

Pelikan, Jaroslav. *Luther the Expositor*. St. Louis, 1959.

Pelikan, J., ed. *Interpreters of Luther: Essays in Honor of Wilhelm Pauck*. Philadelphia, 1968.

Prenter, Regin. *Spiritus Creator*, trans. John M. Jensen. Philadelphia, 1953.

Preus, James S. *From Shadow to Promise: Old Testament Interpretation from Augustine to the Young Luther*. Cambridge (Mass.), 1969.

Richmond, James. *Faith and Philosophy*. New York, 1966.

Rupp, Gordon. *Luther's Progress to the Diet of Worms*. New York, 1964.

————. *The Righteousness of God: Luther Studies*. London. 1953.

Schmid, Lothar. *Paul de Lagardes Kritik an Kirche, Theologie und Christentum*. Stuttgart, 1935.

Schultz, Robert C. *Gesetz und Evangelium in der lutherischen Theologie des 19. Jahrhunderts*. Berlin, 1958.

Spitz, Lewis W., ed. *The Reformation: Material or Spiritual?* Boston, 1962.

Stephan, Horst. *Luther in den Wandlungen seiner Kirche*, 2nd ed. Berlin, 1951.

Stern, Fritz. *The Politics of Cultural Despair: A Study in the Rise of the Germanic Ideology*. New York, 1965.

Stupperich, Robert. "Die Rechtfertigungslehre bei Luther und Melanchthon, 1530-1536," in *Luther and Melanchthon*, ed. Vilmos Vajta (Philadelphia, 1961), pp. 73-88.

Stupperich, R., ed. "Briefe Karl Holls an Adolf Schlatter (1897-1925)," *Zeitschrift für Theologie und Kirche* 64 (1967): 169-240.

Torrance, Thomas F. *Kingdom and Church: A Study in the Theology of the Reformation*. Fair Lawn (N.J.), 1956.

Watson, Philip. *Let God Be God: An Interpretation of the Theology of Martin Luther*. Philadelphia, 1947.

Wolf, Ernst. "Luthers Erbe?" *Evangelische Theologie* 6 (1946/47): 82-114; 310-12.

Wolff, Otto. *Die Haupttypen der neueren Lutherdeutung*. Stuttgart, 1938.

211

INDEX OF NAMES